A DOZEN LIPS

Eavan Boland • Clodagh Corcoran • Carol Coulter
Gretchen Fitzgerald • Maureen Gaffney
Trudy Hayes • Edna Longley • Gerardine Meaney
Ruth Riddick • Helena Sheehan
Ethna Viney • Margaret Ward

Attic Press
DUBLIN

First published in Ireland in 1994 by
Attic Press
4 Upper Mount Street
Dublin 2

British Library Cataloguing in Publication Data
Dozen Lips
823 [F]

ISBN 1 85594 060 4

The moral right of the contributors to be identified as the authors of this work is asserted

Cover Design: Paula Nolan
Origination: Verbatim Typesetting and Design
Printing: Guernsey Press Co Ltd

This book is published with the assistance of The Arts Council/An Chomhairle Ealaíon.

CONTENTS

1

PORNOGRAPHY
The New Terrorism

Clodagh Corcoran, 1989

FOR BERNIE DWYER

Note: I write here only about heterosexual pornography. I write only of pornography that objectifies women, depicts them as sexually subordinate, enjoying violation and violence and which is produced for men.

Neither have I here addressed the question of child pornography. I do not mean to ignore it, nor do I diminish its significance in any way. Although a related issue, it is also a separate issue, and must have its own space.

Clodagh Corcoran 1989

Introduction

In the spring of 1988 I sat in front of a small television set and watched a video. The following day, with three other women, I was to participate in a press conference about pornography and censorship. The aim of this press conference was to establish that it is indeed possible, even reasonable to be anti-censorship and anti-pornography. It was important to establish this point publicly, because of the refusal of a number of individuals and organisations, who paid attention to liberal values and human civil rights, to understand why pornography denies the very humanity of women.

It is, I believe, pointless to try to change an entrenched system unless you have taken the opportunity to be informed on all aspects of the system, and up to this point the only aspect of pornography I had not examined was 'snuff' films. So here I was, sitting alone in a friend's home, in front of a television set, waiting for this video to begin.

I want to describe it to you in detail. But I cannot, because my mind won't let me. What I can tell you is that on that night I watched a man participate in the act of sex with a woman, and during that act he plunged a large hunting knife into her stomach and cut her open from vagina to breast. He then withdrew the knife and stuck it into her left hand, removing the first joints from three fingers, which fell from the bed. The woman's eyes remained open; she looked at the knife and said, 'Oh God, not me'. It took her approximately three minutes to die. The camera was left running. The film was then canned and put on the commercial market as entertainment.

I left the house that night in an apparently calm state, although with hindsight, I realised I had gone into shock. I was determined to show the video at the press conference but because of faulty equipment this did not happen. However, I attempted to describe what I had watched to the very few journalists who attended. On of them, who turned up halfway through the conference, took no notes whatever, but nonetheless felt able to write about the conference later in *The Sunday Press*, under the banner headline, 'My Night With The Video Ladies'.

Shock dissolved into terror and I didn't sleep for many weeks. I was grateful for the temporary loan of a stun-gun to keep beside my bed. I have lived in fear ever since, knowing that while the rape, degradation and dehumanisation of women is filmed and sold as entertainment, women's status in society is worthless, and our lives within and outside our homes are also without value. One can only await an answer with Andrea Dworkin when she asks, in *Letters from the War Zone*:

> What does it mean that the pornographers, the consumers of pornography, and the apologists for pornography are the men we grew up with, the men we talk with, live with, the men who are familiar to us and often cherished by us as friends, fathers, brothers, sons and lovers? How, surrounded by this flesh of our flesh that despises us, will we defend the worth of our lives, establish our own authentic integrity, and, at last, achieve our freedom?

I
Defining pornography

The word pornography derives from the ancient Greek words *porne* and *graphos*: to write about whores. Specifically, and exclusively, the word *porne* means the very lowest class of whores, which in ancient Greece was the brothel slut available to all male citizens. So, when we use the word 'pornography' we are not talking about sex, or erotica, or the sexual act or nude bodies or many other euphemisms which saturate the conversation of the pornographer. We are talking about the graphic description of 'vile whores'.

It has frequently been my experience to hear men supporting my point of view that pornography diminishes us all and that it is most particularly a civil rights issue for women. Inevitably, without pausing to consider the contradiction in what they are saying, they then ask, 'Of course, you don't really mean those lovely Page 3 girls, now do you?' I do. Why? Because any distinction between softcore and hardcore pornography is false and misleading. Both categories represent women as sex objects, sexually available, inviting sexual access and violation. The photographs of women in Page 3 are essentially no different from the photographs we see in the magazines to be found on the 'top shelf'. They communicate the same negative, sexualised image of women, representing us as pieces of meat for men's sexual titillation and gratification.

The distinction between softcore and hardcore is frequently blurred, but they are both represented in a continuum of violence towards women. However, softcore (women with legs splayed, vaginas and anuses gaping and exposed to the camera, posed 'provocatively' inviting sexual arousal and penetration, subjected to bondage, coercion and even violence) is easily, readily and legally available on the top shelf of newsagents, whilst hardcore (torture, flaying, cannibalism, crushing of breasts in vices, exploding vaginas packed with hand-grenades, eyes gouged out, beatings, dismemberings, and burnings, multiple rape, women engaged in sexual intercourse with animals, the films of real rapes by rapists and the actual killing of women) is easily, readily and, *illegally* obtained from under the counter or the back room of the second-hand magazine sellers and many, many video shops.

When asked by a Dublin journalist why he (secretly) stocked and supplied to favoured customers such hardcore videos, the owner of the shop stated that he 'couldn't afford not to, because that's what people want, and also,' he added, 'every other video shop in the area is stocking it and he would lose business if he didn't.'

There are now a number of definitions of pornography, all

of which provide a framework within which civil rights legislation can be enshrined. The definition below, within which I present my views, is based on that developed by the Campaign Against Pornography and Censorship:

The graphic, sexually explicit subordination of women through pictures and/or words, that also include one or more of the following:

- Women portrayed as sexual object, things or commodities
- Women portrayed as enjoying pain or humiliation
- Women portrayed as enjoying being raped, orally, anally or vaginally
- Women portrayed as enjoying being tied up, cut up, mutilated, bruised, or physically hurt, in postures of sexual submission or servility or display
- Women reduced to body parts
- Women shown being penetrated by objects or animals
- Women presented in scenarios of degradation, injury or torture
- Women shown as inferior
- Women shown bleeding, bruised or hurt in a context which is sexual

Pornography does not include erotica (defined as sexually explicit materials premised on equality) and it does not include bona fide sex education materials, or medical or forensic literature.

Pornography is the theory; rape is the practice.

Objectification of women through pornographic represent-ations has one theme, and one theme only: women are things, objects, receptacles, instruments; their nature is passive, insensate, usable, empty; they exist to comply, submit, offer, serve. Such objectification portrays a deep, aggressive hatred of the female sex and the desire to degrade and hurt womankind.

Pornography is the propaganda of sexual fascism, where sexual conduct is dictated by those in power (pornographers). Like all 'isms' it is another form of totalitarianism, and it stretches across a wide spectrum of human affairs, from outright greed to the subjugation and extermination of a human species.

4

II
The links with violence

> ...the propaganda of pornography promulgates the lie that
> fear is arousing, that terror is orgasmic, that women enjoy
> being afraid because being afraid is women's natural state,
> because nice friendly guys are on the loose in the pub and the
> prep school, and every time another woman dies the rest get
> jumpy, which is the point of the vantage because if women
> are jumpy all the time it must mean that being afraid is their
> natural state, which means they enjoy it, which means give
> them more of the same because fear is arousing and terror is
> orgasmic.
>
> Robin Morgan The Demon Lover

It has been a constant assertion especially among male liberals
that there are no real relationships between pornography and
violence. In the August 1989 issue of *Now*, Tom Cooney,
Chairperson of the Irish Council for Civil Liberties, is quoted
in this context: 'The belief that porn causes sexual violence is
just wishful thinking by those seeking an excuse for
censorship.'

On the other hand I have a young friend, who is about
twenty years of age now. She looks, and is, extremely fragile,
because during that rite of passage known to us all as
childhood, at regular intervals male members of her family
and their friends would pick her up from school, throw her in
the boot of the car (frequently with a dead animal) and take
her to a secret house. There, whilst hardcore pornography
was unendingly played on the video, she was raped, beaten,
degraded, denied and tortured, until these men grew bored.
Then she was taken home, and she went back to school next
day. Until the next time. Now, she has a vested interest in
making us understand that pornography incites men to
violence towards women. But that is precisely the problem—
she has a vested interest. So I suppose she would not be a
reliable witness, bearing reputable evidence. Nor, presumably,
would the anguished, silenced experience of adult women
over the decades be reputable. That experience is, no doubt,
'just wishful thinking'.

Most liberals would agree that education is of primary
importance, and that we learn from what we see around us, in
books, in film, in the newspapers, on the television. If this is

so, then surely they must recognise that pornography too imparts certain lessons and understanding to the consumers. But the problem here is that such a recognition would beg further questions, and indeed answers, from these liberal defenders of pornography. Such a recognition, according to Andrea Dworkin ('Pornography's Part in Sexual Violence' in *Letters from a War Zone)* would demand that they reach conclusions about the quality of life contained in the message of pornography. And it would most certainly demand that when pornography is the theory and rape the practice, and sexual violence against women and children is epidemic, that we ask serious, considered questions about the function and value of material that disseminates the propaganda of sexual fascism and makes it synonymous with pleasure.

Unwilling to acknowledge this simple truth, the male fantasy world, in which violence and sex are creamily interfaced, is constantly reinforced through pornographic images. The ongoing male dilemma is about whether to opt for the real world of adult consensual fucking, or for the wet dream. Men want both, and it was out of this dilemma that the culture of pornography was born. In these circumstances 'war on want' assumes a new meaning.

Addressing this issue, Sheila Jeffreys writes, in *Out of Focus:*

> Feminists are asked to prove our assertion that there is a connection between the view of women in pornography and sexually violent films and the harassment and violence against women which happens in the home, in childhood, at work and on the street. Such a degree of proof is not required to show a connection between sex-stereotyping in school textbooks and television advertisements and men's expectations that women should perform all household tasks. Moreover, such a demand for proof shows a remarkable blindness to the abuse and exploitation of millions of women in the actual production of pornography.

As women, the quality of our lives has been defined by one key factor: male control of our sexuality. As it is currently constructed, our sexuality is based on male experience, desires and definitions. And, as we are already too painfully aware, this control legitimates the use of force within our relationships with men. That we exist to be used by them is, quite simply, the common point of view—it is our natural function. This has been the most significant factor in our oppression.

Whilst such oppression continues, we are an occupied people, our integrity violated on a daily basis, because of this male sexuality which, literally, swells with satisfaction at our subjugation and violation. What justifies this demand for pornography, which annihilates our chance for freedom?

Women who, unaware of any feminist debate around pornography, have refused to have it in their homes, have frequently found themselves isolated by their partners. Their resistance to the sexual subjugation of women portrayed in pornography has itself often resulted in violence to them. In *Surviving Sexual Violence*, Liz Kelly notes:

> They were reacting on the basis of how pornography made them feel. They were resisting attempts to make its presence acceptable within their homes and social life. In making these stands, women took a number of risks. For example, the possibility of being labelled 'prudes' within their friendship network and the probability of prolonged dispute with their male partner, which in some cases ended in violence. For these women, and indeed many of us, pornography not only is sexual violence, but causes it.

In the same book, Liz Kelly concludes that:

> Increasing demands for greater autonomy will inevitably lead to greater violence against women within the private and public domain as men seek to reassert their dominance in their unthinking way. Hence the fight now to increase the flow of pornography can be seen as a patriarchal response to women's liberation.

In the spring of 1989, at the AGM of the National Council for Civil Liberties (NCCL) in the UK, the question of evidence on the links between pornography and violence was addressed in a motion put forward by the executive. In part, this motion reads:

> This AGM, whilst appreciating the methodological difficulties in producing scientific evidence and therefore the ability to say the exact nature and extent of a causal link between certain kinds of pornography and harm to women, considers that there is sufficient evidence to say that it is highly likely that such a link exists both in terms of the aggregate increase of sexual violence against women, some individual sexual attacks against women and subordinate,

unequal status of women. This AGM therefore supports lawful campaigns against certain kinds of pornography as defined below, on the grounds of sex discrimination as a civil liberties issue for women, where such campaigns are aimed at changing public attitudes towards such material. Conference notes that, in any definition of pornography, there must be three main ingredients:

1. It must be sexually explicit.
2. It must depict women as enjoying or deserving some form of physical abuse; and
3. It must objectify women, that is, define women in terms of their relationship to men's lust and desire.

There is an abundance of evidence on the links between pornography and violence, which can roughly be classified into four different categories:

- Academic evidence
- Clinical evidence
- Personal testimony
- Legal (and quasi-legal) evidence

It is impossible to ignore this evidence. It exists as a tangible body of work. The pro-pornographers are aware of it. The Irish Council for Civil Liberties (ICCL) is aware of it. Yet they all persist in denying its validity, because to do so would be to acknowledge a terrible truth: women are being denied their human and civil rights.

> We know that men like hurting us.
> We know it because they do it all the time,
> one way or another,
> and we watch them liking it,
> And men don't do things that they don't like,
> generally speaking.
> They like doing it and they like watching it
> and they like watching other men do it
> and it is entertainment
> and men pay money to see it
> and that is one of the reasons why
> men make pornography.
>
> It's fun for God's sake.
>
> **Andrea Dworkin**

III
Anti-pornography Anti-censorship

I am a woman.	I am a woman.
I am a feminist.	I am a feminist.
I am an author.	I am an author.
I am a bookseller.	I am a bookseller.
I am anti-censorship.	I am anti-pornography.

While busily dismissing the evidence of links with violence from victims and researchers on the grounds that such evidence is not reputable, the defence of liberals against those campaigning against censorship but, nevertheless, against pornography, is expressed in a number of predictable, dreary, uninformed myths.

Myth 1
It is not possible or logical to be anti-pornography and anti-censorship.
Women do not oppose pornography for religious or moral reasons, or on the grounds of taste or decency or because they disapprove of sex or have a warped view of sex, as is so often alleged. We do not oppose sexually explicit material per se. Erotica, for example, (sexually explicit material premised on equality) is not considered pornographic.

Our objections to pornography are based on real concerns that while such representations of women exist, they constitute a clear incitement to violence and hatred of all women. Pornography discriminates against us in our everyday lives, in our homes, in our workplace, in our leisure-time. It discriminates against us because of a condition of birth.

Pornography represents the censorship of women. It censors women by depicting us as one-dimensional, as sexual objects, as sub-human beings, existing solely for the purpose of meeting men's sexual desires. Such representations play a key part in both reproducing and reinforcing sexual discrimination and oppression. Certain pornography represents sexual violence, often extreme, to women, and contributes to sexual violence towards other women.

Those who cling desperately to the myth that anti-pornography and anti-censorship are incompatible positions, are frequently the same people who, knowing no sense of ambiguity, express a righteous outrage at evidence of racism and fascism in society, which they see as civil rights issues.

But, introduce pornography, the undiluted existence of anti-female propaganda, embracing issues of sexism, racism, freedom and violation of civil rights, and which informs the consumer that women are 'inferior', unintelligent, worthless, stupid, altogether less able than our male counterparts, and suddenly we are 'censoring freedom of expression'.

Who do these people think they are fooling?

Myth 2
The existing legislation is perfectly adequate to deal with pornography. Any further legislation will increase the power of the state to control society through censorship.

The (Irish) Video Recordings Bill, 1987, which was never translated into legislation, was allegedly drawn up to protect society from 'video nasties'. Extraordinarily, nowhere in this clumsy, ill-considered bill were the words pornography, women or children mentioned. Not once.

It is pointless for politicians to tell us that the bill was meant to tackle pornography. How can it tackle something it has neither identified nor attempted to understand?

Few records are kept about the known importation and sales of pornography in Ireland. However, estimates of customs seizures, which must represent only the tip of a huge trade, reveal that from 1986 to 1988 just under 2,000 videos and approximately 22,000 magazines were confiscated.

It is alarming to note that during this time the number of videos seized fell from 960 (1986) to 244 (1988), while magazine seizures fell from 8,500 to 5,837. This failure in detection corresponds to a significant increase in the number of video shops opening throughout the country, and a significant increase in reported violence against women and children, as highlighted in police statistics, and Rape Crisis Centre and family centre reports.

No prosecutions under the existing legislation (Censorship of Publications Act 1946 and Customs Acts) took place during these three years. Does this reflect confusion about interpretation of the current law or something else altogether? Perhaps just enough seizures and confiscations are being made to keep the politicians and public reassured that the protection of public morals and sensibilities is in good hands?

Any legislation which relies on malestream subjective interpretations of 'obscenity', 'blasphemy' and 'depravity and

10

corruption' to curb availability of pornography actually contributes to its continued use and abuse. Pornography is concrete and objective and can be described and defined specifically. Legislation must acknowledge this and seek to curtail its availability on the grounds of what it is and what it does:

- It perpetuates the oppression of women
- It denies human and civil rights
- It denies women's rights to autonomy and personhood

Earlier this year, the NCCL (UK) addressed itself to this line of (un)reasoning as follows:

> Even the most perfectly drafted legislation cannot alone provide the solution. The limitations on legislation and its enforcement are substantial which means that the control of the legislation would have to be carefully devised and campaigned for—for example, a revamped Equal Opportunities Commission with the power to take cases. Legislation can only be seen as one element in a range of changes needed to tackle the problem. The essential question is whether by legislation more will be gained than lost? For example, although the Sex Discrimination Act and Equal Pay Act have proved disappointing in terms of their effect, even inadequate legislation helps change general attitudes, influences women's own expectation and encourages them to fight for their rights. Campaigning against pornography without the backing of laws comes up against a particularly significant obstacle: the powerful pornography business. As America has witnessed, this can be effectively mustered to defeat campaigns especially when it is allied with the 'free speech' lobby.

Myth 3
Anti-pornographers are a reactionary force in alliance with the 'new right'.

A traditional stance of liberalism is that pornography is sex and therefore good, whilst the stance of conservatism is that pornography is sex and therefore bad.

Pornography, of course, is not sex. Pornography is sexual abuse of and violence towards women.

The Right wants secret access to its pornography, while the Left wants public access. The Right wants to hide it on the top shelf, while the Left wants to hide its meaning. But understand, both sides want access to pornography, and both sides are encouraged and energised by it.

The only alliance which we seek is with those who understand how pornography oppresses both men and women, and while the real fundamentalists seem to have been able to pick up our rhetoric, it appears that some of them have come to a new understanding in this area. Our vigilance, our past experiences and our work at other levels, will ensure that we don't get corrupted by fundamentalism. The real unholy alliance is that of the civil libertarians aligning with the pornographers.

Myth 4
Feminists are threatening/censoring freedom of speech.

Whose freedom of speech is being threatened? What freedom is being protected here? The freedom to portray women as objects who can be beaten, raped, tortured, killed. The freedom to express, through pornography, a deep-seated hatred and fear of all women? The freedom to translate this speech into action within the home through violence to partner and children?

It appears that this 'right' to freedom of speech is held and accessed only by the producers and consumers of pornography. This is the democratisation of pornography.

When women state clearly that they believe that pornography seriously discriminates against us on the grounds of sex, this, apparently, is threatening freedom of speech!

The fact of the matter is that if this concept of freedom of speech does not work for women, it simply does not work.

If the defenders of pornography can understand and accept that their myths have as much substance as the emperor's new clothes, then maybe the good men and boys will put away their dirty pictures and figure out a way to make freedom of speech a reality for women. Maybe these good men and boys will acknowledge the blindingly obvious fact, that eliminating pornography would in fact serve to increase the freedom of women, not to limit it.

What is not embraced in any of these charges is an analysis of the true meaning of pornography for all of us, women and men.

> The notion of a universality of human experience is a confidence trick and the notion of a universality of female experience is a clever confidence trick.
>
> Angela Carter, *The Sadeian Woman*

IV
The Liberals' response

Pornography turns sex inequality into sexuality and turns male dominance into the sex difference. Put another way, pornography makes inequality into sex, which makes it enjoyable, and into gender, which makes it seem natural. By packaging the resulting product as pictures and words, pornography turns gendered and sexualised inequality into 'speech', which has made it a right. Thus does pornography, cloaked as the essence of nature and the index of freedom, turn the inequality between women and men into those twin icons of male supremacy, sex and speech, and a practice of sex discrimination into a legal entitlement.

Catherine A Mackinnon,
Feminism Unmodified: Discourses on Life and Law

It makes an interesting comparison to note the different approaches taken by three different civil rights organisations to the question of redefining pornography or denying women their right to freedom.

The Irish Council for Civil Liberties set out their position in their discussion document on the Video Recordings Bill, as follows:

The essential condition of liberal democracy is that Government show equal respect to its citizens. To have equal respect for adult citizens is to have respect for their capacity to live independent lives. Government must therefore protect the equal liberty of citizens to express themselves, and this protection should cover expression which moral or political convention considers wrong or offensive. However, we do not say that free expression is an absolute value; the State may curtail expression, but it should not do so save only to the extent that particular expressions are directly invasive of the rights of determinate people.

Moving on, it states:

In our view, the canons relating to what might be read, or heard, or seen, derive from a religiously guided mind-set—the (Video Recordings) Bill, is after all, a present to the Knights of St Columbanus—and seeks ultimately to define what is unthinkable by closing off to us what is deemed to be unwatchable.'

Irish Council for Civil Liberties,
'Video Recordings Bill 1987—A Noxious Form of Paternalism',
Position Paper, Dublin: undated.

'To have equal respect for adult citizens is to have respect for their capacity to live independent lives.' Does this not apply to women too? Does the ICCL not know that women are also human beings? Are they saying that it is safer to deny us our human right to freedom from sexual objectification, subordination, violation and violence, rather than seem to be bed-fellows with Knights of Columbanus? Does the concept of 'liberal democracy' not also apply to women's quality of life?

That women continue to embrace such spurious tolerance is recognition of a system which has carefully manipulated and groomed us to see ourselves as 'acceptably' oppressed, economically, politically and sexually. Today, society's two-tiered attitude to pornography is the acceptable face of appeasement. Man disposes. Woman is disposed of.

On 22 January 1986 as the US Attorney General's Commission on Pornography drew to a close, and the conclusion was unavoidable that there were indeed links to be found between pornography and violence towards women, Andrea Dworkin gave her evidence.

In the course of her testimony, she spoke of the things done to women in the name of freedom of expression and freedom of speech. She spoke of the profits made from the consequent films make around their degradation, rape, mutilation and death.

She spoke of 'the collusion of the American Civil Liberties Union with the pornographers, which includes taking money from them. It includes using buildings that pornographers own and not paying rent, it includes using pornography in benefits to raise money. It includes not only defending them in court but also doing publicity for them, including organizing events for them, as the Hugh Hefner First Amendment Awards is organized by ACLU people for Playboy.' (Letters from a War Zone).

Andrea Dworkin, in her evidence, describes how these civil libertarians took real pride, and earned great financial rewards, working to protect the pornographers' trade in women and children, while publicly seeming to be disinterested protectors of civil liberties and free speech.

She asserted that 'they have convinced many of us that the standard for speech is what I would call a repulsion standard. That is to say, we find the most repulsive person in society and we defend him.' Subsequently, one million dollars were spent by the pornography industry creating hysteria about freedom of expression, censorship and feminists interfering in the sexual rights of men.

In Britain, following two years of deliberations and consultation with other groups, in 1989 the Executive Committee of the UK National Council for Civil Liberties voted democratically to put forward at their AGM a motion on pornography already referred to. Part of this motion reads:

> This AGM recognises that, because pornography represents deep-seated sexism, and because of the nature of the power of the pornography industry itself, the campaign against pornography is unlikely to be successful through public debate alone. It therefore resolves that NCCL should consider the kinds of specific legislation (both civil and criminal) which could be enacted to curb the production and distribution of pornographic material; material which should be narrowly defined as that which sexualises violence and the subordination of women.

> NCCL, London, 1989

NACROPA (The National Campaign for the Reform of Obscene Publications Act) are a group affiliated to the NCCL, who have been loud and dogmatic in their anti-censorship stand. They had their own motion, to be debated at the 1989 AGM. But their motion stated, succinctly:

Catherine Itzin; Termination of membership of NCCL.

This was a tactic designed to undermine and, if possible, overturn the executive's motion on Pornography. Catherine Itzin is an elected member of the NCCL executive, and a member of their Women's Rights Committee. As co-founder of The Campaign against Pornography and Censorship, she has long held the belief that pornography promotes sexual inequality towards women and is therefore a civil rights issue which should be addressed by the NCCL.

During NACROPA's presentation to the AGM of their motion on Catherine Itzin's 'termination' they launched into an unprecedented personal attack on her to which Catherine Itzin herself bears witness. NACROPA lost the motion.

The next day, during the debate on the pornography motion, NACROPA again tried to discredit and intimidate NCCL (UK) members who spoke in favour of the motion. An audience of almost 200, completely alienated, hissed and booed the NACROPA representative. It was an extraordinary incident, underlined by the final vote in favour of the NCCL (UK) motion—104–89 in favour.

The motion on pornography put forward by the NCCL (UK) Executive is now official NCCL (UK) policy. It is a major, historic victory, not only for women, but also for men. In the straightforward choice between two censorships: censorship of women and women's civil liberties, or the censorship of pornography, in a democratically taken vote, women's freedom was deemed to be the priority.

During the course of the debate, it was revealed to the AGM that one of the committee members of NACROPA was the managing editor of Penthouse. So there we are; history once again repeats itself. The forces marshalled against both Andrea Dworkin in the USA and Catherine Itzin in the UK were born of the same seed. Hell hath no fury like a vested interest (masquerading as an anti-censorship lobby) scorned.

> Pornography is the graveyard where the Left has gone to die. The Left cannot have its whores and its politics too.
>
> Andrea Dworkin

V

A civil rights issue for women

> All citizens shall, as human persons, be held equal before the law. **Article 40.1**
>
> The State guarantees in its laws to respect, and, as far as practicable, by its laws to defend and vindicate the personal rights of the citizen. **Article 40.3**
>
> No citizen shall be deprived of his personal liberty save in accordance with law. **Article 40.4.1**
>
> The State shall strive to promote the welfare of the whole people by securing and protecting as effectively as it may a social order in which justice and charity shall inform all the institutions of the national life. **Article 45.1**
>
> *Bunreacht na hEireann/The Constitution of Ireland.*

Down through history, men have celebrated their feelings about women through subjugation, slavery, rape, battery, murder, unable to differentiate their feelings about women from their feelings about sex and violence. They don't express these feelings verbally. Instead, liberals intellectualise vaguely about 'freedoms', human 'rights', 'freedom of expression'. They speak of these 'freedoms' as though they were a common experience for women, and they hope we won't see through such hypocrisy. In public they address large meetings on censorship and pornography, pointing (always pointing) an index finger at the audience as they insist that the existence of pornography is the lesser of the two evils, and therefore, (of course) must be permitted to exist. What they don't state to their audience, but what they mean is that, anyway, sex and violence and women go together.

Like Rambo? and 007? and *Presumed Innocent* and and and and and and and.

And because we don't disagree they assume we agree. They read our silent dissent as silent assent.

Pornography is the theory; rape is the Practice

Others attack and, frequently, murder women to express the interfacing of these feelings. Through daily actions they tell us we are worthless. ('She was nothing' said a fourteen year old, part of a large gang, who had just raped and beaten a young woman in Central Park, New York. *The Sunday Times*, 30 April, 1989). They love death, celebrating it on the streets, in the cinema, at the art gallery, in the books they read, on the battlefield. Life without death would be life without meaning. Ted Bundy killed many, many women, and before he went to his own death he laid the blame for his actions squarely on his addiction to hardcore pornography.

Pornography is the theory; rape is the Practice

But when is murder not murder? Yes, you've got it! When it is freedom of speech and expression. thus, while it is illegal to actually kill a woman in the course of making a 'snuff' film, (and if you're found, and if you are charged, and if you are convicted, you can be jailed for life,) it is most certainly not illegal to market that movie as entertainment for men. The killing is illegal, but the film of the killing is protected as 'freedom of speech', These are interesting 'freedoms' to have access to, and clearly you have access to them only if you are male, because what these freedoms are expressing is mysogyny. Their message is succinct: we hate women, we hate women enough to rape them, degrade them, subjugate them and exterminate them.

Apparently, the victims of these freedoms have no rights whatsoever. Isn't this an odd thing? How can this be?

Pornography is the theory; rape is the practice.

Whether we like it or not, Irish society is organised on an assumption that men are altogether better at most things than women. In other words we live in a male supremacist culture. Male supremacy is either divine or natural, depending on whether you are hearing the story from the Catholic Church or your next door neighbour. In our woman-hating society, which marginalises us beyond contempt ('Get married again... you're young enough and good looking enough to get married again' said our Taoiseach/Prime Minister to a widow seeking a small increase in the widow's pension. *The Irish Times* 10 June, 1989), rape is well-established, systematically practiced and ideologically endorsed.

Irish social standards and Irish legislation have never embodied principles and behaviours that respect the sexual rights of women. Nowhere, in recent times, has this been more clearly highlighted than in 1985. Then we watched, in total helplessness and desperation, the degradation and humiliation and psychic extermination of Joanne Hayes, spelled out in clear judicial language in the Kerry Babies Report. Following a decade of progress brought about by the women's movement, this was the light at the end of the tunnel for the mysogynists, and they haven't looked back since. Not once. Since then, the sexual colonisation of our bodies has been enshrined in male-dominated legislation and legislators:

- who refuse us the IUD
- who refuse us non-directive pregnancy counselling
- who refuse us the right to choose abortion
- who drafted a Video Nasties Bill which omits to define or even investigate pornography
- who refuse to fund, with degrading but but buts, our Rape Crisis Centres
- who refuse our homeless children shelter and support
- who advise battered wives that they must have 'real' bruises (and not just sexually abused children) before they can be admitted to a refuge
- who support a political and legal infrastructure which tells us, contrary to what has been our experience, that there is not such a things as rape within marriage
- who closed down the Sexual Assault Unit for children, where immediate and sympathetic identification, help and

support was on offer whether the child had been sexually abused inside her home or outside

Pornography flourishes in such fertile soil.

We have social subordination, because women are not equal in this society and one of the ways that you can tell this is by the quality of our silence. We do not protest as we are forced to watch our bodies, and bits of our bodies, exploited and violated hour by hour, in newspapers, on advertisement boardings, on television, in magazines, from the top of buildings, in the workplace, in the parks, as we walk, drive, jog or sit at home. What are we to do as we sit with loved ones who cheer and clap and grunt as they view the violation of our bodies?

If such things were done to cats and dogs there would be uproar, and demands for legislation to curb such practices. If such things were done to men they would certainly be called 'unnatural' and 'perverted'. But the male-supremacist assumption is that the use of women in pornography is the sexual will of women, expressing their sexuality, their character, their nature. But our silence is not the silence of consent. Through our silence we register our despair at the quality of our everyday environment.

Pornography is the theory, rape is the Practice

No issue concerning women can be discussed as if we had contributed to the development of law, to the enforcement of law, or to the ethics of the law. The law does not work in our interests. It does not support our civil rights and liberties as sexually self-determined people, participating in culture, power and the creation of values, because we do not have any such civil rights or liberties. We do not have bodily integrity, or inviolability, or even, for god's sake, equality before the law. And, knowing this, our neo-leftist liberals, staunch upholders of basic human rights, defend the 'rights' of the pornographer and his clientele.

Fundamental to this male defence of pornography is the placing of an enemy in the anti-pornography anti-censorship camp, and, inevitably, in Irish society, we have women who, collaborating with the enemy, defend pornography and its representation of freedom of speech and freedom of expression. Of such women Susanne Kappeler writes:

They speak the language of liberalism, protecting the liberties men take in their free self-expression at the expense of women's human rights. She speaks the language of conservatism which conserves the privileges of men. But she does not speak the language of the experts. Because here the experts are the victims, and they have vocally and graphically defined what pornography is, what it concerns and does not concern. And it is here that the civil rights issues is most easily clarified. And the pornographers who put forward a woman to speak out for male rights and then quote her as an example of 'a fully liberated woman' are dealing in nothing more than tokenism. It is tokenism at its worst and most illogical and it is of no great consequence as an argument of 'counter-examples.'

Women defending pornography symbolise the internalisation of male oppression.

If we, as a society, are to combat the racism, sexism and oppression inherent in pornography, we must treat it as a civil rights issue for women, demanding appropriate legislation. We need this legislation because it tells us that, as a body of women, we have worth in this society. Otherwise, as Dworkin writes, when your rape is entertainment, your worthlessness is absolute. You have reached the nadir of social worthlessness.

> We dreamed that women might be taken to be so extremely human that one would know, even without laboratory evidence, that where a woman is diminished in her integrity, in her rights, humankind is diminished because of it.
> And we thought that it might even be possible that a woman could be so human that even the law, which is not big on recognising human beings, might recognise her as being human enough to deserve equal protection under the law.

> Just that.
> Human.
> Not a smidgen more.
> Just that.

> Andrea Dworkin, *Letters From A War Zone*

References

Brownmiller, Susan. *Against Our Will*. Harmondsworth: Penguin, 1976.
Cameron, Deborah and Elizabeth Frazer. *The Lust To Kill*. London: Polity Press, 1987.
Caputi, Jane. *The Age of Sex Crime*. London: The Women's Press, 1988.
Carter, Angela. *The Sadeian Woman*. London: Virago, 1979.

Chester, Gail and Julienne Dickey. *Feminism and Censorship*. London: Prism, 1988

Dworkin, Andrea. *Pornography: Men Possessing Women*. London: The Women's Press, 1981.

Dworkin, Andrea. *Letters From A War Zone*. London: Secker and Warburg, 1988.

Everywoman. *Pornography and Sexual Violence: Evidence of the Links*. London: Everywoman, 1988.

Gamman, Lorraine and Margaret Marshment. *The Female Gaze*. London: The Women's Press, 1988.

Griffin, Susan. *Pornography and Silence*. London: The Women's Press, 1981.

Greer, Germaine. *The Madwoman's Underclothes*. London: Picador, 1986.

Gubar, Susan and Joan Hoff. *For Adult Users Only*. Indiana: Indiana University Press, 1989.

Jeffreys, Sheila. *Out of Focus*. (K. Daniels ed.) London: The Women's Press, 1987.

Kappeler, Susanne. *The Pornography of Representation*. (K. Daniels ed.) London: Polity Press, 1988.

Kelly, Liz. *Surviving Sexual Violence*. London: Polity Press, 1988.

McCafferty, Nell. *A Woman To Blame: The Kerry Babies Case*. Dublin: Attic Press, 1987.

Morgan, Robin. *The Demon Lover*. London: Methuen, 1989.

Steinem, Gloria. *Outrageous Acts and Everyday Rebellions*. London: Fontana, 1984.

Walsh, Deirdre and Rosemary Liddy. *Surviving Sexual Abuse*. Dublin: Attic Press, 1989.

A note on the author

Clodagh Corcoran is a writer, bookseller and political activist, especially in sexual politics in Ireland. She lives in London, is divorced and has two daughters.

2

HAS THE RED FLAG FALLEN?

The Fate of Socialism in the 1990s

Helena Sheehan, 1989

For those who have struggled for socialism
when the days were dark
when the tide went out
Who have resisted the pressures to recant
who were still there when others were gone.

For those who are still there
who have the clarity and courage
to come to terms with the times
without succumbing to its deceptions and seductions

For those who have been
and may yet be
my comrades.

Introduction

The eighties have been hard times for the left. On a world scale, the tide seemed to have gone out on us. We sometimes felt washed out and left high and dry on abandoned shores, while a tidal wave of reaction threatened to overtake all the progressive advances of recent decades in a blatant backlash against socialism, feminism, secularism and virtually every cause ever championed by the left. The red flag began to look tattered and torn and trampled into the dust by the relentless rush of the new right levelling whatever stood in its path.

For my generation, who moved to the left in a time of upsurge and felt that the world was ours to reshape, these have been dark days. History, which once seemed so malleable in our hands, suddenly became so recalcitrant and resistant to our touch. No matter how hard we continued to struggle, the world moved on in a direction disdainful of our desires.

On the days when I felt most acutely the weight of our defeat, a poem of Brecht[1] came often to my mind:

You tell us
It looks bad for our cause.
The darkness gets deeper.
Our powers get feebler.
Now, after we have worked for so many years,
We are in a more difficult position
        than at the start.

But the enemy stands there,
        stronger than ever before.
His powers appear to have grown.
Indeed, he has taken on
        an aspect of invincibility.

We, however, have made mistakes.
There is no denying it.
Our numbers are dwindling.
Our slogans are in disarray.
The enemy has twisted our words
beyond recognition.

But what is now false of what we said?
        Some of it? All of it?
Whom can we still count on?

Are we just left over,
        thrown out of the living stream?
Shall we remain behind?
Understanding no one
        and understood by none?

Or have we just got to be lucky?

This you ask.

Expect no other answer than your own.

These questions I have asked. The answers I am struggling to
set forth, although they draw on sources far larger than
myself, are none other than my own. This is not to say they
might not be those of others as well. I write in the hope that it
might be so.

The odds against socialism
Brecht's poem, written in an earlier decade when the tide also
seemed to have gone out, captured so acutely the stress I have
felt as a socialist in these times when the odds against
socialism seem to have mounted, sometimes to the point of
insurmountability. Capitalism has never seemed a more

formidable force and socialism has never seemed in a weaker position to challenge it.

Indeed, the mass media daily have presented a picture of socialism being dismantled on a grand scale. The socialist experiment has been portrayed as having played itself out and finally thrown up leaders who have seen the superiority of the capitalist way and decided to go for it. The world is going our way, the leaders of the free world have declared. The iron curtain has come tumbling down. The Kremlin has been conquered without a single marine opening fire, without a single ICBM being launched.

It unravels before me like a nightmare. No more the red flags flying. No more the heads held high and the fists clenched and voices raised to the strains of 'The Internationale'. No more the larger-than-life murals of workers and soldiers and peasants marching into the future shaping the world with the labour of their hands and hearts and minds. Now it is to be Mickey Mouse and Coca Cola and Michael Jackson and Saatchi & Saatchi.

Within the capitalist world, the socialist voice challenging from within seemed to have gone silent. We have been presented with one-time socialists seeing the error of their ways and singing the praises of capitalism, with left-wing parties moving so far to the right as to jump centre. They have learned, not only to live with the market, but to love it. The electorate, they say, dont want to hear all this dreary talk about production and labour and collective solidarity and class struggle. They are individuals who shop at Next and wear designer labels and buy shares. They identify themselves more as consumers than producers in a pluralist, post-modernist, post-Fordist world.

So the story goes: the old left has failed. The new left has failed. The next left that is taking shape is determined not to fail, but how left is it? Would it leave capitalism intact? Has it given up on socialism? This I ask. To come to terms with the present and future, is it necessary to be so over-anxious to shake off the socialist past? Must the next left be so dismissive of the last left?

Designer socialism
In Western Europe, I witness the debut of designer socialism in sections of this new look left. I don't mind the clipboards

and Filofaxes and Amstrads and attention to sophisticated televisual techniques. In fact, I welcome these things. There is nothing in our socialist principles requiring us to be tacky. We need the best design and the most efficient techniques that are compatible with the sincerity of our convictions. I don't mind the ads for mugs and T-shirts and video cassettes in *Marxism Today*. However, I do mind the deeper shift from production to consumption, from a politics of class struggle to a politics of declassed citizenship.

They scoff at men who drink pints in pubs and have stains on their ties who think that the working class has some special role to play on the stage of history. The working class is disappearing and class consciousness is evaporating even faster, they say; therefore we must make our appeal to those who do not see themselves as members of a class, to milieu groups whose material needs have all been met. The male, manual worker is yesterday's man, says today's man, as he rolls up the sleeves of his baggy Miami Vice suit with such smugness on his stubbled face. Meetings and agendas and resolutions and wage claims and GNPs are so boring, says today's woman, clad in the latest post-everything pastiche. They give off such an air of knowingness. After all, they have read Pynchon novels and they have seen Paris, Texas. They can discourse about Derrida and deconstuction, about floating signifiers with no signified. They know that grand narratives are out and market segmentation is in.

But do they know what class actually is? Do they know anything about the fundamental connection between production and consumption? Do they know from where the standard of living they take for granted has actually come? Must acknowledging the ascendency of the yuppie ethos entail assimilating its perceptions and accepting its values?

Perestroika and glasnost

In Eastern Europe, I see the spoiled children of socialism.They take for granted everything that socialism has given to them and turn on it for everything that it has not given to them. They long for everything that is other than what socialism has been until now. They idealise free enterprise and pop culture; indeed, they idealise capitalism itself, seeing only the consumer luxury and closing their eyes to the exploitation on which it is based.

The policies of glasnost and perestroika have brought

ferment to spheres that had gone stagnant and brought masses of people to believe that their society was theirs to create and re-create. But must this mean evaluating negatively everything that has been evaluated positively until now? Does the Soviet Union really need Mickey Mouse and McDonald's hamburgers? I know that we live in an interconnected world and I believe in the flow from one culture to another, but when they look from east to west, do they have to take the worst of our world? Why do they ignore feminism and go only for beauty contests and first ladies?

The frontlines of the south
I also feel the force of the long dark struggle echoing from the south of the world and the questions it poses to the north. I look into deep dark eyes that wonder if the beacon they have seen shining before them is going dim. I hear voices asking what de-ideologised foreign policy means for their sisters and brothers crossing borders under cover, awaiting trial or serving life sentences in South Africa, what it means for fragile frontline states striving towards socialism against all the pressures of a world capitalist order bearing down on them and amidst constant sabotage in a regional war zone.

Are they to be abandoned by both east and west as third world liberation movements are no longer in fashion? Will first world socialism seek only to redistribute from within the social product taken from the third world? Will second world socialism become so preoccupied with its own security and standards of living as to turn away from its practice of inter-nationalist duty?

Will the new emphasis on universal human rights be a bland blanket to smother the burning exigencies of class/gender/racial struggle? Will the euphoria over market forces block out the sight of the devastation they engender? Will the lists of piecemeal, short-term reforms replace the objective of expropriating the expropriator?

Was it for this, I ask myself, that men and women gave their sweat, their tears, their blood, their lives? Was it for this that they led clandestine hunted lives or were shot in the streets? Was it for this they endured prison or exile or died of dysentery in the bush? Was it for this that they stormed the Winter Palace? Was it for this that they buried their dead in the valleys of Spain? Was it for this that they battled in the hills of Hercegovina?

Was it for this that my own generation marched on the Pentagon, picketed the Miss America contest, cut sugar cane in Cuba, had our heads battered in Chicago or were fired upon at Kent State? Was it for this that we have marched so many times to Leinster House, to the US Embassy, to the Department of Foreign Affairs? Was it for this that we have risked our careers and our security, endured the wear and tear of an endless round of meetings in cold rooms, spent so much of our adult lives studying and writing and attending weekend schools?

Left on the left
So many have fallen by the wayside. Those of us who are left on the left have to ask ourselves so many hard questions. The world has moved on, but what exactly has changed? What is now false of what we said? Some of it? All of it? We may have been marginalised, but were we wrong? Capitalism has prevailed, stronger than ever, and has proved to be a far more resilient system than we ever imagined, but has our critique of capitalism been refuted? Socialism may seem to be falling apart and pushed off the agenda, but has the need for it been superseded?

To answer such questions, I retrace my steps. I push myself to sort out what socialism is, what brought me to it, what has sustained me in it and what I am to make of it now. Apprehensively I ask: Has the red flag fallen? What has become of that tradition which turned my world upside down and set my mind racing and my blood surging? Will my generation be the last to sing:

> The people's flag is deepest red.
> It shrouded oft our martyred dead,
> And ere their limbs grew stiff and cold,
> Their hearts' blood dyed its every fold.
>
> Then raise the scarlet standard high.
> Beneath its shades we'll live and die.
> Let cowards flinch and traitors sneer.
> We'll keep the red flag flying here.

Dyed with the blood of women and men who set out to expropriate the expropriators, the red flag has been for generations the symbol of hope that a new world could be built from the ashes of the old. Must we abandon that hope now?

27

The red flag

Although I grew up under the star-spangled banner and then the tricolour, the red flag has come to be the central symbol of my own hopes. It was the cause of socialism which seized my imagination and stirred my blood as nothing else could and became the fundamental loyalty of my life.

Why?

Everyone who has come to socialism has come to it in their own way, rooted in the experience of their own lives, their own time, their own place. The trajectory of my own transformation was not altogether atypical, given the axis from which I began to explore the terrain of the times and to see my own story within a larger story. In its broad outlines, it is the story of the sixties generation.

It began with specific issues. First it was racism. We joined our white hands with black ones and we sang 'We Shall Overcome'. Then it was sexism. We raised consciousness and we raised tempers and we called ourselves Ms. Then it was ghetto poverty and then it was the Vietnam war and then it was the whole third world. It was, as we came to see it, a seething scenario of an inequitable division of labour and distribution of resources at home and imperialist wars to maintain the same abroad.

For those of us who were Catholic, all of this was underpinned by the relativisation effect of Vatican II in which so much of what had been considered absolute was suddenly discovered to be relative, so much of what had been thought immutable was suddenly made mutable. This atmosphere of rethinking and adapting to modernising modes and mores within the church was crucial to those of us who were its children, even if we took it far beyond the boundaries of what even the most liberal theologians ever intended and many of us soon found ourselves outside its doors altogether.

A momentum was building and gathering mass and velocity. We were no longer just civil rights supporters or feminists or agnostics or anti-war activists. We were no longer liberals who wanted to reform the system. Shocking not only our elders, but even ourselves, we began to think of ourselves as revolutionaries who wanted to transform the system in a most fundamental way. Questioning that began in response to particular injustices swelled into a critique of capitalism, a critique which saw racism, sexism, poverty and war, no longer as isolated phenomena occurring in spite of the system, but as interconnected manifestations emerging because of it.

From this critique of capitalism came a new curiosity about socialism, which brought various strands of the new left into a new relation to the old left. In America, the cold war had created a chasm very difficult to bridge. In Europe, however, where I have lived since the early seventies, the gap between the old and new narrowed considerably. Ireland may have seemed an unlikely place to have become a socialist, but the political subculture of the Irish left has provided an atmosphere in which I have grown, argued and struggled, a base from which I have reached out to a wider world and refined my understanding of what socialism is and its place in the agenda of our times.

So what is it and where does it fit into the world looming ahead of us?

There is a crying need for clear definitions, both of socialism and capitalism. There is so much loose and lazy talk which identifies capitalism with buying a house and wearing a suit and socialism with concern for the poor, higher social welfare payments and increasing aid to the third world. There is also such complexity in our world and such a clutter of contending theories all analysing it in such contradictory ways, many of them doing more to mask the underlying realities than to shed light on them. It has never been so difficult to see structures and to see them clearly and to see them whole. There is a need for definitions which penetrate to the most fundamental structures and not flit about on the periphery, which convey what capitalism is and what socialism is in structural terms.

Capitalism: crisis and contradiction

Capitalism is a mode of production based on the private ownership of the means of social production, distribution and exchange. It is a system giving primacy to the free play of market forces propelled by the drive for maximum profitability with minimum risk in the shortest time.

Capitalism generates a fundamental class division between those whose wealth comes from ownership of the means of production and those whose livelihood depends on their labour.[2] The illusion of equivalent exchange on the free market masks the structural inequality of class between those who produce and those who appropriate that production, between those whose position in the marketplace is based on what they are paid for their labour and those whose position is based on what they own, which is the accumulation of what the surplus value created by labour has produced.[3]

Capitalism came into being with the struggle of the revolutionary bourgeoisie to free production from feudal restriction. Capitalism gradually replaced feudalism, a social order in which ownership and power were founded on blood and land, with a social order in which ownership and power were based on buying and selling.

Capitalism achieved an unprecedented concentration of productive forces and advanced civilisation, creating institutions of parliamentary democracy, mass literacy, scientific and technological development and the highest standards of living that the world has ever known.

Capitalism achieved this and continues to achieve this at the cost of the most severe inequalities that history has ever known. Capital accumulation in Europe and North America was built upon the expropriation of land and raw materials from Africa, Asia and Latin America and on the exploitation of labour both at home and abroad. Colonialism has given way to neo-colonialism, an even more efficient system of expropriation, which no longer depends on state power. It is not really nations that are colonised by other nations anymore. It is the earth and the majority of its people that are colonised by international finance capital.

Capitalism is engaged in one of the most radical phases of its history of periodic restructuring. It is embarked on a whole new cycle of capital accumulation, based on the international-isation of the world economy, the deregulation of market forces and the reconstruction of the productive process through new technology. In order to restore capital's rate of profitabity, which had been eroded through compromises forced by labour and liberation movements and through challenges to the first world's hold on land, labour and resources in the third world, capitalism is reorganising itself.

The economic crisis of recent years has been the result of a massive struggle over the re-allocation of the world's productive resources and a re-negotiation of the international division of labour. Cuts in public expenditure have been forced by the pressure to dismantle the public sector in so far as capitalism has outgrown its need for it and it has become an obstacle to futher profitability. The economic crisis is not the result of sudden scarcity in the world. The cuts are not caused by the world no longer being able to afford the same standards of education and health care as it previously had. The fact is that there is more wealth in the world than ever there was. The fact is that there has never been such enormous inequality in how that wealth is allocated.

The disparities in the distribution of the world's wealth can be indicated by the following statistics. According to figures based on a World Bank report in 1987[4], if we list the percentage share of the world's gross product according to the world's population in five groups ranging from the poorest to the richest:

poorest	20% have	1.8% of world's GNP
2nd	20%	2.4%
3rd	20%	3.6%
4th	20%	13.9%
richest	20%	77.9%

The developing world has 75% of the world's population,[5] but only:

17 % of the world's GNP
15 % of the world's energy consumption
30 % of the world's grain consumption
 6 % of the world's educational expenditure
 6 % of the world's health expenditure
 5 % of the world's scientific & technological capacity
 8 % of the world's industrial capacity

One man, Rupert Murdoch, owns more than eighty newspapers and magazines (not to mention film studios and television stations), whereas eight African countries don't even have one newspaper.[6]

In the most underdeveloped countries of the world, where land is the main source of wealth, 79% of the land is owned by 3% of the population.[7]

In Ireland, a neo-colonial country in an intermediate position between the developed and developing world, the twenty third richest country in the world, 5% of the population owns 72% of the wealth.[8]

These inequalities are inherent in the very structure of capitalism. The free play of market forces allocates $550,000,000 a year to a dealer in junk bonds in the US and $276 a year to a teacher in Tanzania. The free play of market forces generates a global system of trade in which the price of imported manufacturing goods rise and commodity prices fall, in which shareholders, who need never leave their swimming pools in Santa Barbara, live in luxury, while copper miners in Zambia and tea pickers in Sri Lanka struggle for subsistence.

Parasitic elements thrive effortlessly, consuming what they do not produce, while primary producers toil like Sisyphus rolling the rock up the hill, producing more and more to consume less and less. Some reap what they do not sow and leave others to sow more and more to reap less and less. Those who give least to the world take most. Those who give most take least. The theory is that each individual pursuing their own individual interests results in the greater good of all. It may seem that way on the floor of the stock exchange in New York, London or Tokyo, but that is not the way it looks from the fields and factories of Nicaragua, Nigeria or Nepal.

Capitalism of its very nature creates contradictions which cannot be overcome within its boundaries. It generates crises of overproduction and underconsumption caused by the drive to expand production and maximise profits and at the same time to minimise wages, resulting in the production of goods which the workforce who are also consumers cannot afford to buy. It creates massive unemployment in societies where there is work crying out to be done. It uses accumulated surplus value created by human labour to invest in technology to reduce its need for human labour and to cast out the class whose ancestors produced it from participating in its fruits. It wreaks havoc upon the earth whose resources have provided the basis for all it has produced. It destroys the very forces that have formed the very foundations of its creativity. Acknowledging all that capitalism has achieved, while realising that it is structurally incapable of utilising fully and fairly the constructive forces it has itself brought forth, socialism came into being.

Socialism: the way beyond

Socialism is a social order organised according to the principle:

From each according to their abilities,
To each according to their work and needs.

Socialism is a mode of production based on the social

ownership of the major means of social production, distribution and exchange. It is a system in which market forces are subordinated to an overall plan, which ensures that what is socially produced will be socially distributed and reinvested in the most efficient and equitable fashion.

Socialism has reduced the massive inequalities that exist in the world. It eliminates the class division between those whose standard of living comes from ownership and those whose standard of living comes from work. All live by their labour, except those who are unable to work who are subsidised according to their need. It ensures equality at the starting line, but not necessarily at the finish. It need not produce wage or status levelling, but should reward hard work and creative achievement and penalise parasitism and passivity in a system of material and moral incentives.

Socialism deals with the surplus value created by labour in a fundamentally different fashion from capitalism. Profit is not diverted into private accumulation and parasitic consumption, but reinvested in social production or redistributed in social consumption. Everything that is created by collective effort is collectively distributed, whether as wages, as social services or as social investment.

Socialism also is engaged in one of the most radical phases in its history of periodic restructuring. Perestroika represents the refinement of the relationship between central planning and market forces and the adaptation of socialism to an increasingly internationalised world economy. Experiments with new forms of social ownership are necessary to eliminate the log jams created by particular methods of planning riddled with inefficiencies and disincentives. Reassessment of the role of nationalisation is obviously necessary in a world in which the nation state is no longer what it once was, if for no other reason.

Capitalism and socialism are fundamentally different modes of production which generate fundamentally different social orders and fundamentally different world views. They are alternative ways of structuring not only our economy, but also our political institutions, our social customs, our cultural creations, our educational systems, our moral codes, our aesthetic values, our domestic lives, our sexual roles, our personal relationships, our psychological development, our patterns of thought and behaviour. The entire social order in which a person lives is given characteristic shape by the dominant mode of production, which has profound implications for the prevailing division of labour and the whole complex ideological apparatus flowing from it.

Capitalism has generated an increasingly specialised division of labour, which is not confined to the organisation of a factory, but reaches into the very formation of personality, shaping the very patterns of perception that prevail, giving rise to patterns of thought and behaviour that are ever more fragmented and distorted. It is a social order based not only on the maximum expropriation of surplus value but on the maximum dissolution of social bonds, decreasing access to totality, increasing atomisation of thought processes and behavioural norms. Capitalism begets the craziness endemic to our age.

Postmodernism in particular bears witness to the disintegrative power of late capitalism.[9] It is something in the very essence of our present social order which structurally inhibits integrated thinking, which undermines the very foundations of rationality and sanity and morality. It is something at the very core of contemporary experience which blocks access to totality, which keeps theory flying so far apart from experience and keeps experience groping so helplessly in the dark. Only by breaking its boundaries, only by penetrating to the very source of this societys inner tensions, only by perceiving the very mechanism generating this fragmentation, only by naming the system and taking it on, can the way beyond it be discerned.

Socialism is the way beyond. Integrated thinking, which touches all the bases, is not possible within the logic of capitalism. A vision of an alternative social order is a necessary matrix for alternative thinking. Only socialism, as a radical tranformation of our relations of production, as the foundation for a fundamental reorganisation of human energies, gives us the possibility of human wholeness.

Although capitalism and socialism need to be seen as strongly contrasting structural alternatives, it must be said that neither exists in pure form. There are many intermediate and transitional forms. Most existing capitalist societies have made concessions to socialist ideas under pressure from labour and liberation movements. The post-war edifice of nationalised industry and the welfare state in such countries as Britain and Ireland are such hybrids, as is even the USA, in so far as some regulatory mechanisms constraining the market are still in place. Social democratic regimes such as

Austria and Sweden are futher along the spectrum, combining more radical redistribution within a mixed economy of public and private ownership of the means of production.

Other countries such as Zimbabwe and Mozambique have chosen the socialist path, but are constrained in moving as far or as fast along it as they would choose, because of such obstacles as foreign control of the economy, sabotage and underdevelopment. Even countries further along that path such as Cuba and Vietnam have to contend for a long time to come with the legacy of underdevelopment and disruption. Not even the socialist countries in Eastern Europe, including the Soviet Union as the world's first socialist state with the longest history of socialist construction, are free from the pressures and constraints imposed by functioning within a world order still dominated by the capitalist mode of production.

It is possible to go only so far and no further in building socialism in one country as long as capitalism controls the commanding heights of the world economy. In a world more interdependent than ever this has never been more true.

It is not only countries that are intermediate or transitional forms. So are socialist movements within capitalist countries and so even are individual psyches within those movements and those countries.

Building global socialism
The strategy for achieving socialism must begin within ourselves and encompass the whole terrain that must be contested... from the struggle for the individual soul to the challenge to the citadels of world capitalism. It must be taken on in all of its dimensions.

Ideological struggle is a primary task. Capitalism rules most powerfully, not through coercion, but through consent, not through its armies and police forces and guns and nuclear weapons, but through its ability to define reality, to make its view of the world appear to be common sense. The task of socialists is to challenge its hegemony, its power to exercise intellectual, moral, political and economic leadership and to make its particular view of the world appear to be immutable and universal truth. The building of socialism begins with breaking that consent, undermining that hegemony, and winning consent for an alternative view of the world, gaining hegemony for alternative intellectual, moral, political and

35

economic norms.

Socialists need to break with old paradigms for achieving power. Old strategies of social democratic evolutionism or revolutionary insurrectionism are both obsolete.

The social democratic programme of piecemeal reforms only redistributes within severe limits and does not address the questions of taking on power at the commanding heights of the world economy. It also lacks a strong inner core and the vision to create a full blown socialist society and not just a socialist state.

The insurrectionist model, which involved seizing factories and storming government buildings, is an anachronism now. First of all, because real power isn't actually there any more, neither in locally or nationally based enterprises nor in nation states. Secondly, while parliamentary democracy is not an end point of human political evolution, it has been an advance in human history that must be built upon rather than destroyed. Thirdly, a real revolution must pervade the whole of civil society and reach deep into the psyche and not confine itelf to industry and institutions of state. This is a much more sustained and subtle struggle for power than a coup d'etat, but it is also far more solid.

Socialism must be built through making the long march through all the institutions of our society, our schools, our universities, our farms, our factories, our offices, our homes, our unions, our newspapers, our publishing houses, our radio and television, our theatres, both before and after achieving state power. We need to build the new within the shell of the old. We must not believe that socialism will suddenly spring into being full blown *ex nihilo* on the day we elect a socialist majority to the Dáil. Between now and then, and in order to bring that about, we need to bring the clarity and warmth of socialism into every dark and cold space within ourselves, within our own movement, within every corner of our society.

Our political culture in Ireland has been far too statist in its terms of political discourse, distracting from the complex political tasks within civil society on the one hand and from the power of global capital on the other. On the other hand, there has been a populist anti-statism that is more in the interests of those stripping the state from above than those looking for power from below. Unprecedented decentralisation at the top has been masked by a flurry of decentralisation at the bottom, squeezing out the middle level of institutions which have heretofore been at the centre of power. Simultaneous globalisation and localisation have displaced nationalisation on a grand scale, bringing the pressure for the dismantling of nationalised industry and the privatisation of the public sector in education, health, broadcasting, etc, indeed the erosion of the power of the nation state itself in the face of the power of stateless money. However, the nation state is not yet powerless and the defence of the nation state and the public sector is a vital bulwark of resistance in the present situation.

State power should be an important intermediate object-ive. The left in Ireland should build on the steady advances it has made in achieving socialist representation in Dáil Éireann and Seanad Eireann with a view to achieving an eventual majority and forming what might be a Labour Party/Workers Party government. It cannot simply take over the existing state apparatus, but must enter upon a course that will trans-form the state and the public sector in a socialist direction. But a socialist government and even a socialist transformation of civil society will not be enough to achieve socialism.

In Zimbabwe, for example, there is a socialist government and there is a process of socialist transformation underway encompassing its social, educational and cultural institutions. While a Marxist-Leninist party, ZANU-PF, has won massive popular support in elections and controls the state apparatus and exercises considerable (but not complete) hegemony within civil society, they do not control the economy. There is not social ownership of the major means of production, distribution and exchange, which are not only in private, but largely foreign, ownership.

There remains the problem of expropriating the expropriators, which cannot be done on any meaningful scale any more within the nation state, not even in the most powerful developed nations. Of the fifty greatest economic powers in the world today, only half are nation states and in the future it will probably be less.[10] Quite a few transnational corporations, such as General Motors, rank far ahead of nations such as Ireland. With capital flows being what they are and with power becoming increasingly more remote and impenetrable, how can what has been taken be taken back? We must tackle this most difficult question in detail, but certain things should be clear.

The answer to it must be on a global scale and involve

global forces. Nation states are still capable of functioning as power bases to regulate and mitigate the effect of global forces and ways to do so more effectively need to be explored. Generally, however, we cannot and should not resist internationalisation. We are already connected to the wider world in a different way than our ancestors, in a way that is positive as well as negative. We should struggle for a progressive internationalisation against an exploitative internationalisation We need to strengthen existing countervailing forces as alternative power bases to international capitalism: the existing socialist countries, the non-aligned countries, the socialist group in the EC, the OAU, SADCC and so on. If the world's debtor countries were to unite against the conditions of the IMF and to insist that more was owed to them in reparations than they could ever possibly owe, what might happen?

The new world situation has brought a reduction of world tensions, but the prevailing attitude is that it is the socialist world that must make all the concessions and will only become acceptable in so far as they are moving, like children taking their first feeble steps, in the direction of democracy, which is ludicrously used as a synonym for capitalism. The attitude of west to east is that it is they who must change and they are judged as getting it right only in so far as they approximate western practice. This must be turned around.

It has been perhaps the primary objection raised against socialism that it is undemocratic. Although this image of socialism has not been without foundation, it has nevertheless been a gross distortion. The smug identification of democracy with capitalism has masked the reality of a system in which real power has never been so far from people's grasp. The facile identification of socialism with denial of democracy and the representation of the new flourishing of democracy in the Soviet Union as a move away from socialism confuses distortions of socialism with socialism itself and the process of restoring socialism with destroying it. Gorbachev, truly one of the great leaders of our times, has been at pains to clarify this:

> We are not abandoning socialism…What we are abandoning is everything done in past decades that was not socialist.[11]

> If anyone thinks we are leading socialism to the ashtip of history, they are wrong.[12]

Socialists have been arguing for decades, not only that there is no real socialism without democracy, but also that there is no real democracy without socialism. How can there be democracy in a society in which there is private ownership of the means of social production? Even in the narrow terms of reference of parliamentary discourse, where there is most democratic ferment... in the US Congress, in the UK House of Commons, in Dáil Éireann or in the USSR Congress of Peoples Deputies? Who exercises greatest freedom of speech... a Fianna Fáil TD on *Questions and Answers* or a Communist Party deputy talking to the western press?

The new turn of socialism in Eastern Europe has been perhaps the strongest surge of promise breaking through the bleak eighties. If capitalism can restructure and renew itself, so can socialism. It is a process fraught with dangers, because formidable reactionary forces have been let loose. It must be so. They must be let loose and defeated by socialism for real and in the open. There is only an even chance of winning, given the seething underground resentment building up during years of repression, the dynamic of over-reaction that has set in now that they are above ground and the very real pressure of capitalist co-optation.

The failure of nerve of the party leadership in China in dealing with reactionary forces politically has resulted in the repression of progressive and reactionary forces alike. No doubt the west was moving in and playing its part in shaping the pro-democracy movement in China, but the leading edge of the movement was full of energy that was there to be harnessed for socialism and not against it. The problem is: The next time around, will they still be waving red flags and singing *The Internationale*?

The past and recent history of socialism has been full of both triumphs and tragedies. However, anyone who persists in saying that socialism has failed is either deceived or deceitful. The current wave of criticism and self-criticism of socialism is obscuring its enormous achievements. Even though it may lag behind capitalism in material productivity, because of its legacy of previous underdevelopment, and even though it is full of defects and self-inflicted disasters, it still represents a historically more advanced stage of human development that cannot be reduced to a historical cul de sac from which there is need to retreat and to catch up with capitalism. It has brought material and social equality on a vast scale such as history has never before known. It has put a considerable part of the world in the hands of the people who work in it. It is striving to evolve ways of building on this to make it ever more open, democratic and efficient.

In the meantime, the rest of the world is not in the hands of those who work in it. Those who say that class struggle is outdated are wrong. Those who say that the working class is disappearing are wrong. It is true that the workforce is dramatically changing, that it is less dominated by the salt-of-the-earth, grease-on-the-hands, spanner-in-the-back-pocket, donkey-jacketed male proletariat, that it is encompassing women using wordprocessors or teaching school, leaving their children at playschool after returning from maternity leave. The workforce may be better paid, more highly skilled, more educated, more female, more complex than it was before, but a computer programmer still stands in the same basic relation to the means of production as a labourer on a construction site. As long as one class works and another appropriates the fruit of their work, there will be reason to engage in class struggle. As long as there is capitalism, there will be a need for socialism.

New social forces coming onto the scene and adding to the complexity of our political culture do not invalidate class struggle or justify a false dichotomy between a workerist caricature of class and class struggle and a declassed pluralism of alternative political subjects with alternative agendas. New social movements growing up around the politics of gender, race and environment should broaden and deepen the socialist agenda and not displace it.

None of the problems they highlight can be decisively resolved within the capitalist mode of production. The ecological agenda, for example, requires social planning on a vast scale and generates imperatives that are antithetical to the fundamental capitalist imperative of maximum profitability.

Socialism and the liberation of women

Feminists often argue that socialism is just one more form of patriarchy. Although patriarchal attitudes persist in some socialists, there is a deep structural relationship between socialism and the liberation of women.

If we do not settle for a shopping list of particular demands on contraception, equal pay, child care and so on, and press to the core of the problem, we come to see that the source of the oppression of women is in the sexual division of labour and the whole ideological apparatus supporting it, which is inherent in class society and intensified under the capitalist form of class society. With increasing specialisation and the increasing separation of the public and private spheres along the lines of the separation of male labour from female labour, patterns of one-sided distortion of personality developed along the fault lines of definitions of masculinity and femininity parallel to the exclusion of women from the public realm and the exclusion of men from the domestic realm.

The liberation of women must be grounded in a radical break with the existing sexual division of labour. Women must re-enter the public realm and demand that men re-enter the domestic realm. There is no real liberation for women without labour, without participation in the realm of collective effort. Until work plays the same part in the lives of women as it does for men and women stop living off the labour and social position of men, things will never be right. It will not do to demand the right to decide whether to work or not to work. To have the right to consume what a society produces and to participate in deciding what a society does, it is necessary to contribute to what a society needs.

The full participation of the full potential labour force in social production and distribution is a structural impossibility under capitalism. Because it is inherently subject to booms and slumps and because its driving force is maximum profitability, it needs a reserve labour force and it needs a division of labour based on class, sex and race. This is not to say that many reforms cannot be achieved under capitalism, but the full liberation of women requires a thoroughgoing revolution in consciousness and in the patterns of everyday life grounded in a revolution in the relations of production. It requires an end to a social division of labour based on class, race and sex.

Exploitation resulting from such a division of labour goes much deeper than is often realised. It is not only that an individual is excluded from control of the labour process and denied the fruits of her/his own labour on the basis of class, race or sex (in the case of black working women, all three). It is being excluded from the whole apparatus of cognitive, cultural, technological power, being deprived of access to what has been produced by the collective labour of centuries, to the knowledge, culture and technology grounded in the surplus value created by generations of human effort.

Emancipation is not only being paid a fair price for individual labour, but being free to make our own the whole web of knowledge and culture and technolgy of the centuries and to recast it according to new norms free of capitalist, racist and sexist values. Only socialism provides the foundations for this.

We must not change its colour now

Socialism is about everything. An economist/reductionist/ soulless caricature of socialism as one enormous conformist factory is the substitution of a badly-drawn, black and white, two-dimensional diagram for the richness, colour and vitality of a full-blooded, three-dimensional life world. Socialism is a movement, not only for the socialisation of the means of production, distribution and exchange, but for the total transformation of human energies. Socialism is not only a different way of organising our economic activity, but a whole different way of thinking, experiencing, creating and coming together. Socialism is the only system able to give full scope to the full flowering of human personality, strong in the dignity that comes only from labour, reconciled to nature and to society. Socialism enables us to come together in our fullness and at our best, instead of preying upon each other in competition, dissipation and despair. Socialism is bread and roses and much more.

Socialism is possible, but it is not inevitable. History is an open process, full of real risk and real surprise. It is up to us. It is up to everyone to decide: Which side are you on? Capitalism or socialism?

The obstacles have multiplied and the stakes have never been so high, but perhaps our determination can rise to meet them. Hopefully, the song sung both at the Labour Party conference and in the Workers' Party election broadcast may be indicative of our strength:

> The higher you build your barriers
> The taller I become...
> Something inside so strong
> I know that I can make it
> Though you're doing me wrong, so wrong
> You thought that my pride was gone
> Oh no, something inside so strong

The more you refuse to hear my voice
The louder I will sing
You hide behind walls of Jericho
Your lies will come tumbling
Deny my place in time
You squander wealth that's mine
My light will shine so brightly
It will blind you...

Brothers and sisters
When they insist we're just not good enough
We know better
Just look them in the eyes and say
'We're going to do it anyway.
We're going to do it anyway.'

Perhaps, after all the difficulties and disappointments and defeats, we are going to do it anyway. Perhaps our time will come again. Perhaps from the living stream still flowing from the old left and the new left a great burst of a newer left will rush forth into the next decade. Perhaps it comes in thirty year cycles. The thirties was a red decade and so was the sixties... so might be the nineties.

The red flag is tattered and torn, but it still flies.

It waved above our infant might
When all ahead seemed dark as night
It witnessed many a deed and vow
We must not change its colour now.

Notes

1 Bertolt Brecht, 'To a Waverer', *Poems 1913-1956*. London: Eyre Methuen, 1976.
2 Class is a category referring to the relationship to the means of production, distribution and exchange. It is a term for specifying someone's place in the social division of labour and distribution of resources. The great divide under capitalism is ownership or non-ownership of the means of production, distribution and exchange.
3 Surplus value is value produced by labour over and above wages paid for that labour and after the costs of production have been met.
4. *World Development Report*. Washington, DC: World Bank, 1987.
5 *Ireland in an Unequal World*. Dublin: Congood, 1984.
6 *Capitalism, Socialism and Development*. Gweru: Mambo Press, 1986.
7 *Land*. Gweru: Mambo Press, 1986.
8 Sean Byrne, *Wealth and the Wealthy in Ireland: A Review of the Evidence*. Dublin: Combat Poverty Working Paper, 1989.
9 Postmodernism is a cultural/intellectual trend rejecting modernist ideals of historicism, progressivism, rationalism, humanism. It

proclaims the end of grand narratives (eg, Christianity, Enlightenment, Marxism) and the collapse of the capacity of the contemporary subject to organise past, present and future into any sort of coherent experience, whether as biography or history. It celebrates incoherence, fragmentation, randomness, depthlessness, meaninglessness.

10 *Moto* May 1989.

11 Mikhail Gorbachev, *The Irish Times*, 16 June 1989.

12 Mikhail Gorbachev, *The Irish Times*, 18 May 1989.

A note on the author

Helena Sheehan was born in Philadelphia, lives in Dublin and holds dual Irish and American citizenship. A political activist, philosopher and socialist, she works as a freelance lecturer and writer. Her publications include *Communism and the Emancipation of Women* (1976); *Marxism and the Philosophy of Science: A Critical History* (1985); *Irish Television Drama: a Society and its Stories* (1987).

3

ANCIENT WARS
Sex and Sexuality

Ethna Viney, 1989

Introduction

When you stop to think about it, the extent to which sexuality rules a woman's existence is remarkable. Ever present in her adult life is evidence of her sexuality—the physical evidence of menstruation, contraception or pregnancy; childcare; and more abstractly, importunate love (romantic or lustful) and the price she has got to pay for its satisfaction—a lifetime of service unless she struggles against her fate. These are the obvious, despotic effects of sexuality, and ones that society considers 'natural'—hard luck on women, and all that. If, however, women are to do something about their inequality then they must understand the reasons for it. These reasons are not simple and they emerge from a culture of ancient lineage, which is full of misconceptions and prejudices. To express or articulate criticism of this culture is to be called 'manhating' (for, as we all know, it is a male culture), and it is impossible to avoid the slander, from both women and men, if one writes about the structure and component parts of women's inequality. The problem is that many women accept men's warped perception of womankind, or refuse to see the elements of oppression in it, either because the realisation would be too hard to bear, or because they insulate themselves within the cocoon of a personal relationship which is satisfactory for them.

Sexuality is a subject not easily or readily discussed in Ireland and when the word is used it takes on a variety of meanings. For the purposes of this pamphlet, and so that we all know what we mean, I use the word 'sexuality' in its dictionary definition of relations between the sexes, especially with reference to mutual attraction and to gratification of resulting desires. I intend to use both parts of this definition, and to show that the wider interpretation of 'relations between the sexes'—the general acts and attitudes of men towards women because they are women, and women towards men because they are men—is considerably influenced by the narrower one of sexual attraction and activity. It could be said that this is encroaching on the territory of the word 'gender', which means the cultural characteristics of the sexes, and around which a controversy—'Is gender biological or is it cultural?'—rages. However, gender is rooted in sexuality and I intend to show that sexuality is not only biological, but that it is also heavily cultural and governs the way the sexes treat each other. I also intend to show that while the high point of male sexuality is penetration and ejaculation, the climax of women's sexuality is the earth-shattering orgasm of giving birth, the Big O.

Culture

Our culture envelops us like an old and comfortable coat—no, more like a warm familiar room. It is hallowed by living, dear to us as part of our routine and our past, it is right. We are slow to change its organisation, because that is the way it has always been; we are used to the arrangement. It can exist side by side with change, new ideas and the search for truth. During periods of change, we cling to large portions of our culture, even the awkward or useless bits, almost unconsciously, because it is familiar. It gives us social stability and security, and a framework for our lives. By culture I mean not just art and literature, but a broader context of the customs, practices and beliefs of the society in which we live: the way we communicate with each other; our working habits and leisure pursuits; religion, politics; how we solve problems and celebrate success; in a word, our attitudes to everything.

Culture is absorbed by all of us, as we grow up and as we grow older, from the society in which we live. The process of socialisation could be called 'conditioning', or more pejoratively 'brainwashing', but I prefer to call it 'internalising': we take in ideas and attitudes from the prevailing culture and make them our own, internalise them. I prefer that term because we co-operate, indeed concur, with the process, and it is therefore something over which we can exercise control. Debriefing oneself, however, is not easy; you need an overriding drive to do so. Even after a successful debriefing flashes of the old conditioning can return like the hallucinogenic relapses experienced by addicts.

Rooted deep within our culture is an attitude to women which can only be described as misogyny, a degrading and downgrading of women, which is based on their sexuality. In the course of this pamphlet I will make some tough criticism of our culture, of male culture, of men who maintain it and of the support we women give it. Many women will say that the men they know are not fiends who degrade or oppress women. They may be right. Some men do not; and it is likely that many of the women who are concerned about the problem of oppression, and who will read this text, will tend to know and favour those men who treat women with fairness. Indeed the oppressors and the degraders avoid engagement with women who challenge their position, or read pamphlets like this; they give them a wide berth when seeking a 'wife' or female companion. At the same time, let us not forget that even the fairest of men do little to challenge the prevailing culture which is the medium through which the subordination of women works.

For those who do not believe that there is a deeply ingrained streak in our culture that defines and degrades women in terms of their sexuality, I will recount an incident which happened to a friend of mine last summer. She was taking the bus from Heuston railway station to the centre of Dublin, and alongside her bus stood another, full of ten-year-old girls on a school outing. Seated behind her on the bus were two yobbos who carried on a conversation in revolting detail about the pleasures of raping these schoolgirls when they were ten years older. It is immaterial whether they really meant what they said, or whether they were merely chest-thumping for each other's benefit: they had the ideas and the vocabulary of sexual oppression, and a cultural context in which to express them.

Sexuality in Ireland
We are a society ambivalent about sexuality—we have celibate priests, a religion which forbids pre-marital sex and until the recent past, had generations of bachelors. Sexual expression is so narrowly confined to what is known as 'the sex act' or 'sexual intercourse', which is penile penetration of the vagina, that other expressions of sexuality such as affectionate touching and kissing are virtually dismissed; they are marginalised. This was not always the case. In the importunate youth of half the population of this country (the older half)—before the advent of the permissive society, the Pill and commonplace pre-marital sex—sexual expression

took a form which ranged from mild affectionate touching, such as holding hands, to heavy petting which stopped short of 'the sex act'.

Now male readers from that era will dispute the virtues of that period. They will tell of the pain of thwarted passion. But did they not talk themselves up to that passion in the first place? Did the passion not often start in competitive, macho male conversations; and did expectations not also play a major part in the arousal of these passions?

In Ireland, in the second half of this century, cultural attitudes to sexuality have undergone change. From the days of parish priests beating the hedgerows for courting couples when sex outside marriage was the paramount sin, and of women being castigated in confession for refusing intercourse to their husbands, there is now a somewhat more rational view of this human condition and its functions. However, with some people, a certain amount of prurience still attaches to the subject, a hangover from the severe repression of those bygone days. At the same time the state, on behalf of society, and even more so, the Catholic Church, try to regulate women's sexuality by controlling their fertility; there is legislation limiting the use of contraceptives, and an article in the Constitution forbidding the introduction of legislation relating to abortion. The contraception debate and the abortion referendum are the nearest this country has ever got to a long overdue discussion of sexuality; and these subjects are merely symptoms of a very narrow interpretation of what sexuality is really about.

Feminists are taking a close, sharp look at the role of women in our society, at their inferior status and oppression in a world of male supremacy, and at their apparent acquiescence in this situation. Are we oppressed because we are of the female sex, or because we are physically weaker? If the latter, why has there not been a mass rebellion in the ages when weapons provide an equaliser? And if being female is the reason, has it to do with our gender, which is the sum of our womanly characteristics; or is it because of our sexuality, our particular hormonal make-up and our ability to bear and feed children? Are men, perhaps, really superior?

What have feminists found in their quest for truth? They found that the roots of our oppression lie deep in our culture and in our psyches. It has been learned and imposed, assimilated and internalised, and condenses into a simplistic message: *men have needed to believe that they are superior to women, and we have been brainwashed into believing it too.* (If you don't believe that you have been brainwashed, ask yourself why you feel contempt for a man who dresses as a woman, and not for a woman who dresses as a man.) Our consent to this state of affairs has been obtained by socialisation which starts from the moment we are born and which operates through the components of our early small world—parents and friends, teachers, books and pictures, toys and clothes; and later on through the mass media (including advertising), and professionals such as doctors and psychologists. A few women, and fewer men, have gone some distance in debugging their minds; but overwhelmingly life rolls on with the caste of women regarded as inferior to the caste of men. Why?

Let's look first at our culture as it depicts and affects us, women and men. It is, in fact, two cultures, a pair of twins, complementary but not identical. The nature of women's culture is regarded as passive, weak, emotional, caring, helpful, co-operative, valuing friendship, not into dominating others, life-giving, inferior. Although some exceptions are allowed, women who depart from this image suffer disapproval or even punishment. Men's culture, on the other hand, is regarded as assertive, strong, unemotional, hierarchial, independent, death-dealing, superior. Again exceptions are allowed, but men who do not conform are generally despised. These different characteristics are regarded by the culture as given, and from them are derived the roles allotted. Women are the child-rearers, homemakers, servers and servicers; men are the providers, protectors, lawmakers: man, head; woman, heart.

Women's re-evaluation of themselves and of their culture is part of a process that has been going on for more than a century. Unfortunately, because feminism suffers generational recessions, at every re-emergence of their movement, women must again 'reinvent the wheel'. Over the past twenty years, in the current cycle of feminism, this process has been occurring in stages. Stage one began when women looked for equal rights with men, and found that control of their own fertility was essential. In stage two women started to invade the 'male world'. This meant adopting a male value system which did not always rest comfortably on their shoulders. It also meant doing two jobs because men did not make any significant attempt to enter the 'female realm'. Stage three is the cultural struggle now in progress, or more precisely in the process of discussion, which is women consolidating their own value system, accepting some values from 'male culture' and discarding others. Stage four will be designing a new culture, a revolutionary concept for women to undertake because it means redesigning personal lives and relationships.

For the past twenty years wherever a women's movement emerged, the main preoccupation has been with sexual politics. The emphasis has been on one or other aspect of biological sexuality—women's fertility, the mechanics of sexuality, sexual abuse and violence towards women—and the narrow interpretation of sexual preference. Sexual politics cover all areas of women's exploitation. Women are exploited and oppressed because of their sex, because they are biologically different from men, and therefore, can be grouped, tagged and treated in a particular manner. Persecuting identifiable groups is a power tactic that occurs with depressing regularity in history, and most dramatically in instances of racism; in the case of the African and Red Indian peoples and many others in colonial times; and, closer in time and place, in the case of the Jews in Nazi Germany, Blacks in South Africa and current sectarian killings in Northern Ireland.

But why do men want to exploit women? Why do men ridicule women and usually in reference to their sexuality? *What is it in the essence of women, in their sexuality, that has aroused a misogyny and antagonism which stretches back through history?*

History of Misogyny

A brief look back through human history reveals a strong, steely core of misogyny throughout the surviving records. The Old Testament of the Bible, the Homeric epics and the Tables of Ancient Rome are among the oldest historical writings, and together with our own Annals are the foundation on which European culture (including ours) grew. The Old Testament begins with the story of Eve in the Garden of Eden, and continues with one account after another of the exploitation of women. The story of Eve's role in 'the Fall' has been used as a stick with which to beat women for at least four thousand years. Yet, a careful examination of the Bible shows Adam to be just as much to blame as Eve for their separate sins of disobedience. The Bible account does not say that she knocked him down and forced the apple into his mouth. He succumbed to temptation just as much as Eve did. If he was unable to resist the temptation, that was his fault. Where was his much vaunted superiority?

The Bible story of the Fall was interpreted by the early Church fathers as an allegory in which partaking of the fruit from the tree of knowledge of good and evil was the discovery of sexuality, whereupon the eyes of Adam and Eve were opened and they knew that they were naked and they sewed fig leaves together to cover themselves. When God appeared, Adam ran whining to him: 'It was all her fault. She gave me the apple.' And He cursed both of them, laying sorrow and pain in childbirth on Eve because of her sexuality, and making her subordinate to Adam; and sentencing Adam to hard labour for his sexuality. For thousands of years po-faced priests, like Adam, have been laying blame on women, as daughters of Eve, for 'the Fall', and for everything else that went wrong since then. Are men not sons of Eve, and women daughters of Adam? What has happened to logic?

The Bible is full of horrendous tales of the oppression and exploitation of women, and of misogyny directly related to sexuality. For example, menstruating and post-natal women were (and in Jewish practice still are) considered unclean and unfit to enter the synagogue. Out of the hundreds of instances of disregard for and antagonism to women I will mention just two: Moses ordered the death of the sexually active (married) Midianite women captured in battle, and the sexual enslavement of the virgins (all males had been killed). Both Lot and the man of Gibeah sought to appease thugs who called at their house seeking to sodomise their male guests, by offering their virgin daughters to them instead, to satisfy their lust. Few interpret the Old Testament literally. It is regarded as an amalgam of folklore and stories handed down by word of mouth and, more than likely, distorted from the original facts by the time it came to be written. What is certain is that when it was written it reflected the culture of the time, a culture which has formed the basis of our own culture.

Jesus preached a kinder religion with equality for all believers whether women or men. In the persecuted Christian church of the early centuries women were accepted as leaders, priests and teachers of congregations. But in every century there were powerful and articulate male leaders who kept alive the misogyny of the Old Testament and of the Hebrew tradition, from Paul (who dipped his pen in his own brand of vitriol) Tertullian, Jerome, and Ambrose to John Chrysostom and Augustine. They all had a pathological aversion to sexuality, for the existence of which they blamed women.

As Christianity spread over Europe, it encountered other cultures with traditions of subordinating women, thus reinforcing a tendency of its own which had never really disappeared. Before and during the early Christian period in Ireland, women were classed with captives, slaves and drunks as 'senseless'; but in later centuries, and through to the end of the Middle Ages, Irish women, at least among the upper and educated classes (who kept the records), made political and legal gains—in property rights, equality in marriage, the right to divorce—rights which were limited by Norman influence and ended by the advent, in the seventeenth century, of English law.

Meanwhile Thomas Aquinas, at the centre of Christian power during the Middle Ages, added his tuppenceworth to keep the pot boiling, with a contempt for women's sexuality that has poisoned our society ever since. He decreed that the power of grace could never be transmitted to the female creature. Hence, being female came first among the disabilities which automatically disqualified a person from the priesthood, before being insane, enslaved, a murderer, illegitimate or crippled. The resounding echo of his prejudice still rings loudly through the Christian churches today when the Pope and other Churchmen try lamely to justify their own prejudice and misogyny. The Council of Trent, which established the rule of clerical celibacy, did so to preserve the clergy from 'the filth of impurity and unclean bondage'. Women's sexuality is still being used to keep them out of positions of authority in the Roman Catholic Church, and to maintain a celibate clergy.

But, said Aquinas, if women took vows of chastity, and foreswore sex, pregnancy and childbirth, they could achieve the dignity of men. And many women of that period, those from the better-off families, followed that advice. They banded together in convents; not for the reasons the Church Fathers believed, I am sure, but to be free of the daily interference of men, to take charge of their own future and have dignity and honour.

They were the lucky ones; the women who didn't, and who were assertive, presumptuous or 'uppity', became the object of the greatest wave of lethal misogyny, that ever swept Europe—the witchhunts of the fifteenth and succeeding centuries. *Malleus Malificarum* (Hammer of the Witches), a document drawn up by two Dominican priests at the behest of the Pope at the end of the fifteenth century, became a powerful instrument of woman hatred. It contained all the traditional condemnations of women, their inferiority, evil inclinations and uncleanness, and then linked them to witchcraft, sorcery, heresy and demonology.

Women were sexually insatiable, they said, they copulated with the devil and he then gave them formulas for potions to cast spells on men. The two monks described in pornographic detail the orgies and lewdness of the witches' activities with the devil, and their fevered imaginings led them into even greater paroxysms of hatred for women. During a period of two centuries following their endeavours, hundreds of thousands of women, perhaps more than a million, were tortured and killed.

Today, someone exhibiting such mental antics would be termed psychopathic; and although to a large extent (except perhaps among fundamentalists) such demented fantasies have no public acceptance, the cultural attitudes that they encouraged remain. Paradoxically, in the two religions which evolved from Judaism and influenced attitudes to women in our hemispheres—Christianity and Islam—the founders intended equality for all followers. There are no texts in the Gospels of the New Testament or in the Koran calling for the suppression of women. In both religions the patriarchs went back to the Old Testament for their authorisation, subverting the intentions of the founders.

As in the centuries before the witch hunts, an unbroken tradition of misogyny can be traced through the social records of the intervening centuries. When women emerged from a period of severe oppression into one of comparative freedom, they may have thought that the improvement was permanent, as did the women of Iran before the fundamentalists took control. Historically, women's freedom has risen and fallen like the waves on the sea, or like the tides, making only imperceptible gains against the land with each flow and losing much of that gain at the ebb.

Take but one of the sexual oppressions visited on

women—rape. As we have seen, it has impeccable Biblical provenance, an accepted history, and it still flourishes. Considered feminist analysis sees rape as the product of male power, and its function the control of all women's sexuality by men. That is not a surprising conclusion when a successful act of intercourse is regarded in our culture as an effective remedy for female discontent. Many believe that a woman's psychic problems or unusual behaviour show a desire for rough sex ('a good fucking'). Once she has had it her exaggerated ideas will dissolve of their own accord.

It would seem at first glance that there are two types of rape: sex-inspired and power-inspired. But on closer examination power is at the core of both. The man who believes that a woman had been leading him on ('a cock teaser'), rapes her partly because he is aroused but also to show 'who is boss', to control her, to take revenge on her. Rape is a punishment for women who express their sexuality; and also for women who challenge men in what men consider their own areas of superiority. It can also be a simple declaration of men's superiority and power over women.

There are lesser examples of male control of women's sexuality which, in all societies, is surrounded by legal and cultural restraints. These are manifested in many different ways from Italian bottom-pinching to the chador of Islam; in the contempt for, and dismissal of, non-child-bearing women—'spinsters' and the old; in pornography and prostitution; coercive sex everywhere and laws regulating reproduction; the commercial use of women's bodies in advertising; in the inescapable promotion of sexuality and eroticism in pop music, films, advertising and pulp fiction. You will find it even in the nicknaming of Dublin's sculptures of women: 'the floozie in the jacuzzi', 'the tart with the cart', 'the hag with the bag'. Everywhere male sexuality is represented as dominant, female sexuality as passive and exploitable. Women's acceptance of this control is evident in the way that some have internalised it even at the expense of their health: for instance in the way they walk—hiding breasts in concave chests, walking from the thighs to keep their buttocks stationary. The free-striding, confident woman is a challenge to male pride and sexuality because he interprets her bearing as sexual, and he wants to suppress it.

In the midst of this sex-laden atmosphere, women must not be assertive, because their assertiveness is linked automatically to their sexuality and is seen as a challenge to men. 'Keep you heads down, girls!' is the message. Male reaction has always been either the arrogant, 'How dare such an inferior creature, whose functions are related to blood and guts, assert herself before the cleanness and integrity of my superior and cerebral person?' or the more aggressive. 'I'll show her who's boss; she needs a good fucking.'

Dependency, deference, discrimination, derision, despotism, unpaid service, rape and violence are the continuing, camouflaged characteristics of relations between men and women. Some say that this astonishing edifice of misogyny, of antagonism. of disdain towards and exploitation of women arose from the desire of men to know their own children; and some say that it derives from the monopoly that women have on childrearing. Others claim that the problem is caused by envy of women's role in reproduction (womb envy).

Most certainly, men's desire to know their children inspired actual, physical subjection of women; the only way men could be sure of knowing their own offspring was to hold the mothers in as close captivity as was practicable. Some researchers say that men resent the power that their mothers had over them in their infancy, and that they retaliate for that early impotence. If men were equally involved in child nurture, they say, then women would not be marked out for revenge.

The theory about womb-envy goes as follows: men, it says invented war as an antidote to womb-envy, giving themselves a role more important than that of women in the community: its protection against annihilation. Women might be important to the continuation of the species, but their efforts would come to nought if they were wiped out by enemies. It is a persuasive idea. Since records began, men's history glorifies war and martial cultures; and women's history, the history of social civilisation, has been ignored. We have got the evidence of our own eyes that female subordination is taught, and then becomes accepted as natural—a hallowed tradition—which is reinforced by warfare. We also observe that men, and only men, are taught to be aggressive in ordinary life, and rigorously trained in aggression for war. Humans are the only species that have institutionalised hostilities against each other. There are easier ways for men to know their children and to offset womb-envy than by war and exploitation. If these two conditions are its side effects, it is time we examined human sexuality in greater detail.

Human sexuality

When the campaigners of the Irish women's movement (and also those in other countries) began their struggle in the early 1970s, they found that their demands for equality of status and opportunity led back to factors relating to their sexuality. Man-serving, child-bearing and rearing, and the structure of the family within which these occupations took place, were what kept women dependent and poor. And women bought their place within that structure with their sexuality.

That was one way of putting it. Another way to define the situation was to say that the role of women in life was to rear children and provide sexual and personal service to a man; and this was best achieved in the family structure. (One can only say that the desire of men to know their children seemed to be matched by the great biological drive in women to have children, and both perpetuated an exploitative family structure.)

These were harsh definitions. They took no account of romance or love, or of the fact that when people lived off the land, in a primitive, cashless, subsistence economy, equality was possible between men and women in the family. In the twentieth century, economics had changed, and whatever way one looks at it, women lost out in the family situation, for when the rising tide of romantic love which swept them into it receded, they were like castaways on a desert island. Their responsibilities to their children (and in Ireland these were numerous) were as impassable as a trackless, craftless ocean. Rafts had to be built.

With great courage and daring, in 1971, fifty Irish women organised a trip by train from Dublin to Belfast to buy and bring back contraceptives which were then illegal in the Republic of Ireland. It was a public protest and carried out in a glare of media attention. The objective was to highlight the enslavement of women to a life of repeated pregnancies and the rearing of large families and to show that the law banning contraception was hypocritical and affected mainly the poor. Many who could afford it travelled regularly to Belfast to buy supplies of contraceptives; and the traffic and illegal importation of banned goods was ignored by Irish customs.

During the following years, one by one the issues emerged: contraception, divorce, abortion, sexual harassment, rape, violence. The women's movement found that resistance to equal pay and equal opportunity to, and at, work were also linked to woman's sexuality. Her child-bearing and rearing, it was said, were factors that would interfere with a woman's ability to hold down a job outside the home; her child-bearing and rearing would suffer if she worked outside the home. That old Biblical phobia, menstruation, was again trotted out; this time it was said to impair a woman's ability to do a proper job. These reasons for discriminating against women are not openly declared very often now; but that does not mean that they are not held. Women have at least, for the present, won a climate in which articulating such ideas attracts derision. But let's take a closer look at sexuality.

We owe our present ability to discuss and analyse sexuality to the women's movement of the past two decades. Society's attitudes towards women's sexuality, which includes the moral and censorious, the prurient and exploitative, make it difficult for women to discuss the subject, or even to find the right words in which to debate it, without sounding crude or technical. However, the consciousness-raising sessions of the 1970s, in which women explored the roots of their oppression, cleared the way for a clarity of language which must have shocked some. Since then, feminist thinkers have sought to tease out the biological from the cultural and social aspects of this human phenomenon.

If human sexuality were not beset by so many cultural agglutinations it is likely that it could take its place as neither more or less important, than some other pleasurable aspects of life, both physical and mental. Basic human needs (which are also pleasures) can be graded in three groups of declining importunity:

- hunger, thirst and warmth. These are essential for life and the survival of the individual.
- sexual activity, fitness, the activity impulse. These are of secondary importance, but necessary for the survival of the species and important for the wellbeing of the individual.
- use of the senses, speech, achievement of purpose, appreciation of beauty. These enhance the life of the individual.

It is a monumental myth that sexuality as we know it—an imprisoned animal, partly domesticated, used and abused in a whole spectrum of ways and for a multitude of purposes, sometimes pathological, and sometimes out of control—is true human sexuality. Let us first look at the general perception of human sexuality.

At its most basic, and in its narrowest sense, human sexuality, like that of all mammals, exists in the interest of reproduction, but it has evolved and developed beyond its mammalian base just as, and because, humans have evolved. Sexual activity is now a social (and leisure) pursuit with economic connotations, as well as a biological phenomenon; it concerns intimacy as well as reproduction. Even the Roman Catholic church accepts that matrimonial sexual activity while primarily for reproduction, is also an exercise which is important to the happiness of the couple.

Human sexuality cannot be compared to the behaviour of other mammals principally because of the development of human intelligence and memory, but also because of other factors such as the psychological effects of our long childhood and the fact that we have contributed to our own evolution by the changes which we have made in our environment—the transcendence of humans, in which some would deny women a part. Other species procreate purely by instinct, but the human species has an awareness of its own continuity and a conscious interest in both its own past and the future of its progeny. The pleasure or relief from tension that induces other mammals to procreate in response to oestrus is also present in humans; but in humans these are urges that are controlled by their intelligence, not instincts to which they are blindly obedient. Their sexual encounters involve thoughts and feelings that are infinitely more complex than the instinctive coupling of other species.

Well, so far, there are no obvious reasons to be found, in the basic function of sexuality, as to whether, or why, it should be an instrument of women's oppression. The females of other species are not subjugated by the males; and sexual activity does not have the ever-present influence on their lives that it seems to have in the human species. The reasons must lie elsewhere, perhaps in the differences between the species, of which the principal one is intelligence.

Anthropologists, psychoanalysts and other behavioural scientists have been rummaging around in their fields of interest seeking explanations for male supremacy, and two main schools of thought have emerged, both based on human sexuality. The first is biological determinism. Because women

58

and men have physically different reproductive systems, some behavioural scientists believe that they have other biological differences which are reflected in their characters. For example, man is aggressive and woman is passive; and therefore as man is physically stronger than woman, it is inevitable that she should be oppressed by him. This credo (which I shall return to later) relies heavily on human biology and instinct, and leaves no room for the role of intelligence in power relations between the sexes. It may well have female protagonists, but I have only come across its male proponents. And it raises the hackles of most women I know.

In the second school of thought, a growing number of scientists and philosophers hold that sexuality, (the relations between the sexes, as opposed to human relations which disregard sex), is socially and culturally constructed, that it is a series of attitudes and emotions which are learned, and that sexual activity, even the forms which reproductive sexual activity take (apart from the basic drive), are also learned. This conclusion is supported by masses of evidence, and it gives intelligence a central role in relations between the sexes.

In conventional wisdom, male sexuality is compulsive, aggressive, not necessarily linked to emotion. It goes further than that: men define their identity, their masculinity, in terms of their sexuality, and identify their sexuality with power and prestige. These are cultural imperatives. All over the world, there are cultural pressures for males to prove their masculine sexuality (to have balls), by being aggressive, not showing the gentler emotions, being sexually active, and aspiring to power (which in its least manifestation is the control of a woman), as evidence of their masculinity. Human culture allows men a very limited range of feelings and emotions in public; they can be angry, aggressive, courageous, competitive, exhilarated, arrogant, proud or imperious; all emotions that relate to ability, status and power. Above all they should not show fear, submission, or any of the softer feelings or caring emotions. These are not manly.

On the other hand, women's sexuality is regarded as passive, existing only as a response to male sexuality, related to emotion, and a trap for unwary men. There is a lot of double-think on the question of women's sexuality. Side by side with this image of a quiescent libido, paradoxically, women are also supposed to be sexually insatiable (the arousal of a woman probably frightens men because, as will become evident later, it is outside their control). Their carnality is considered a danger to men, diverting them from higher things (note again the Eve syndrome); and everything to do with women's sexuality is regarded as dirty. By whom are these views held? Not overtly or consciously by the vast majority of us, women or men; but these attitudes run like a deep seam in human culture, and they submerge and resurface again at intervals throughout history. There are multitudes of records testifying to their existence, and one may think that they have disappeared in modern times in our developed society. but while sanitary pads are publicly displayed in supermarkets and magazine advertisements, menstruation is still regarded as if it were a guilty secret. Fertility and childbirth are messy considerations which women should confine among themselves (except for the lucrative practice of gynaecologists). A recent article in *The Irish Times* recorded the antipathy of many men, even trade unionists and politicians, to married women of childbearing years in the workforce. These revelations were followed by a letter in the same paper from a retired primary school teacher who recalled an incident in the 1960s when her principal, a nun, remarked to her about a pregnant married colleague, how inappropriate and unseemly morally it was for an obviously pregnant woman to stand in front of a class.

Only in the last two decades has the Roman Catholic church abandoned the ritual of Churching (purifying) women after childbirth. And only over the same period has the custom of fathers attending the birth of their children become an accepted (if not general) practice. Celibacy among clergy and opposition to women priests rests on these same prejudices, as does the scandal attached to sexual dalliance by highly placed public figures.

This is where we come to the double standard in attitudes to women's and men's sexuality. There are different sets of rules for male and female sexual behaviour (as indeed in other areas of life): men are allowed to be sexually promiscuous, while women are not. Present day breaches of this bastion of male privilege are more apparent than real. Research has shown that women who have emulated the sexual behaviour of men find it personally unsatisfactory; while at the same time men retain the categorisation of women: those who sleep around are sluts, nice women don't.

The double standard has internal illogicalities, eg

prostitutes are dirty. What makes them dirty? Men's penises. So why are men who go to prostitutes not dirty? Dorothy Dinnerstein, an American analyst, replies:

> The messiness allowed men in our own culture does not really contradict this point (that men are clean and women dirty). Their proverbial unfastidious lust, their tolerance of filthy public toilets, their foul language and slovenly ways, all of this is accepted because it does not touch upon their central, clean humanity. It is washed off, like dirt off healthy skin, when they turn to serious matters. In woman messiness of this kind would convey that an intrinsic, inherent uncleanliness, which she is counted to keep under her control, has broken out of bounds.

The sexual revolution

Here, I'll give a brief tabulated account of two revolutions of the recent decades—the sexual and the feminist:

1. Sexual radicalism, sleeping around, facilitated by the Pill, was the sexual revolution of the '60s. The Pill changed the character of the sexual revolution. The separation of intercourse from reproduction brought new freedom to women. It also brought benefits to men by releasing them from some responsibility for their sexual acts. Women soon realised that it was freedom only to say 'yes', not to say 'no'; they were 'frigid' if they said no! This knowledge partly gave rise to the present wave of feminism.
2. The role of motherhood and childcare, in keeping women economically dependent and deprived, became another issue. The key to men's control over women, they found, lay in their control of female sexuality and, as a direct consequence, women's domestic labour. Patriarchy (male dominance) was defined as the first and most basic aspect of all power relations; and the family came under attack.
3. Women came to realise that femaleness was defined by men; that they had adopted and internalised a male interpretation of their sexuality, and that purging themselves of it would be difficult. Even today definitions of female sexuality are still afflicted by the virus of male perceptions. At first women questioned the language and practice of sexuality which assigned activity and control to men, and passivity and surrender to women.
4. Next came anger against the beliefs, ideas and arrangements surrounding reproduction. Women's fertility,

61

they found, and ultimately their lives, were in men's hands. They sought control of their own fertility—hence the demands for safe contraception and abortion. (They were still defining their sexuality in male terms.) Health care became an issue and the question of authoritarian (mainly male) doctors.

5. Frigidity had engaged the interest of sexologists in the early years of the century. It was the diagnosis offered by men to women who failed to reach orgasms. Later they decided that virtuosity in sexual activity was the cure, and female satisfaction was made dependent on male resourcefulness. Then in the seventies a discovery was made. Enter the clitoral orgasm.

6. Women gained self-confidence in the assault on the double standard; and, for some, a new era of sexual enjoyment had arrived. But others found that adopting male attitudes to their sexual activity was unsatisfactory; their emotional requirements were left unsatisfied; they wanted men to love in a more intimate and caring way, like women. Furthermore, they found that men still designated them as 'birds', 'strokes', 'tail', 'broads', 'pussy', and other degrading labels; and women who 'slept around' were still 'sluts'.

7. Radical feminists maintained that men's sexuality was directed towards the conquest of women. Some saw intercourse as a political act of submission, and any dealings with men as traffic with, or giving succour to, the enemy. Hence the emergence of political lesbianism and separatism.

8. The uncovering of male violence towards women and the declaration 'the personal is political'.

9. The search continued for women's true sexuality—and men's. It was found that women's sexuality is muted, diffuse, more sensual than a man's, and inextricably identified with love; that, for a woman, love is inseparable from emotion, tender and intimate; while love, for men, meant sexual activity, not necessarily involving any emotion.

Some of these discoveries were made during the early consciousness-raising sessions of the '70s, and others were the result of academic work. While more detailed studies, in subsequent years, uncovered new insights, these were made within that same basic framework.

Controversies broke out in defence of various theories: principally the one between biological determinism and cultural conditioning. Women are passive by nature, said the determinists. Women are not passive by nature, countered the cultural school, otherwise they would all be passive, just as, in principle, all women can have children; men are not dominant by nature, otherwise they would all be dominant, just as all men can have erections.

Internationally, various factions developed in feminism. There were those who believed in gradual reform so as not to antagonise men and the majority of women. Some visualised an androgynous type of equality and sexuality; and there were those who were prepared to fight on the barricades. For some (radical) feminists the barricades were drawn between the sexes and patriarchal heterosexuality became a target. A new category of sexual being emerged—political lesbians, women who refused to have sexual, or any other kind of relations with men. Political lesbianism was a rejection of heterosexuality, used as a tactic in the battle for equality, and not necessarily a positive desire for sexual engagement with women, or for freedom of sexual choice.

Some believed that the question of sexuality was overshadowing other pressing matters; that feminists were in danger of falling into a trap. They had protested against being cast as sex objects, yet they were involved in discussions of their sexuality to the point of obsession. Is sexuality really the arena, many asked, in which our well-being is determined in power-structures in modern society? What is the function of an ideology that keeps everyone looking for the meaning of life between their own or someone else's legs? On the contrary, said other, we have had our purpose in life tied to our sexuality; we have been made to suffer for it, and be ashamed of it, yet not allowed to enjoy it, or permitted to rise above a nearly exclusively sexual existence. We must understand our sexuality if we are to break free.

Later, other factions developed, including reactionary groups, such as cultural feminists who are defined differently in different countries. Their philosophy is basically opposed to the androgyny of earlier times. they celebrate the differences between women and men and believe that women's sexuality is biologically constructed (contradicting their title) and a resource rather than a handicap. Some want to return to the earlier values of respect for women (which they say the sexual revolution destroyed), as a solution to male lasciviousness, dominance and violence. They want to encourage development of a women's culture separate from that of men, because they believe that men will never change.

While these discussions were engaging the minds and energies of feminists in other developed countries, things took a different turn in Ireland. When internal tensions and personality differences broke up the Irish Women's Liberation Movement, some of the original members returned to work on their own lives in keeping with the motto, 'the personal is political'. You hear some of them now refer to a 'post-feminist era'. Some campaigned in the workplace, to ensure the implementation of equality and anti-discrimination legislation. Others sought, in the traditional caring role of women, to relieve the sufferings of women in particular situations of violence and oppression; battered women, rape victims, family planning and health. Difficult as it was, it was easier to struggle for equality in a series of specific battles against economic discrimination and violence than to challenge the deep cultural attitudes relating to sex. But general organisation of women to oppose their oppression, and the education of the mass of women, and of the next generation, eventually petered out.

While sexuality came out into the open in other societies, here it remained in the closet. Irish women (and men) have not involved themselves to any great extent in the agonising over sexuality which has occurred in other Western countries. While the feminist literature of other countries has endless dissertations on sexuality, discussion of the subject among Irish feminists was never able to surface into the public domain. Throughout this century, when research into sexuality became first a daring venture, and later became an accepted academic study, there was no public debate in this country on the theories of Freud (his name was whispered with prurient overtones), nor on the books of the sexologists—Kinsey, or Masters and Johnson, or Foucault, or Hite. These were all studies in one form or another of sexuality, female and male, and contributed to a better understanding of its complexity. Central to the deliberations of the sexologists was the vexed problem of the female orgasm. This elusive pimpernel was sought here, there and everywhere. With a seriousness that cannot but amuse, sexual gymnastics were devised to coax it out of hiding. Then, eureka, they discovered the clitoral orgasm. But wait! There was a snag! The clitoral orgasm was not dependent on penile penetration, or even on a man! A new theory of women's sexuality was emerging, inching slowly away from the male perspective.

Defining women's sexuality

Well, what is the true definition of women's sexuality? The answer is that a woman's sexuality, and her physical enjoyment of it, has a much wider context than that defined as, or confined to, vaginal or clitoral orgasms, sexual intercourse, or erotic actions whether carried out alone or with another. The climax of female sexuality is giving birth, not intercourse which is only one milestone on the road to a woman's fulfilment. That is only the physical dimension. Manifestations of a woman's sexuality extend into her life in a way that influences all her behaviour and attitudes.

It is a cultural construct that birthing and child nurturing are divorced in our minds from sexual pleasure; that birth is associated with pain and treated as an illness. (By whom could it possibly be regarded as an illness except perhaps by men?) Some lucky women experience ecstatic physical pleasure—those who are healthy and fit, and who go with the rhythms of labour rather than against them. Some women have experienced the paroxysm of delivery as an orgasm surpassing the genital one that gets such a high profile in the lexicon of sexual pleasure. *Giving birth is the logical climax in the essential sequence of a woman's sexuality, if one stops defining it in the male terms of intercourse.* It remains only for women to insist on conditions in the physical, social and political (the politics of the medicalisation of childbirth) environment of pregnancy and birth, and in the attitudes towards them, which would allow women to enjoy their pleasures.

This is not a new idea. I have come across it in feminist literature because I have been looking for it. On the zigzag path to awareness, it is easily missed if your mind is not open to it. Because motherhood has been used to suppress women, and has been a major factor in their oppression, many of the early feminists wanted to deny it, curtail it, excise it from the female consciousness. But, if I might be pardoned the pun, it was like throwing out the baby with the bath water.

Still, some recognised birthing for what it was. Dora

Russell (1927) described intercourse for a woman as 'the merest incident in the satisfaction of the older impulse to gain power and abundant and eternal life by multiplying her own body'. When Germaine Greer (1984) saw the pleasure Tuscan women took in their children, and began to revise her earlier ideas about sexuality to include motherhood, she was castigated by less perceptive feminists, who had become entrenched at an earlier stage along the road of self-discovery. Mary Evans (1982), accused gynaecologists of practices 'which, like those of pornography, [seem] incapable of seeing sexuality and reproduction as constituent elements of a complex system of responses.' In *Our Bodies Ourselves*, by the Boston Women's Health Collective, the authors describe the second stage of labour as 'joyful, not painful, to the over-whelming majority of women' even in the regular practice of routine obstetrics. Adrienne Rice quotes from several establishment researchers who have documented the erotic sensations experienced by women giving birth, and goes on to declare that there are strong cultural forces at work to desexualise women as mothers and to deny the orgasmic sensations felt in childbirth or while suckling infants. Today we might ask ourselves if the latent sexuality of childbirth and child nurturing has not had some part in the increasing numbers of single mothers raising their children.

It is true that birth has been strictly segregated from sexuality. In pregnancy and parturition women's sexual parts have been desexualised: the vagina becomes the birth canal. The atmosphere in a modern labour ward, the technology, the brisk impersonal attendants, the unnecessary use of drugs, also conspire to divorce childbirth from sexuality. It does not have to be like that; the current arrangements are solely for the convenience of the medical personal. The up-ended-beetle position of the perinatal mother, lying on her back with her feet suspended in stirrups, allows medical personnel more ease of access to regulate the birth, often to suit their own purposes. Birth is accomplished more easily for the mother if she squats, kneels or stands; yet few labour wards allow these positions.

Modern gynaecological and obstetrical practices, which historically have been oppressive and anti-woman, are male constructed. In the last century, male doctors displaced traditional midwives in what they undoubtedly saw as a lucrative field. Early on they developed anti-woman practices, such as clitoridectomy (yes, in civilised northern countries!) to cure female masturbation, and removal of the ovaries to cure insanity. These and other unbelievable surgical remedies were followed by manipulation of the birthing process: the more insidious one of drug administration, and routine, mechanical, and often unnecessary, interventions such as induction, forceps delivery, episiotomies and Caesarean sections, which continue to the present day. Women gynaecologists are trained by men and only a minority of them develop systems of their own, out of their own experience, like the English woman, Wendy Savage, who fell foul of the male gynaecological establishment for her woman-oriented practices.

Women cannot be blamed for experiencing childbirth as painful. Poor health, overwork, lack of fitness, bad posture, medical practices and cultural conditioning are basic causes of perinatal pain. The culture has decreed it; didn't God lay that curse of Eve in the Garden of Eden? Nobody has said that it need not be so, that giving birth can be a highly pleasurable part of their sexuality.

Male sexuality

If female sexuality is more than it is said to be, where then does that leave male sexuality? Well, for a start, it is much more narrowly defined than female sexuality. Men have a reductionist approach to sexuality, pruning it down to the bare essentials necessary for reproduction; but, paradoxically, engaging in the residual, perfunctory act principally for gratification. But is it the compulsive, aggressive, exploiting phenomenon that it is held to be? Many of us might say: no, not necessarily 'aggressive' or 'exploiting'. 'Compulsive'? Well, everyone knows that men's sex drive is a biological imperative, that they have no control over their erections. But is that a fact or merely an assumption?

One of the factors that cause differences between human sexuality and that of other mammals, as was said earlier, is human intelligence which regulates the instincts. Is male sexuality the only maverick instinct, unchecked by intellect? I think not. If that were so then no woman would ever be safe. Economic activity would grind to a halt; our workplaces would be snake-pits of incapacitated males in the grip of engorged desire. No, our culture imposes limits which are invigilated by the intellect on the range of male sexuality. And from one culture to another there are different rules.

If a woman walks alone at night, if she dresses in what is deemed a 'sexy' manner, she is said to be giving provocation to men, then she is to blame if she is attacked. (Shades of Adam and 'It's all her fault.') In our society a glimpse of female breast can rouse a man; yet among some African tribes women go bare-breasted without causing a male flutter. If that is the case among primitive peoples, then breast fetishism, or arousal at the shape of the female figure or the sight of a woman alone, must be a learned response among our more cultivated and civilised tribesmen. Or, conversely, Africans have learned mammary indifference. One way or another there is a learning process. Furthermore, in our culture chastity is practised among groups of men without undue physical stress (or else hordes of Roman Catholic priests are leading lives of rabid desperation). Obviously, they learn control of their sexuality. In millions of marriages men practise restraint, or have sexual equanimity that belies the idea of an uncontrollable biological imperative; but because of the cultural attitude towards male sexuality they would be slow to admit it. Sexual equanimity is unmanly; only the sexual activist can claim respect: 'a man's gotta do what a man's gotta do'.

If we can show, as I have just done, that there are cultural pressures on people to behave in a certain way, that the culture informs males that they should be excited by certain images, and in certain circumstances, then we cannot assume that sexual behaviour is only biological. It must be deduced logically that sexual responses can be learned and become cultural as well as biological imperatives. Therefore it can be unlearned. (I am not saying that cultural imperatives are always wrong. I only protest in this instance at carving them in stone, at misrepresenting male sexual responses as solely, unalterably biological.) And if male sexuality can be controlled by the intellect, as it undoubtedly can, then why in the name of sanity is it allowed untrammelled sway in relations between the sexes? Why has periodic male continence never been seriously considered in the context of contraception? The Rhythm and Billings methods of family planning are popularly derided as unworkable. The 'biological compulsion' of male sexuality is given, and taken, as the reason why life is organised to provide a man with a regularly available woman, and why contraceptive devices are necessary if women are not to be eternally pregnant. To satisfy the importunate sexual demands of men, women have had to introduce hardware (sometimes lethal) into their bodies, and take drugs that are dangerous to their health, consoled by doctors who say that on balance the risk is worth it. The answer is that men will not agree, and those who act reasonably and equitably don't publicly admit to it, and definitely don't urge that code of conduct on others. The myth of biological compulsion has been the greatest single instrument for the sexual oppression of women; and, astonishingly, it has gone unchallenged, even in these comparatively enlightened, questing and questioning times.

Where do we go from here?
It may seem glib to say, as some radical feminists have declared, that sexual violence and the sexual oppression of women are instruments of power that benefit all men, whether or not they are involved in their practice, or even approve of them. That may be so, although there is no doubt that the subordination which results from the oppression of women at least satisfies male pride, and also provides them with personal service and support that smooth their way in life. But it is an unsatisfactory answer when one seeks ways to change prevailing attitudes. And how does one tackle the problem of misogyny when it is other women—secretaries, shop assistants, other men's partners, colleagues, cleaning women, 'the woman in the street', old women, unmarried women—that men put down, generally not their own sisters, mothers, partners or daughters?

What can be done to change the situation? Many suggestions have been made, many policies tried. Political lesbians and cultural feminists have decided on courses of action; each group in their own way have set about creating a culture which ignores male culture. For many that is not a realistic or feasible solution. Half the population of the planet is male, and most women find them interesting in themselves as well as necessary for procreation. Women also have sons.

There is another dimension to the matter: it would benefit men to shed some of their cultural conditioning, such factors as their marital rites, their power hunger and competitiveness; to free their emotions and learn to care; to share in the nurture of their children, whether or not it would affect the way their male offspring regard women. How can the mould be broken? A starting point could be, perhaps, if women tried to wean their children away from the worst excesses of male culture despite the pressures for young males to conform.

Should the family be abolished? It has come under fire from feminists as the locus of women's oppression; but what would replace it? Such an overwhelming majority of people find satisfaction and emotional security in the family that abolishing it is neither feasible nor desirable until a better structure can be devised. It can, however, be reformed into an institution that is user-friendly, especially to women.

I have shown that female and male sexuality have been distorted and restricted by the prevailing culture from their natural form. I make no claim to have discovered what the aggressive reality of that natural form is, beyond establishing that sexuality, as we interpret and know it, is distorted and stunted because it is used as an instrument of oppression.

It is warped and stunted because its definition is limited to the activity which constitutes the male role in reproduction, and which has been designated as the core of sexuality—a sexist definition and one that diminishes loving intimacy between people of either or the same sex, and denies the sexuality of giving birth. Homosexuality and self-stimulation are deprecated as unnatural and unclean. Childbirth becomes a medical problem; and both childbirth and child nurture are regarded as burdens.

This almost universally accepted definition of sexuality ignores, even denies, the reality of female sexuality which exists on a different plane and in a different dimension to male experience. While female sexuality has been repressed, male sexuality has been allowed, indeed encouraged, to run rampant within its narrow definition, because masculinity is identified with sexuality. This restricted activity has become an addiction; men have developed into copulation junkies and they try to convince women that they should do the same.

In proposing that women set about changing the culture, are we seeking Utopia? Perhaps. It takes an enormous internal struggle to change cultural attitudes in oneself without ever attempting to change the perception of others, especially sexual recidivists like men. It is easier for a subjugated group to recognise their oppression for what it is, than for the oppressors to admit, even to themselves, that they have fostered injustice, and constructed a culture and an

70

interpretation of sexuality to support that injustice. On the other hand great strides have been made by women in the past twenty years in altering their perceptions of themselves and the world they live in.

The obsession of society with things sexual arises from several causes. An important one is the sexual oppression of women. With that, and one or two other causes out of the way, we could relegate sex to its rightful place in our lives—one that is neither obsessive nor neglected—and get on with the other exciting things there are to do, like changing the world and making it a better place for everyone.

References
Boston Health Collective. *Our Bodies Ourselves*. Harmondsworth: Penguin, 1979 (Rev. edition, 1989).
Dinnerstein, Dorothy. *The Rocking of the Cradle and the Ruling of the World*. London: The Women's Press, 1987.
Rich, Adrienne. *Of Woman Born*. London: Virago, 1977.
Greer Germaine. *Sex and Destiny*. London: Secker & Warburg, 1984.

A note on the author
Ethna Viney is a writer and journalist and a regular contributor to *The Irish Times*. She lives in County Sligo.

A KIND OF SCAR
The Woman Poet in a National Tradition

Eavan Boland, 1989

…who neither
knows nor cares that
a new language
is a kind of scar
and heals after a while
into a passable imitation
of what went before.

Mise Éire

The Achill Woman

She pushed the hair out of her eyes with
her free hand and put the bucket down.

The zinc-music of the handle on the rim
tuned the evening. An Easter moon rose.
In the next-door field a stream was
a fluid sunset; and then, stars.

I remember the cold rosiness of her hands.
She bent down and blew on them like broth.
And round her waist, on a white background,
in coarse, woven letters, the words 'glass cloth'

And she was nearly finished for the day. *Difference*
And I was all talk, raw from college—

week-ending at a friend's cottage
with one suitcase and the set text
of the Court poets of the Silver Age.
We stayed putting down time until
the evening turned cold without warning.
She said goodnight and started down the hill.

The grass changed from lavender to black.
The trees turned back to cold outlines.
You could taste frost

but nothing now can change the way I went
indoors, chilled by the wind
and made a fire
and took down my book and opened it
and failed to comprehend

the harmonies of servitude,
the grace music gives to flattery
and language borrows from ambition

and how I fell asleep
oblivious to

the planets clouding over in the skies,
the slow decline of the spring moon,
the songs crying out their ironies.

I

Years ago, I went to Achill for Easter. I was a student at Trinity
then and I had the loan of a friend's cottage. It was a one-
storey stone building with two rooms and a view of sloping
fields.

April was cold that year. The cottage was in sight of the
Atlantic and at night a bitter, humid wind blew across the
shore. By day there was heckling sunshine but after dark a
fire was necessary. The loneliness of the place suited me. My
purposes in being there were purgatorial and I had no
intention of going out and about. I had done erratically, to say
the least, in my first year exams. In token of the need to do
better, I had brought with me a small accusing volume of the
Court poets of the Silver Age. In other words, those sixteenth-
century English song writers, like Wyatt and Raleigh, whose
lines appear so elegant, so off-hand, yet whose poems smell of
the gallows.

I was there less than a week. The cottage had no water and
every evening the caretaker, an old woman who shared a
cottage with her brother at the bottom of the field, would
carry water up to me. I can see her still. She has a tea-towel
round her waist—perhaps this is one image that has become
all the images I have of her—she wears an old cardigan and
her hands are blushing with cold as she puts down the
bucket. Sometimes we talk inside the door of the cottage.
Once, I remember, we stood there as the dark grew all around
us and I could see stars beginning to curve in the stream
behind us.

She was the first person to talk to me about the famine. The first person, in fact, to speak to me with any force about the terrible parish of survival and death which the event had been in those regions. She kept repeating to me that they were great people, the people in the famine. Great people. I had never heard that before. She pointed out the beauties of the place. But they themselves, I see now, were a sub-text. On the eastern side of Keel, the cliffs of Menawn rose sheer out of the water. And here was Keel itself, with its blonde strand and broken stone, where the villagers in the famine, she told me, had moved closer to the shore, the better to eat the seaweed.

Memory is treacherous. It confers meanings which are not apparent at the time. I want to say that I understood this woman as emblem and instance of everything I am about to propose. Of course I did not. Yet even then, I sensed a power in the encounter. I knew, without having words for it, that she came from a past which affected me. When she pointed out Keel to me that evening when the wind was brisk and cold and the light was going; when she gestured towards that shore which had stones as outlines and monuments of a desperate people, what was she pointing at? A history? A nation? Her memories or mine?

Those questions, once I began to write my own poetry, came back to haunt me. 'I have been amazed, more than once' writes Hélène Cixous, "by a description a woman gave me of a world all her own, which she had been secretly haunting since early childhood.' As the years passed, my amazement grew. I would see again the spring evening, the woman talking to me. Above all, I would remember how, when I finished speaking to her I went in, lit a fire, took out my book of English court poetry and memorised all over again—with no sense of irony or omission—the cadences of power and despair.

II

I have written this to probe the virulence and necessity of the idea of a nation. Not on its own and not in a vacuum, but as it intersects with a specific poetic inheritance and as that inheritance, in turn, cuts across me as woman and poet. Some of these intersections are personal. Some of them may be painful to remember. Nearly all of them are elusive and difficult to describe with any degree of precision. Nevertheless, I believe these intersections, if I can observe them at all properly here, reveal something about poetry, about nationalism, about the difficulties for a woman poet within a constraining national tradition. Perhaps the argument itself is nothing more than a way of revisiting the cold lights of that Western evening and the force of that woman's conversation. In any case, the questions inherent in that encounter remain with me. It could well be that they might appear, even to a sympathetic reader, too complex to admit of an answer. In other words, that an argument like mine must contain too many imponderables to admit of any practical focus.

Yet I have no difficulty in stating the central premise of my argument. It is that over a relatively short time—certainly no more than a generation or so—women have moved from being the subjects and objects of Irish poems to being the authors of them. It is a momentous transit. It is also a disruptive one. It raises questions of identity, issues of poetic motive and ethical direction which can seem almost impossibly complex. What is more, such a transit—like the slow course of a star or the shifts in a constellation—is almost invisible to the naked eye. Critics may well miss it or map it inaccurately. Yet such a transit inevitably changes our idea of measurement, of distance, of the past as well as the future. Most importantly, it changes our idea of the Irish poem; of its composition and authority, of its right to appropriate certain themes and make certain fiats. And, since poetry is never local for long, that in turn widens out into further implications.

Everything I am about to argue here could be taken as local and personal, rooted in one country and one poetic inheritance; and both of them mine. Yet, if the names were changed, if situations and places were transposed, the issues might well be revealed as less parochial. This is not, after all, an essay on the craft of the art. I am not writing about aesthetics but about the ethics which are altogether less visible in a poetic tradition. Who the poet is, what she or he nominates as a proper theme for poetry, what self they discover and confirm through this subject matter—all of this involves an ethical choice. The more volatile the material— and a wounded history, public or private, is always volatile— the more intensely ethical the choice. Poetic ethics are evident and urgent in any culture where tensions between a poet and her or his birthplace are inherited and established. Poets from such cultures might well recognise some of the issues raised here. After all, this is not the only country or the only politic where the previously passive objects of a work of art have, in a relatively short time, become the authors of it.

So it was with me. For this very reason, early on as a poet, certainly in my twenties, I realized that the Irish nation as an existing construct in Irish poetry was not available to me. I would not have been able to articulate it at that point, but at some preliminary level I already knew that the anguish and power of that woman's gesture on Achill, with its suggestive hinterland of pain, was not something I could predict or rely on in Irish poetry. There were glimpses here and there; sometimes more than that. But all too often, when I was searching for such an inclusion what I found was a rhetoric of imagery which alienated me: a fusion of the national and the feminine which seemed to simplify both.

It was not a comfortable realisation. There was nothing clear-cut about my feelings. I had tribal ambivalences and doubts; and even then I had an uneasy sense of the conflict which awaited me. On the one hand I knew that as a poet, I could not easily do without the idea of a nation. Poetry in every time draws on that reserve. On the other, I could not as a woman accept the nation formulated for me by Irish poetry and its traditions. At one point it even looked to me as if the whole thing might be made up of irreconcilable differences. At the very least, it seemed to me that I was likely to remain an outsider in my own national literature, cut off from its archive, at a distance from its energy. Unless, that is, I could repossess it. This essay is about that conflict and that repossession; and about the fact that repossession itself is not a static or single act. Indeed this essay, which describes it, may itself be no more than a part of it.

III

A nation. It is, in some ways, the most fragile and improbable of concepts. Yet the idea of an Ireland, resolved and healed of its wounds, is an irreducible presence in the Irish past and its literature. In one sense, of course, both the concept and its realisation resist definition. It is certainly nothing conceived in what Edmund Burke calls the 'the spirit of rational liberty'. When a people have been so dispossessed by events as the Irish in the 18th and 19th centuries an extra burden falls on the very idea of a nation. What should be a political aspiration becomes a collective fantasy. The dream itself becomes freighted with invention. The Irish nation, materialising in the songs and ballads of these centuries, is a sequence of improvised images. These songs, these images, wonderful and terrible and memorable as they are, propose for a nation an impossible task: to be at once an archive of defeat and a diagram of victory.

As a child I loved these songs. Even now, in some moods and at certain times, I can find it difficult to resist their makeshift angers. And no wonder. The best of them are written—like lyrics of Wyatt and Raleigh—within sight of the gibbet. They breathe just free of the noose.

In one sense I was a captive audience. My childhood was spent in London. My image-makers as a child, therefore, were refractions of my exile: conversations overheard, memories and visitors. I listened and absorbed. For me, as for many another exile, Ireland was my nation long before it was once again my country. That nation, then and later, was a session of images: of defeats and sacrifices, of individual defiances happening off-stage. The songs enhanced the images; the images reinforced the songs. To me they were the soundings of the place I had lost: drowned treasure.

It took me years to shake off those presences. In the end, though, I did escape. My escape was assisted by the realisation that these songs were effect not cause. They were only the curators of the dream; not the inventors. In retrospect I could accuse both them and the dream of certain crucial simplifications. I made then, and I make now, a moral division between what those songs sought to accomplish and what Irish poetry must seek to achieve. The songs, with their postures and their angers glamourised resistance, action. But the Irish experience, certainly for the purposes of poetry, was only incidentally about action and resistance. At a far deeper level—and here the Achill woman returns—it was about defeat. The coffin ships, the soup queues, those desperate villagers at the shoreline—these things had actually happened. The songs, persuasive, hypnotic, could wish them away. Poetry could not. Of course the relation between a poem and a past is never that simple. When I met the Achill woman I was already a poet. I thought of myself as a poet. Yet nothing that I understood about poetry enabled me to understand her better. Quite the reverse. I turned my back on her in that cold twilight and went to commit to memory the songs and artifices of the very power systems which had made her own memory such an archive of loss.

If I understand her better now, and my relation to her, it is not just because my sense of irony or history has developed over the years; although I hope they have. It is more likely because of my own experience as a poet. Inevitably, any account of this carries the risk of subjective codes and impressions. Yet in poetry in particular and women's writing in general, the private witness is often all there is to go on. Since my personal experience as a poet is part of my source material, it is to that I now turn.

IV

I entered Trinity to study English and Latin. Those were the early sixties and Dublin was another world—a place for which I can still feel Henry James' 'tiger pounce of homesickness'. In a very real sense, it was a city of images and anachronisms. There were still brewery horses on Grafton Street, their rumps draped and smoking under sackcloth. In the coffee bars, they poached eggs in a rolling boil and spooned them onto thick, crustless toast. The lights went on at twilight; by midnight the city was full of echoes. After the day's lectures, I took a bus home from College. It was a short journey. Home was an attic flat on the near edge of a town that was just beginning to sprawl. There in the kitchen, on an oilskin tablecloth, I wrote my first real poems: derivative, formalist, gesturing poems. I was a very long way from Adrienne Rich's realisation that 'instead of poems about experience, I am getting poems that are experiences'. If anything, my poems were other people's experiences. This, after all, was the heyday of the Movement in Britain and the neat stanza, the well-broken line were the very stuff of poetic identity.

Now I wonder how many young women poets taught themselves—in rooms like that, with a blank discipline—to write the poem that was in the air, rather than the one within their experience? How many faltered, as I did, not for lack of answers, but for lack of questions. 'It will be a long time still, I think' wrote Virginia Woolf 'before a woman can sit down to write a book without finding a phantom to be slain, a rock to be dashed against.'

But for now, let me invent a shift of time. I am turning down those streets which echo after midnight. I am climbing the stairs of a coffee bar which stays open late. I know what I will find. Here is the salt-glazed mug on a table-top which is as scarred as a desk in a country school. Here is the window with its view of an empty street, of lamplight and iron. And there, in the corner, is my younger self.

I draw up a chair, I sit down opposite her. I begin to talk—no, to harangue her. Why, I say, do you do it? Why do you go back to that attic flat, night after night, write in forms explored and sealed by English men hundreds of years ago? You are Irish. You are a woman. Why do you keep these things at the periphery of the poem? Why do you not move them to the centre, where they belong?

But the woman who looks back at me is uncomprehending. If she answers at all it will be with the rhetoric of a callow apprenticeship: that the poem is pure process, that the technical encounter is the one which guarantees all others. She will speak about the dissonance of the line and the necessity for the stanza. And so on. And so on.

'For what is the poet responsible?' asks Allen Tate. 'He is responsible for the virtue proper to him as a poet, for his special arête: for the mastery of a disciplined language which will not shun the full report of the reality conveyed to him by his awarenes.'

She is a long way, that young woman—with her gleaming cup and her Movement jargon—from the full report of anything. In her lack of any sense of implication or complication, she might as well be a scientist in the thirties, bombarding uranium with neutrons.

If I try now to analyse why such a dialogue would be a waste of time, I come up with several reasons. One of them is that it would take years for me to see, let alone comprehend, certain realities. Not until the oilskin tablecloth was well folded and the sprawling town had become a rapacious city, and the attic flat was a house in the suburbs, could I accept the fact that I was a woman and a poet in a culture which had the greatest difficulty associating the two ideas. 'A woman must often take a critical stance towards her social, historical and cultural position in order to experience her own quest'. writes the American poet and feminist, Rachel Blau du Plessis. 'Poems of the self's growth, or of self-knowledge may often include or be preceded by a questioning of major social prescriptions about the shape women's experience should take.' In years to come, I could never be sure whether my poems had generated the questions or the questions had facilitated the poems. All that way ahead. 'No poet' says Eliot 'no artist of any kind has his complete meaning alone.' In the meantime, I existed, whether I liked it or not, in a mesh, a web, a labyrinth of associations. Of poems past and present. Contemporary poems. Irish poems.

V

Irish poetry was predominantly male. Here or there you found a small eloquence, like 'After Aughrim' by Emily Lawless. Now and again, in discussion, you heard a woman's name. But the lived vocation, the craft witnessed by a human life—that was missing. And I missed it. Not in the beginning, perhaps. But later, when perceptions of womanhood began to redirect my own work, what I regretted was the absence of an expressed poetic life which would have dignified and revealed mine. The influence of absences should not be underestimated. Isolation itself can have a powerful effect in the life of a young writer. 'I'm talking about real influence now,' says Raymond Carver. 'I'm talking about the moon and the tide.'

I turned to the work of Irish male poets. After all, I thought of myself as an Irish poet. I wanted to locate myself within the Irish poetic tradition. The dangers and stresses in my own themes gave me an added incentive to discover a context for them. But what I found dismayed me.

The majority of Irish male poets depended on women as motifs in their poetry. They moved easily, deftly, as if by right among images of women in which I did not believe and of which I could not approve. The women in their poems were often passive, decorative, raised to emblematic status. This was especially true where the woman and the idea of the nation were mixed: where the nation became a woman and the woman took on a national posture.

The trouble was these images did good service as ornaments. In fact they had a wide acceptance as ornaments by readers of Irish poetry. Women in such poems were frequently referred to approvingly as mythic, emblematic. But to me these passive and simplified women seemed a corruption. Moreover, the transaction they urged on the reader, to accept them as mere decoration, seemed to compound the corruption. For they were not decorations, they were not ornaments. However distorted these images, they had their roots in a suffered truth.

What had happened? How had the women of our past—the women of a long struggle and a terrible survival—undergone such a transformation? How had they suffered Irish history and inscribed themselves in the speech and memory of the Achill woman, only to re-emerge in the Irish poetry as fictive queens and national sibyls?

The more I thought about it, the more uneasy I became. The wrath and grief of Irish history seemed to me—as it did to many—one of our true possessions. Women were part of that wrath, had endured that grief. It seemed to me a species of human insult that at the end of all, in certain Irish poems, they should become elements of style rather than aspects of truth.

The association of the feminine and the national—and the consequent simplification of both—is not of course a monopoly of Irish poetry. 'All my life,' wrote Charles de Gaulle, 'I have thought about France in a certain way. The emotional side of me tends to imagine France like the princess in the fairytale, or the Madonna of the Frescoes'. De Gaulle's words point up the power of nationhood to edit the reality of womanhood. Once the idea of a nation influences the perception of a woman then that woman is suddenly and inevitably simplified. She can no longer have complex feelings and aspirations. She becomes the passive projection of a national idea.

Irish poems simplified women most at the point of intersection between womanhood and Irishness. The further the Irish poem drew away from the idea of Ireland, the more real and persuasive became the images of women. Once the pendulum swung back the simplifications started again. The idea of the defeated nation being reborn as a triumphant woman was central to a certain kind of Irish poem. Dark Rosaleen. Cathleen Ni Houlihan. The nation as woman; the woman as national muse.

The more I looked at it, the more it seemed to me that in relation to the idea of a nation many, if not most, Irish male poets had taken the soft option. The irony was that few Irish poets were nationalists. By and large, they had eschewed the fervour and crudity of that ideal. But long after they had rejected the politics of Irish nationalism, they continued to deploy the emblems and enchantments of its culture. It was the culture, not the politics, which informed Irish poetry: not the harsh awakenings, but the old dreams.

In all of this I did not blame nationalism. Nationalism

seemed to me inevitable in the Irish context; a necessary hallucination within Joyce's nightmare of history. I did blame Irish poets. Long after it was necessary, Irish poetry had continued to trade in the exhausted fictions of the nation; had allowed these fictions to edit ideas of womanhood and modes of remembrance. Some of the poetry produced by such simplifications was, of course, difficult to argue with. It was difficult to deny that something was gained by poems which used the imagery and emblem of the national muse. Something was gained, certainly; but only at an aesthetic level. While what was lost occurred at the deepest, most ethical level; and what was lost was what I valued. Not just the details of a past. Not just the hungers, the angers. These, however terrible, remain local. But the truths these details witness—human truths of survival and humiliation—these also were suppressed along with the details. Gone was the suggestion of any complicated human suffering. Instead, you had the hollow victories, the passive images, the rhyming queens.

I knew that the women of the Irish past were defeated. I knew it instinctively long before the Achill woman pointed down the hill to the Keel shoreline. What I objected to was that Irish poetry should defeat them twice.

'I have not written day after day' says Camus 'because I desire the world to be covered with Greek statues and masterpieces. The man who has such a desire does exist in me. But I have written so much because I cannot keep from being drawn toward every day life, toward those, whoever they may be, who are humiliated. They need to hope and, if all keep silent, they will be forever deprived of hope and we with them.'

This essay originates in some part from my own need to locate myself in a powerful literary tradition in which until then, or so it seemed to me, I had been an element of design rather than an agent of change. But even as a young poet, and certainly by the time my work confronted me with some of these questions, I had already had a vivid, human witness of the stresses which a national literature can impose on a poet. I had already seen the damage it could do.

VI

I remember the Dublin of the sixties almost more vividly than the city which usurped it. I remember its grace and emptiness and the old hotels with their chintzes and Sheffield trays. In one of these I had tea with Padraic Colum. I find it hard to be exact about the year; somewhere around the middle sixties. But I have no difficulty at all about the season. It was winter. We sat on a sofa by the window overlooking the street. The lamps were on and a fine rain was being glamourised as it fell past their cowls.

Colum was then in his eighties. He had come from his native Longford in the early years of the century to a Dublin fermenting with political and literary change. Yeats admired his 1913 volume of poetry, *Wild Earth*. He felt the Ireland Colum proposed fitted neatly into his own ideas. 'It is unbeautiful Ireland,' Yeats wrote. 'He will contrast finely with our Western dialect-makers.'

In old photographs Colum looks the part: curly-headed, dark, winsome. In every way he was a godsend to the Irish revival. No one would actually have used the term peasant poet. But then no one would have needed to. Such things were understood.

The devil, they say, casts no shadow. But that folk image applies to more than evil. There are writers in every country who begin in the morning of promise but by the evening, mysteriously, have cast no shadow and left no mark. Colum is one of them. For some reason, although he was eminently placed to deal with the energies of his own culture, he failed to do so. His musical, tender, hopeful imagination glanced off the barbaric griefs of the nineteenth century. It is no good fudging the issue. Very few of his poems now look persuasive on the page. All that heritage which should have been his— rage robbed of language, suffering denied its dignity— somehow eluded him. When he met it at all, it was with a borrowed sophistication.

Now in old age he struggled for a living. He transited stoically between Dublin and New York giving readings, writing articles. He remained open and approachable. No doubt for this reason, I asked him what he really thought of Yeats. He paused for a moment. His voice had a distinctive, treble resonance. When he answered it was high and emphatic. 'Yeats hurt me,' he said. 'He expected too much of me.'

I have never been quite sure what Colum meant. What I understand by his words may be different from their intent. But I see his relation with the Irish Revival as governed by corrupt laws of supply and demand. He could only be tolerated if he read the signals right and acquiesced in his role as a peasant poet. He did not and he could not. To be an accomplice in such a distortion required a calculation he never possessed. But the fact that he was screen-tested for it suggests how relentless the idea of Irishness in Irish poetry has been.

Colum exemplified something else to me. Here also was a poet who had been asked to make the journey, in one working lifetime, from being the object of Irish poems to being their author. He too, as an image, had been unacceptably simplified in all those poems about the land and the tenantry. So that—if he was to realise his identity—not only must he move from image to image-maker, he must also undo the simplifications of the first by his force and command of the second. I suspect he found the imaginative stresses of that transit beyond his comprehension, let alone his strength. And so something terrible happened to him. He wrote Irish poetry as if he were still the object of it. He wrote with the passivity and simplification of his own reflection looking back at him from poems, plays and novels in which the so-called Irish peasant was a son of the earth, a cipher of the national cause.

He had the worst of both worlds.

VII

Like Colum, Francis Ledwidge was born at the sharp end of history. An Irish poet who fought as a British soldier, a writer in a radical situation who used a conservative idiom to support it, Ledwidge's short life was full of contradiction. He was in his early twenties when he died in the First World War.

Despite his own marginal and pressured position, Ledwidge used the conventional language of romantic nationalism. Not always; perhaps not often. But his poem on the death of the leaders of the Easter Rising, 'The Blackbirds', is a case in point. It is, in a small way, a celebrated poem and I have certainly not chosen it because it represents careless or shoddy work. Far from it. It is a skilful poem, adroit and quick in its rhythms, with an underlying sweetness of tone. For all that, it provides an example of a gifted poet who did not resist the contemporary orthodoxy. Perhaps he might have, had he lived longer and learned more. As it was, Ledwidge surrendered easily to the idioms of the Irish Revival. This in turn meant that he could avail himself of a number of approved stereotypes and, chief among them, the easy blend of feminine and national. Even here he could exercise a choice although, it must be said, a limited one. He could have had the Young Queen or The Old Mother. As it happens, he chose the Poor Old Woman. But we are in no doubt what he means:

The Blackbirds

I heard the Poor Old Woman say
'At break of day the fowler came
And took my blackbirds from their song
Who loved me well through shame and blame.

No more from lovely distances
Their songs shall bless me mile from mile,
Nor to white Ashbourne call me down
To wear my crown another while.
With bended flowers the angels mark
For the skylark the place they lie.
From there its little family
Shall dip their wings first in the sky.

And when the first surprise of flight
Sweet songs excite, from the far dawn
Shall there come blackbirds, loud with love,
Sweet echoes of the singers gone.

But in the lonely hush of eve
Weeping I grieve the silent bills'
I heard the Poor Old Woman say
In Derry of the little hills.

I am not sure this poem would pass muster now. There are too many sugary phrases 'loud with love' and 'shame and blame'—evoking the very worst of Georgian poetry. But Ledwidge was young and the impulse for the poem was historical. The 1916 leaders were dead. He was at a foreign front. The poem takes on an extra resonance if it is read as a concealed elegy for his own loyalties.

What is more interesting is how, in his attempt to make the feminine stand in for the national, he has simplified the woman in the poem almost out of existence. She is in no sense the poor old woman of the colloquial expression. There are no vulnerabilities here, no human complexities. She is a Poor Old Woman in capital letters. A mouthpiece. A sign.

Therefore the poem divides into two parts; one vital, one inert. The subject of the poem appears to be the woman. But appearances deceive. She is merely the object, the pretext. The real subject is the blackbirds. They are the animated substance of the piece. They call from 'lovely distances'; their 'sweet songs' 'excite' and 'bless'. Whatever imaginative power the lyric has, it comes from these birds. Like all effective images, the blackbirds have a life outside the poem. They take their literal shape from the birds we know and to these they return an emblematic force. They continue to be vital once the poem is over.

The woman, on the other hand, is a diagram. By the time the poem is over, she has become a dehumanized ornament. When her speaking part finishes she goes out of the piece and out of our memory. At best she has been the engine of the action; a convenient frame for the proposition.

The question worth asking is whether this fusion of national and feminine, this interpretation of one by the other, is inevitable. It was, after all, common practice in Irish poetry: Mangan's 'Dark Rosaleen' comes immediately to mind. In fact the custom and the practice reached back, past the songs and simplifications of the 19th century, into the bardic tradition itself. Daniel Corkery refers to this in his analysis of the aisling convention in *The Hidden Ireland*. 'The vision the poet sees' he writes there 'is always the spirit of Ireland as a majestic and radiant maiden'.

So many male Irish poets—the later Yeats seems to me a rare exception—have feminised the national and nationalised the feminine that from time to time it has seemed there is no other option. But an Irish writer who turned away from such usages suggests that there was, in fact, another and more subversive choice.

In the opening of *Ulysses* Joyce describes an old woman. She climbs the steps to the Martello tower, darkening its doorway. She is, in fact, the daily milkwoman. But no sooner has she started to pour a quart of milk into Stephen's measure than she begins to shimmer and dissolve into legendary images: 'Silk of the kine and poor old woman, names given her in old times. A wandering crone, lowly form of an immortal, serving her conqueror and her gay betrayer, their common cuckquean, a messenger from the secret morning. To serve or to upbraid, whether he could not tell; but scorned to beg her favour'.

The same phrase as Ledwidge uses—poor old woman—is included here. But whereas Ledwidge uses it with a straight face, Joyce dazzles it with irony. By reference and inference, he shows himself to be intent on breaking the traditional association of Ireland with ideas of womanhood and tragic motherhood. After all, these simplifications are part and parcel of what he, Joyce, has painfully rejected. They are some of the reason he is in exile from the mythos of his own country. Now by cunning inflations, by disproportions of language, he takes his revenge. He holds at glittering manageable distance a whole tendency in national thought and expression; and dismisses it. But then Joyce is a poetic moralist. Much of *Ulysses*, after all, is invested in Dedalus's search for the ethical shadow of his own aesthetic longings. He has a difficult journey ahead of him. And Joyce has no intention of letting him be waylaid, so early in the book, by the very self-deceptions he has created him to resolve.

VIII

It is easy, and intellectually seductive, for a woman artist to walk away from the idea of a nation. There has been, and there must continue to be, a great deal of debate about the energies and myths women writers should bring with them into a new age. Start again, has been the cry of some of the best feminist poets. Wipe clean the slate, start afresh. It is a cry with force and justice behind it. And it is a potent idea: to begin in a new world, clearing the desert as it were, making it blossom; even making the rain.

In any new dispensation the idea of a nation must seem an expendable construct. After all, it has never admitted of women. Its flags and songs and battle-cries, even its poetry, as I've suggested, make use of feminine imagery. But that is all. The true voice and vision of women are routinely excluded.

Then why did I not walk away? Simply because I was not free to. For all my quarrels with the concept, and no doubt partly because of them, I needed to find and repossess that idea at some level of repose. Like the swimmer in Adrienne Rich's poem, 'Diving Into the Wreck', I needed to find out 'the damage that was done and the treasures that prevail'. I knew the idea was flawed. But if it was flawed, it was also one of the vital human constructs of a place in which, like Leopold Bloom, I was born. More importantly, as a friend and feminist scholar said to me, we ourselves are constructed by the construct. I might be the author of my poems; I was not the author of my past. However crude the diagram, the idea of a nation remained the rough graphic of an ordeal. In some subterranean way I felt myself to be part of that ordeal; its fragmentations extended into mine.

'I am invisible' begins the prologue of Ralph Ellison, the black writer's novel *The Invisible Man*. 'I am invisible, understand, because people refuse to see me. Like the bodiless heads you see sometimes in circus side shows it is as though I have been surrounded by mirrors of hard, distorting glass. When they approach me they see only their surroundings, themselves, or figments of their own imagination—indeed everything and anything except me.'

In an important sense, Ellison's words applied to the sort of Irish poem which availed of that old potent blurring of feminine and national. In such poems, the real woman behind the image was not only explored, she was never even seen.

It was a subtle mechanism; subtle and corrupt. And it was linked, I believed, to a wider sequence of things not seen. A society, a nation, a literary heritage is always in danger of making up its communicable heritage from its visible elements. Women, as it happens, are not especially visible in Ireland. This came to me early and with personal force. I realised when I published a poem that what was seen of me, what drew approval, if it was forthcoming at all, was the poet. The woman, by and large, was invisible. It was an unsettling discovery. Yet I came to believe that my invisibility as a woman was a disguised grace. It had the power to draw me, I sensed, towards realities like the Achill woman. It made clear to me that what she and I shared, apart from those fragile moments of talk, was the danger of being edited out of our own literature by conventional tribalisms.

Marginality within a tradition, however painful, confers certain advantages. It allows the writer clear eyes and a quick critical sense. Above all, the years of marginality suggest to such a writer—and I am speaking of myself now—the real potential of subversion. I wanted to relocate myself within the Irish poetic tradition. I felt the need to do so. I thought of myself as an Irish poet, although I was fairly sure it was not a category that readily suggested itself in connection with my work. A woman poet is rarely regarded as an automatic part of a national poetic tradition; and for the reasons I have already stated. She is too deeply woven into the pasive texture of that tradition, to intimate a part of its imagery, to be allowed her freedom. She may know, as an artist, that she is now the maker of the poems and not merely the subject of them. The critique is slow to catch up. There has been a growing tendency in the last few years for academics and critics in this country to discuss women's poetry as subculture, to keep it quarantined from the main body of poetry. I thought it vital that women poets such as myself should establish a discourse with the idea of a nation. I felt sure that the most effective way to do this was by subverting the previous terms of that discourse. Rather than accept the nation as it appeared in Irish poetry, with its queens and muses, I felt the time had come to re-work those images by exploring the emblematic relation between my own feminine experience and a national past.

The truths of womanhood and the defeats of a nation? An improbable intersection? At first sight perhaps. Yet the idea of it opened doors in my mind which had hitherto been closed fast. I began to think there was indeed a connection; that my womanhood and my nationhood were meshed and linked at some root. It was not just that I had a womanly feeling for those women who waited with handcarts, went into the sour stomachs of ships and even—according to terrible legend— eyed their baby's haunches speculatively in the hungers of the 1840s. It was more than that. I was excited by the idea that if there really was an emblematic relation between the defeats of womanhood and the suffering of a nation, I need only prove the first in order to reveal the second. If so, then Irishness and womanhood, those tormenting fragments of my youth, could at last stand in for one another. Out of a painful apprenticeship and an ethical dusk, the laws of metaphor beckoned me.

I was not alone. 'Where women write strongly as women' says Alicia Ostriker, the American poet and critic, in her germinal book, *Stealing the Language*, 'it is clear their intention is to subvert the life and literature they inherit'. This was not only true of contemporary women poets. In the terrible years between 1935 and 1940, the Russian poet Anna Akhmatova composed 'The Requiem'. It was written for her only son, Lev Gumilev, who at the start of the Stalinist Terror had been arrested, released, re-arrested. Then, like so many others, he disappeared into the silence of a Leningrad prison. For days, months, years Akhmatova queued outside. What is compelling and instructive is the connection it makes between her womanhood and her sense of a nation as a community of grief. The country she wishes to belong to, to be commemorated by, is the one revealed to her by her suffering.

And if ever in this country they should want
To build me a monument

I consent to that honour
But only on condition that they

Erect it not on the sea-shore where I was born:
My last links with that were broken long ago,

Nor by the stump in the Royal Gardens
Where an inconsolable young shade is seeking me

But here, where I stood for three hundred hours
And where they never, never opened the doors for me

Lest in blessed death I should ever forget
The grinding scream of the Black Marias,

The hideous clanging gate, the old
Woman wailing like a wounded beast.

Translation D M Thomas

IX

I want to summarise this argument. At the same time I am
concerned that, in the process, it may take on a false
symmetry. I have, after all, been describing ideas and
impressions as if they were events. I have been proposing
thoughts and perceptions in a way they did not and could not
occur. I have given hard shapes and definite outlines to
feelings which were far more hesitant.

The reality was different. Exact definitions do not happen
in the real life of a poet; and certainly not in mine. I have
written here about the need to repossess the idea of a nation.
But there was nothing assured or automatic about it. 'It is not
in the darkness of belief that I desire you' says Richard Rowan
at the end of Joyce's *Exiles* 'but in restless, living, wounding
doubt.' I had the additional doubts of a writer who knows
that a great deal of their literary tradition has been made up
in ignorance of their very existence; that its momentum has
been predicated on simplifications of their complexity. Yet I
still wished to enter that tradition; although I knew my angle
of entry must be oblique. None of it was easy. I reached
tentative havens after figurative storms. I came to understand
what Mallarmé meant when he wrote: 'Each newly acquired
truth was born only at the expense of an impression that
flamed up and then burned itself out, so that its particular
darkness could be isolated.'

My particular darkness as an Irish poet has been the subject of this piece. But there were checks and balances. I was, as I have said, a woman in a literary tradition which simplified them. I was also a poet lacking the precedent and example of previous Irish women poets. These were the givens of my working life. But if these circumstances displaced my sense of relation to the Irish past in Irish poetry, they also forced me into a perception of the advantages of being able to move, with almost surreal inevitability, from being within the poem to being its maker. A hundred years ago I might have been a motif in a poem. Now I could have a complex self within my own poem. Part of that process entailed being a privileged witness to forces of reaction in Irish poetry.

Some of these I have named. The tendency to fuse the national and the feminine, to make the image of the woman in the pretext of a romantic nationalism—these have been weaknesses in Irish poetry. As a young poet, these simplifications isolated and estranged me. They also made it clearer to me that my own discourse must be subversive. In other words, that I must be vigilant to write of my own womanhood—whether it was revealed to me in the shape of a child or a woman from Achill—in such a way that I never colluded with the simplified images of woman in Irish poetry.

When I was young all this was comfortless. I took to heart the responsibility of making my own critique, even if for years it consisted of little more than accusing Irish poetry in my own mind of deficient ethics. Even now I make no apology for such a critique. I believe it is still necessary. Those simplified women, those conventional reflexes and reflexive feminisations of the national experience; those static, passive, ornamental figures do no credit to a poetic tradition which has been, in other respects, radical and innovative, capable of both latitude and compassion.

But there is more to it. As a young poet I would not have felt so threatened and estranged if the issue had merely been the demands a national programme makes on a country's poetry. The real issue went deeper. When I read those simplifications of women I felt there was an underlying fault in Irish poetry; almost a geological weakness. All good poetry depends on an ethical relation between imagination and image. Images are not ornaments; they are truths. When I read about Cathleen Ni Houlihan or the Old Woman of the Roads or Dark Rosaleen

I felt that a necessary ethical relation was in danger of being violated over and over again; that a merely ornamental relation between imagination and image was being handed on from poet to poet, from generation to generation; was becoming orthodox poetic practice. It was the violation, even more than the simplification, which alienated me.

Once the image is distorted the truth is demeaned. That was the heart of it all as far as I was concerned. In availing themselves of the old convention, in using and re-using women as icons and figments, Irish poets were not just dealing with emblems. They were also evading the real women of an actual past: women whose silence their poetry should have broken. They ran the risk of turning a terrible witness into an empty decoration. One of the ironic purposes of my argument has been to point out that those emblems are no longer silent. They have acquired voices. They have turned from poems into poets.

Writers, if they are wise, do not make their home in any comfort within a national tradition. However vigilant the writer, however enlightened the climate, the dangers persist. So too do the obligations. There is a recurring temptation for any nation, and for any writer who operates within its field of force, to make an ornament of the past; to turn the losses to victories and to restate humiliations as triumphs. In every age language holds out narcosis and amnesia for this purpose. But such triumphs in the end are unsustaining and may, in fact, be corrupt.

If a poet does not tell the truth about time, her or his work will not survive it. Past or present, there is a human dimension to time, human voices within it and human griefs ordained by it. Our present will become the past of other men and women. We depend on them to remember it with the complexity with which it was suffered. As others, once, depended on us.

A note on the author

Eavan Boland lives in Dublin with her husband Kevin Casey and two daughters. Her collections of poetry include *New Territory* (1967), *The War Horse* (1975), *In Her Own Image* (1980), all published by Arlen House. Her *Selected Poems* was published in 1989 by Carcanet Press.

5

IRELAND:
Between the First and the
Third Worlds

Carol Coulter, 1990

There has been much debate recently about the use of the female image to represent Ireland, ranging from the academic discourse of the Yeats Summer School to the polemical—and banned—film by the Derry Film Video Group, *Mother Ireland*. This could be dismissed as self-indulgence on the part of literary critics or radicals' nostalgia for the language of revolutionary nationalism, were it not for the resurgence of this image in new guise in contemporary political debate. Our political leaders and commentators of today are every bit as ready as our poets and revolutionaries to turn to the language of personal relationships when seeking to express and explain national aspirations. However, the terminology is different.

This is particularly evident in the sphere of Anglo-Irish relations, which are frequently spoken of in language normally applied to the field of marital breakdown. Ronan Fanning writes of 'the bond with Britain', while 'the totality of relationships between these two islands' has come to be a catch-phrase. Speaking of the Anglo-Irish agreement, James Molyneaux described it as 'two nations locked in a loveless marriage which has irretrievably broken down', ironically echoing Seamus Heaney's poem, 'Act of Union'. Equally common are exhortations to forget the past, to forge a new relationship based on new realities and mutual respect, to embrace 'forgiveness' and 'reconciliation'.

All this conjures up an image of a marriage gone wrong, of years of bitterness and discord, certainly, leaving a heritage of suspicion and querulousness. But wiser counsel demands that all this is put behind us and that a new relationship is forged on the basis of mutual, if more limited, cooperation—for the sake of the children.

Fundamental to the concept of marriage is that it is a relationship freely entered into by both parties. If it goes wrong there are faults on both sides and there is no point in recriminations or in apportioning blame. All sensible people agree that the separation should be effected with the minimum of confrontation.

However, if we pursue the image of male-female relations with reference to the history of those between Britain and Ireland, a more appropriate image is that of kidnap and multiple rape—the enforced domination of a nation and centuries of exploitation. This suggests a different trajectory for the relationship which follows the escape of the victim, who should not be expected to behave like an estranged spouse.

This use of language is more than a question of style. It is part of the development of a modern political ideology in this country which seeks to minimise our colonial history and heritage, and therefore ignore the implications of this history for an analysis of our present problems and solutions for the future. If we come to believe in a past unsullied by colonial conquest we can look forward to a future in which we are no less—and no more—than any other Western European nation, entering into a new experience of Europe on the same basis as everyone else.

In this pamphlet I want to argue that any discussion of Irish politics must start from our experience of colonialism and imperialism, which ended in a compromise with the former coloniser which denied true emancipation. This has left us with a heritage which included political institutions designed to prevent significant social change, and it is futile for feminists, socialists, or anyone seeking it to do so through them. To help us understand this, we should look to the experiences of other former colonies and also to our fellow-Europeans in East and Central Europe which also experienced national oppression.

The Irish 'national question' is thus as much at the centre of seeking a solution to the social, economic and political ills of the south as to ending the political crisis in the north. I argue for a reappraisal of the radical and revolutionary content of Irish nationalism, freed from the pseudo-nationalist ideology created by the architects of the southern state, and fused with the new radical thinking now emanating from these other former colonies and subjugated nations.

It is of course undeniable that we are part of Europe, geographically, historically and ethnically. We can neither deny it nor imagine a future outside it. But this must be refracted through our fundamental historical experience, which has formed our political institutions and our consciousness, with all its contradictions and complexities. And that is a colonial experience. Therefore the analogues of our institutions, our culture and our political life and expectations are to be found more in other former colonies than in the old imperialist power of Western Europe. The countries of Central Europe, most of them formerly part of the Austro-Hungarian empire, are another matter.

The suggestion that Ireland should be compared to Third World countries is often met with a combination of derision and indignation. What! Are we not white? And European? And, compared with the countries of the Third World, wealthy? And educated?

These objections are all true, but none of them negate our history and the political heritage it has left us, which has profound implications for the permanence and stability of our institutions and their capacity to permit major reform.

Indeed, we are not alone among former colonies in seeking to deny a family relationship with the lower-class members of this club, those with teeming masses of black or brown uneducated poor, the deserving recipients of our charity and our prayers.

Argentina is a case in point. Like the Irish, the Argentinians are white, well-educated, European in culture and outlook and, until recently, were relatively wealthy. Indeed, they were the biggest consumers of meat in the world in the 1950s and 1960s, with a high consumption of bread, rice, fresh fruit and other components of a balanced diet. Primary education was free and compulsory, and the state also provided free or almost free public secondary and technical schools—somewhat like the situation in Ireland until the end of the 1960s.

Not surprisingly, Argentinians reacted angrily to any attempt to include them in the Third World. However, their political history undermined their claim to be a fully paid-up member of the First. They had an embarrassing tendency towards military coups. And events of the last twelve months show the fragility of their economic prosperity, based as it was, on an economy which developed in total dependence on imperialism, particularly British and North American imperialism.

Interestingly, the Argentinian poet Luis Borges recognised the positive aspects of this experience both for his country and for Ireland:

> Our tradition is all of Western culture ...Veblen says that the Jews are outstanding in Western culture because they act within that culture and, at the same time, do not feel tied to it by any special devotion...and we can say the same of the Irish in English culture...I believe that we Argentines, we South Americans in general, are in an analogous situation; we can handle all European themes, handle them without superstition, with an irreverence which can have, and already does have, fortunate consequences.

I would suggest that it is neither geographical location nor level of economic development which explains our institutions and allows us to plan for the future in a realistic way. Rather it is our historically defined place in international relations and the political institutions we have inherited from the past, themselves the accumulation of battles fought between different social forces.

Irish Nationalism—a many-stranded tradition

The Palestinian writer and critic, Edward Said, has pointed out that there are two distinct political moments during a nationalist revival, the first the assertion of the reality of imperialist domination and the need to escape from it, the second the development of the 'post-nationalist' theme of liberation implicit in the works of Connolly, Garvey, Marti, Mariategi and DuBois.

The struggle for Irish independence has, since the latter part of the nineteenth century, been fused with the struggle for the social emancipation of the most oppressed sections of the Irish population, the tenant farmers and workers. These two strands cohabited in an uneasy alliance and the future of the poor was often sacrificed for the sake of the political aspirations of the nascent Irish middle class.

This was not just an Irish problem. The labour movement which developed in Europe and America in the nineteenth century, and expanded throughout the world in the twentieth century, never saw its own, independent role within the nationalist movement. During the crucial period in Irish history, the Second International, dominated by parties from the major imperialisms of Europe, could offer nothing to tenant farmers and workers in Ireland or anywhere else struggling against colonial exploitation and facing the half-heartedness of their own bourgeoisie.

Women's organisations emerged also at this time, and generally sided with the most oppressed foot-soldiers of the struggle against British imperialism and its local allies. In her thorough study of women and Irish nationalism, *Unmanageable Revolutionaries*, Margaret Ward points out that the women of the Ladies Land League were far more radical than Parnell in pursuing the demands of the tenants; that Inghinidhe na héireann, unlike Sinn Féin, campaigned to support the workers during the 1913 Lockout and the women in Cumann na mBan were among the most radical opponents of the Treaty.

The development of these nationalist women's organisations coincided with that of the suffragette movement and, indeed, there was frequent cooperation between these two strands of the women's movement. This period of national awakening, therefore, saw the emergence of a plethora of groups, movements and organisations operating in the social, political and cultural arenas. Whatever their common national aspirations, they often represented different interests and as the national struggle unfolded some would come to dominate over others.

Modern critics of Irish nationalism represent it as monolithic, a unified ideology which produced as its inevitable embodiment the southern Irish state. This ideology is seen as socially and economically conservative, Gaelic, deeply imbued with catholicism, narrow and inward-looking. The state it would produce would inevitably contain these flaws, it is argued.

This is a kind of retrospective argument. Faced with the modern Irish state it is easy to find in Irish nationalism all the elements which serve as its ideology. (By this I mean the southern state. Only in the southern part of the partitioned country has there been the development of any state. The northern part cannot really be called a state in its own right but is rather an extension of the British state, distinguished from it only by its specially repressive characteristics in the field of personal and civil rights.)

The many other elements which were undoubtedly present in Irish nationalism—not just at the level of ideology, but expressed in living people—ranging from socialism and feminism to religious scepticism and various forms of mysticism, were defeated and their adherents marginalised or forced to keep their dissident views to themselves. This defeat was by no means inevitable. Nor is it irreversible.

The historical point when this occurred was with the Treaty, although there were several other important moments around that, from the formation of the First Dáil, through the Civil War and culminating in the 1937 Constitution, which followed Fianna Fáil's entry into the Dáil and subsequent election victory. This period was marked by social unrest, by strikes, factory and land occupations, in parts of the north as well as the south, involving Protestants in the north as well as the predominantly Catholic workers of the south.

No one should be surprised at this. The decade from the Rising to the British General Strike of 1926 was one of revolutionary activity throughout Europe, with millions of women and men seeking fundamental changes in their circumstances.

The Irish state which came into being in this period was, in Said's words, 'The old colonial structures replicated in new national terms'. In this it can be compared with many other states which were formed following the formal ending of imperialist domination, but without a radical transfer of power between social classes. Indeed, the maintenance of 'old colonial structures' was imperative precisely in order to prevent a transfer of political power to those who bore the brunt of imperialist exploitation. The new ruling class had no structure of its own to put in their place and politics, like nature, abhors a vacuum.to prevent a transfer of political power to those who bore the brunt of imperialist exploitation. The new ruling class had no structure of its own to put in their place and politics, like nature, abhors a vacuum.

Disguising the old

Central to the functioning of the new Irish state was the civil service. This was maintained intact, with the civil servants, including very senior ones, changing masters with equanimity. In his autobiography, *Man of No Property* (Volume Two), Todd Andrews describes the mistrust with which Fianna Fáil viewed the civil service when it came to power. But it did nothing to dismantle it, or even to purge it, thus revealing its eagerness to model the new Irish state on the old colonial one.

This was carried through to the form of the parliamentary system, with its upper and lower houses, and the maintenance of the legal system, even including the absurdity of keeping judges and barristers in wigs and gowns. The laws adopted earlier in England to meet the needs of colonialism and finance capital were kept intact on the statute books, and to this day legal precedent set in Britain is used in Irish courts.

Another institution which survived the transition from British to Irish rule was the Catholic Church. Indeed, it did so with its power enhanced. The special kind of collaboration between the Church and the state which is such a mark of the modern Irish state began under the British administration and was developed when independence was established. Were it not for the roots it had put down in the education and health systems under British rule, it could not play the role in them it does today.

The institutions inherited from Britain reflect the specific character of former British colonies, as opposed to former colonies of other powers, particularly Spain and Portugal. Although, like them, it ruled by military domination, applied when the need arose, its grip was maintained through its administration, and this system survived its departure.

British domination characteristically took the form of a unique combination of a civil service modelled on its own and cooperation with native power structures. India had a ready-made and long-established social structure with which the British system was able to combine. In the case of Ireland, however, Britain's attempt to incorporate the native Irish ruling caste failed very early on. Later it tried to use the Church, and it is interesting to see how Britain cultivated the Catholic Church throughout the nineteenth century, as it became clear that resistance to its rule was becoming more and more widespread.

Spain, despite its extensive colonial possessions, was unable (because of the backwardness of its own society, dominated by an inert and profligate aristocracy) to develop a real colonial administration. It exported to its colonies a habit of seizing and holding vast tracts of land and of raising pillaging armies dominated by this landowning class. Most Latin American countries continue to be dominated by a small class of big landowners, who provided the basis for the development of much of the rest of native capital, and most of them also have huge armies, frequently the only permanent institution in the country apart from the Catholic Church.

So the countries of Latin American, including those, like

Argentina and Brazil, which have controlled great wealth, look very different from Ireland. They are dominated by land-based oligarchies. They have vast armies with a sense of political mission, even if not always fulfilled. We have a tiny army, not linked to any political party or ruling group, which has no will—or capacity—to play a political role.

But this should not lead us to conclude that the Latin American countries are part of post-colonial society and we are not, that they are thus characterised as of the Third World while we are conspicuously of the First. It means only that the colonial structures we have inherited are different. Different, but equally inherited. It could also be pointed out that India, like us a former British colony, has a vast civil and public service and an army which has never played a part in politics.

Societies and states which struggle to find a space between their own history as colonies and the domination of the world by the big imperialist powers, while seeking simultaneously to preserve their social order undisturbed, carry the marks of this on their political institutions and their culture. These marks are different from those borne by the major European countries, including the smaller ones like Holland and Belgium, whose political development, by and large, follows their economic development and needs.

Irish political institutions, political culture, language and habits, have, I would argue, more in common with many Latin American and indeed Eastern European countries than with our Western European neighbours. Poland, Hungary and Czechoslovakia also spent centuries under the domination of a powerful neighbour (or two, in the case of poor Poland). They too suffered from the suppression of their language, culture and, in the case of Poland and Czechoslovakia, of their religion. They also experienced the growth of large nationalist movements in the nineteenth century in which literature and culture played a major role. They won their independence in the revolutionary surge sparked off by the first world war.

Since the end of the second world war, the history of these countries has been very different from ours. But that is a period of only forty-five years, far from being long enough to create a new political culture. Further, their subsequent experience of foreign domination and, in the cases of Hungary or Czechoslovakia, of invasion, have strong echoes of the past, even if their source, and the social system they accompany, is different.

The search for a definition of identity and real sovereignty, the intensity of cultural debate and its fusion with political discussion, albeit linked to the political problem of the fight against totalitarianism, have interesting parallels with the contemporary Irish experience. An attempt to find a European identity on the basis of parallels with France, Holland or even Portugal has far less basis in historical reality.

Turning again to the parallels with Latin America, we find that, like them, our major political parties have their origins in a revolutionary nationalist movement, still reflected, however shamefacedly, in their constitutions and rhetoric. Even Fine Gael pays ritual obeisance to the aim of the establishment of a united and independent Ireland, though the party which has appropriated this objective as its own is Fianna Fáil.

Legitimising the new state

However, unlike the countries of Latin America, Irish independence was not established unequivocally, and it took some years for the new state to gain acceptance among the whole population. Fianna Fáil and the Catholic Church were both crucial to this.

The Church accepted Fianna Fáil only when it indicated its willingness to accept the legitimacy of the Free State, by its decision to take seats in a newly created twenty-six county parliament. The Church's first commitment was to the Free State, whose foundation it supported to the hilt, justifying the draconian measures taken by the Cumann na nGaedheal government to consolidate it.

Thus began the relationship of mutual dependence between the new Irish state and the Catholic Church. From the outset they supported each other and during the early years of the state, the Church established its grip on key parts of the public service, notably education and health, and had its moral and social teaching enshrined in legislation.

In fact, the control the Church exercises on health and education is much more than a moral one. It provides a material base (in terms of property like the valuable site of Carysfort College, recently sold) for the exercise of political power and influence in a broader sphere.

In the beginning, the custodians of the new Irish state were Cumann na nGaedheal, a party of heterogeneous origins. Although born of a split in Sinn Féin, it quickly attracted the remnants of the formerly anti-Sinn Féin forces. Its ideology was defined rather by what it opposed (republicanism, subversion and chaos) than by what it stood for and, although cowed by the Catholic Church, it did not have the self-confidence to establish the intimate relationship with it that de Valera's Fianna Fáil did.

But this came only with de Valera's conversion to constitutional politics. In *The Rise and Decline of Fianna Fáil*, Kevin Boland describes how this came about: 'There was no acceptance of the legitimacy of the Free State, which had been officially characterised at the La Scala [meeting] as a pretence at democracy. It was merely a question of recognising the *de facto* situation for practical reasons.'

He points out that what made the southern state 'legitimate' for Fianna Fáil and their supporters was the adoption of the 1937 (Fianna Fáil) Constitution. From this time on, he writes, 'there could be no doubt, in the mind of any reasonable person, of the legitimacy of the elected government'. It was the election of Fianna Fáil to government, and the subsequent elaboration of a constitution, which rendered the state legitimate in the eyes of the mass of the people, he claims.

There is more than an element of truth in this assertion. Before the decision of de Valera to enter the Dáil, both the Dáil itself and the Cumann na nGaedheal government were viewed with suspicion and hostility by a large proportion of the population, and this party's early rule was accompanied by severe repression of and discrimination against suspected republican sympathisers. Nor was it any better for others who hoped to see liberation after the departure of the British. The rights and conditions of women, workers and the poor generally were pushed into the background or ignored, and a series of laws passed (on divorce, censorship and the like) reflecting the growing hold of the Catholic Church on public life to the detriment of women and the poor. The new government singularly failed to establish popular support.

This was evident in the first post-Treaty election, where the governing party received only 39% of the vote, despite the fact that most of the active opposition was on the run or interned and that the resources of the state it controlled were used to disrupt the Sinn Féin campaign. The latter, in these very adverse conditions, received 26.7% of the vote. Given that this was on the basis of the non-recognition of the state, it was hardly a recipe for political stability.

So the acceptance by Fianna Fáil of the legitimacy of the state in the south was absolutely crucial for establishing its stability. Although people were war-weary and demoralised, and those who sought radical change had been defeated, without the foundation and construction of Fianna Fáil as a bridge between a large dissident minority and the new state, the Free State would have remained as something alien to a large proportion of the population. It would have required constant coercion to ensure political quietude, with the attendant danger of an explosion of discontent—a situation not dissimilar to that which prevailed in the north.

A new past and a new character were created for Mother Ireland, de Valera's metaphorical bride, by Fianna Fáil. If Ireland was a woman, she was also Irish-speaking, Catholic and (paradoxically) a virgin. If she had once been kidnapped and raped, no offspring ensued and thus no provision needed to be made for them and it could all be put behind her and a new, pure life built. History was rewritten to present successive nationalist movements as expressions of an uninterrupted fight for the Catholic faith. Nationality was presented as identical with religion, thus removing any necessity to look closely at the real social, political and cultural content of colonial domination. Doing so might prompt people to make comparisons uncomfortable to the new rulers.

The ideology created in these years, with the enthusiastic support and participation of the Catholic Church, justified the growing grip of Fianna Fáil on the machinery of the state, and on the development of an infrastructure for the fledgling independent economy.

Control of the state also meant control of patronage, and this control was used by both major parties to advance the interests of their supporters. At a national level it meant that supporters had access to jobs in the judiciary and at the head of state-sponsored bodies. Later it might mean a state grant. At local level, which was more important in terms of popular support, a word from a TD could mean a job working with the county council or one of the state companies, the main sources of employment outside agriculture in the 1940s, 50s and early 60s. It was understood that in return, the recipients of the favour, their family and friends, would vote for the obliging TD, and this understanding was usually faithfully honoured. Thus were people bound both to the state and the party.

As Frank McDonald of *The Irish Times* has pointed out, it was a logical step from this to more direct corruption, the exchange of money for favours, which surfaced in the recent Dublin planning scandal. The culture of corruption, a feature of all neo-colonial societies, had already been created, albeit within the framework of legality up to then.

It is true that in other Western European countries—and in the United States of America—senior public appointments often depend on party affiliation. But this is not true at a general level and even where local government officials control access to certain jobs, this has operated in a context where people could find employment elsewhere in the economy. It did not act as political cement, binding people to one or other political party, in the way it did in Ireland.

The Latin American experience
One must look to countries outside Western Europe and the United States of America to find analogies for the way in which the major political parties, particularly Fianna Fáil, operate. While in Colombia, early in 1989, I was surprised to discover how familiar the political scene was. Political life was dominated by two political parties whose history was marked by intermittent war between them, but who had come to a truce on the basis of an agreement that neither of them would seek to monopolise political power and patronage. Both are linked to the big land-owners, big business—and individuals within both parties have links with the drug mafia.

The political system was, and remains, one in which access to any area of public life, to even the most menial job in the public service, is controlled by the major political parties. This has been modified in recent years, but until recently the tendrils of the political parties, especially the Liberal party, reached into trade unions, municipal organisations and the limited public service, binding people to the state far more effectively than any intermittent participation in the electoral process. Serious political questions are not decided in elections, where there is no real choice, and the rigid political and military structures, based on the need to keep the mass of the population out of active political life, will permit of no fundamental change.

Our institutions share this inflexibility. Unlike the political institutions of our Western European neighbours, which evolved out of the changing needs of the indigenous ruling groups, they were born of a compromise between the former colonising power and the native ruling class to whom they were handing over. Essential to that compromise was the maintenance of continuity with the old regime, while giving the appearance of creating a new one, ostensibly the product of years of popular struggle. Hence the green post-boxes, the cúpla focal, the Irish names for parliamentary institutions and parties. But behind the green and Gaelic facade lies the heritage of British legislation, of a two-tier parliament, of a civil service and police modelled on the lines of the colonial power, all upholding a social system entirely in accord with the interests of that power.

For some years now political commentators and politicians from Fine Gael and the pre-Damascus road Progressive Democrats have been bewailing the 'clientelism' of Irish politics. People see their TDs as the donors of favours, as their mediators, and the politicians are therefore forced to spend their time dealing with petty individual problems rather than concerning themselves with affairs of state. Casting longing glances at Britain and Continental Europe, these politicians deplore the blinkered ignorance of the Irish electorate which fails to recognise the lofty tasks to which politicians aspire, and expects them to be errand boys and girls instead.

In September last Padraig Flynn, Minister for the Environment and archetypal Fianna Fáil politician (rural-based, Catholic, conservative), made a spirited defense of clientelism in the pages of *The Irish Times*, arguing that people feel alienated from and fearful of 'bureaucracy'. They feel the need for a more approachable figure to explain its workings and mediate between them and the faceless bureaucrats, to find individual details which might modify uncaring decisions. In his second article he quoted a survey of clientelism which found that rural-based people and the working class were more likely to believe in the efficacy of this kind of political brokerage than those from urban and middle-class backgrounds—significantly, precisely the traditional base of Fianna Fáil.

These are also the people who withheld initial recognition from the state, and who were lured into becoming involved in the political process through this mediating service on behalf of Fianna Fáil. Padraig Flynn rightly fears the danger of removing this conduit between the state and those he describes as suffering from 'isolation, alienation and a sense that you don't matter'. It is the function of politicians, he argued, to lessen people's sense of alienation from the state and political institutions they mistrust.

The foundation of Fianna Fáil and the manner in which it proceeded to organise and involve people in the complex political process, including elements of patronage, clientelism and corporatism, all 'part of what we are', was intended to legitimise the state and make it stable. However, in so doing Fianna Fáil made that state peculiarly unable to accommodate major change. It depends on a fragile balance between different interest groups, whose interests were built into its foundations, and which cannot now be disturbed.

Most conspicuous among them is the Catholic Church whose ownership (literally) of large areas of public life, like education and health, was a cornerstone of the state and sanctioned in the Constitution. Changes have been made, not by the election of a party dedicated to developing and implementing a programme of change, as happens elsewhere in Western Europe, but by negotiation between the government of the day and different interest groups. Which party is in power is largely immaterial, though Fianna Fáil has cultivated a wider variety of interest groups. Questions like social welfare, wages policy, health and education policy have been worked out more in the framework of discussions between the government, employers and unions than through any party implementing a political programme.

The positive side of political disillusionment
Yet all this has not succeeded in removing the vague contempt, the suspicion of impermanence, from the state, its laws and institutions. The lack of respect for the law gives rise to much public hand-wringing, and there is no doubt that the level of defiance of traffic and parking legislation, for example, is far higher here than in Britain. However defiance goes beyond parking on double yellow lines or cycling without a light on your bike. In September 1989 hundreds of people in Waterford kidnapped council workers sent to cut off water for non-payment of water rates.

The 1983 amendment to the constitution provides another example. Although the Society for the Protection of Unborn

106

Children (SPUC) obtained an injunction to prevent the dissemination of abortion information, this was recently defied by several student unions whose leaders indicated their willingness to go to jail in defiance of the law. SPUC suggested that the issue then was one of application of the law, and was no longer one of abortion. But this found few echoes from politicians, who knew full well that in this country the enactment of a law by parliament—or indirectly, by referendum—does not mean it will be obeyed. Endorsement by political institutions alone does not guarantee acceptance. The law must reflect a consensus negotiated outside parliament.

Why should people vote for parties offering them a programme for radical change? Understanding how the system works, they know that this would not happen, that things would go on much as before, with the influence of the powerful interest groups holding sway. So why not vote for a negotiator, a mediator, someone you can badger and blackmail into representing your individual interests?

This gives rise to despair among those politicians, especially on the left, who seek change through the Irish political system. But it has a positive side as well. The relative unimportance of the Dáil in the decision-making process means, not only that forces like industrialists, farmers and lay Catholic organisations can effect change through pressure, but so can other extra-parliamentary groups if they can win support.

A small example is the Rape Crisis Centre, which started off with a handful of women and no resources, but through some sympathy in the media and considerable organisational ability on the part of its organisers achieved changes in the treatment of rape victims by the police and the courts, achieved some state support for its services and influenced the report of the Law Reform Commission on rape, all in a relatively short time. In Britain much bigger pressure groups on various issues have been running around in circles for ages without making the slightest impact on Margaret Thatcher's government, for whom there is only one reality—her majority in parliament. In contrast, many of the changes in social legislation in Ireland have come about as a result of pressure from organised lobbies applied to whatever government was in power. This could be a very positive mechanism for people, especially women, who have little weight in the political system and political parties.

The fact that elections change very little in Ireland implies actual or potential disillusionment with the political system. As I have argued above, Fianna Fáil sought, and succeeded, in acting as a buffer between potentially disillusioned voters and that system. But now that is threatened by the crisis in Fianna Fáil induced by the changes within it, culminating in the leadership's acceptance of coalition.

This should be a cause of rejoicing, not dismay, among those who seek radical change in Ireland, north and south. The political system in this part of the country is not amenable to fundamental change, any more than it is in the north. A crisis in its institutions should prompt all those anxious to see change to reconsider its foundation, the premises on which it is based, its ideology, and to look beyond them to a new framework for the whole island.

Thus, far from the 'national question' being a device to divert the attention of people in the south from their immediate and day-to-day problems, it is intimately connected to the solution of these problems.

The 'national question' concerns the capacity of the people living in the south to live a life free of exploitation and oppression as much as it concerns the need to end the decades of discrimination, repression and warfare in the north, and all that derive from them.

An uneasy, unarticulated suspicion that this might indeed be so has given rise to a fear of nationalism among the southern middle class, expressed in the concern that the 'trouble' in the north will 'spill over' into the south, seeping into our carefully stabilised society like a malign virus.

Of course for the unemployed youth of Darndale and Tallaght there is little hope except that the instability in the north will indeed 'spill over' and threaten the system that has so alienated them, and so among the working class and especially the youth there is considerable, if unformed and inarticulate, support for the Irish Republican Army (IRA). But the uncomfortable recognition of this only serves to reinforce the dominant consensus that the 'trouble' in the north must be contained at all costs, and the IRA, now cast as the source of it all, destroyed.

The creation of an ideology

The past twenty years have seen the growth of a consensus

among politicians and commentators that the northern problem must be contained and, it is hastily added, of course ultimately solved. The first priority, therefore, is to contain and if possible reduce the violence.

Here common cause has been made with Britain, and hence the apologetic downgrading of the history of colonisation, the substitution of language describing colonisers' rapaciousness with that of marital discord. Hence also the embarrassed disavowal of 'old fashioned nationalism', the fear that this will jeopardise the prospects of a new harmony with our estranged neighbours and of 'reconciliation' between the 'two traditions' in the north, and ultimately on this island, necessary to 'peaceful reunification'.

In fact, this developing new orthodoxy is part of a continuum with the 'old nationalism' it seeks to repudiate. The real break in the political thinking in the southern state came, not with the reputed 'revisionism', but with the Treaty, partition and the need for an ideology to legitimate them. For all its bluster, the nationalism used to justify the formation and consolidation of the new state was in fact a carefully constructed bulwark against a resurgence of a radical anti-imperialism that, drawing on the grievances of the artificially-created minority of the north, might fuse with the disappointment of the small farmers, women, workers and also intellectuals in the south who found their circumstances little changed—or changed for the worse—by independence.

Yet for the 'traditional' nationalist ideology to be developed in the 1920s, 30s and 40s, it needed to contain elements of the real experience of the mass of the Irish people, the experience of dispossession, oppression and discrimination which fed the successive nationalist movements of the nineteenth century. The native language and culture really were suppressed, hundreds of thousands of people really were dispossessed of their land and displaced, over a million really did starve during the Famine...and these and other experiences really were the result of British policy at the time. The existence of anti-imperialist sentiment (not surprisingly, predominantly anti-British in form) among Irish people is due, not to a bigoted education, but to this reality.

What the Free State and its ideologists sought to do was take the revolutionary sting out of it, rewrite and oversimplify this experience and represent it as centuries-long struggle for formal independence and for the untrammelled flowering of a Catholic identity, after years of subjugation to the Protestant identity of the conqueror. A Catholic state for a Catholic people indeed. Further, 'patriotism' now became identified with the economic and political consolidation of this state, under the leadership of the 'entrepreneurial class' as described by Kevin Boland when he outlined the early ideology of Fianna Fáil.

It suited this class down to the ground to entrust the education of the youth, and the formulation of social policy, to the Catholic Church. The outlook which it put forward in the 1930s, with its corporate view of society, sought to deny class divisions, to preach satisfaction with the economic status quo and to keep women and young people subordinated to husbands and fathers. The asceticism it preached conformed perfectly to de Valera's vision of rural-based frugal simplicity with the illusory national independence presented as a consolation for the lack of material comforts.

Consciously or not, the nationalist ideology developed at this time was deeply partitionist in nature. Presenting the southern state as the achievement of the fight for national freedom was in fundamental contradiction to a perspective of the freedom and independence of the whole country. It destroyed any common heritage with the Protestant small farmers and working class of the country, most of them living in the northern part of it. It provided unionist politicians with ample ammunition to bolster their contention that Irish independence meant Rome rule and economic backwardness. Unionist ideology among the Protestant working class, weakened during the revolutionary upheavals of the 1913-1923 decade when it appeared that life was about to change fundamentally for everyone, was reinforced so that it is stronger now than ever before.

It was a short step from this for the ideologists of the south to present Protestants and Protestantism (whatever that may be) as the antithesis of Irish nationalism, as foreign in every sense, even, in moments of intense rhetoric, as representing the historical enemy. Meanwhile, with typical hypocrisy, they were slipping privileges to the small number of Protestants who lived in the south in the form of highly subsidised schools and hospitals, and encouraging the continued advance of those among them who held economic power. Thus was bought their silence concerning the suppression of personal liberties promoted by the Catholic Church, and its control over vast areas of public life. The Protestant churches were well-versed in rendering unto Caesar the things that were Caesar's; they had been doing so in Ireland for far longer than their Catholic counterparts. In the north, meanwhile, they enjoyed unrestricted influence in government, with clerics often participating openly in the Orange Order and the Unionist party.

This division of labour in helping to govern the whole country worked perfectly until the 1960s. The necessity of opening up the Irish economy had by then eroded the old kind of nationalism and its rural, Catholic values. But its crisis came with the outbreak of open rebellion in the north.

So now it is succeeded by talk of the necessity of 'reconciling' the 'two traditions', retrospectively legitimising partition by representing it as the inevitable outcome of the presence on this island of two distinct ethnic, cultural and political entities. No-one stops to ask—what two traditions? It is assumed that they refer to realities behind the rural, Gaelic, Catholic ideology of Irish nationalism and the urban, 'British' protestant ideology of unionism.

This is a total falsification of reality. The rural, Gaelic model of Irishness, itself an artificial construct, means far less to a child of a Catholic working class family from Dublin's inner city than it does to a Protestant child from a rural background in the West of Ireland. I had personal experience of this when I discovered how baffled my friends from Dublin working class background were by their primary school Irish and English textbooks, with their stories like 'A Day on the Bog', which had a deep resonance for me. As a Protestant I had less empathy with Jimín Mháire Thadhg's religious vocation, but even then more of my neighbours probably entered Catholic religious life than did the children of Ballyfermot or Finglas.

If that is true for the (Catholic) working class of the south, how much more alien is this ideology to the Catholic working class of Belfast and Derry? Although their religion is a badge of nationality, and in recent years learning Irish has become a mark of political consciousness, neither of these lead the people of the ghettoes to identify with the southern state.

This is less true of the northern Catholic middle class, frequently rural in origin, whose advancement in the northern state was always blocked by discrimination. As the long

111

association of the Nationalist Party, and now the SDLP, with the main parties in the south attests, they could readily find a common identity with those who created, built and now sustain the southern state. Austin Currie found no difficulty in transplanting himself south and becoming a Fine Gael TD in Dublin.

The Protestant population is not homogeneous either. In the south there are big cultural and political differences between people from urban and rural backgrounds, between the relatively poor members of the Protestant churches who integrated with their Catholic neighbours and those, richer, ones who did not. In the north too there are important social and cultural differences between Protestants from different social and geographical backgrounds, though these are either latent or have been largely submerged by the recent developments of different degrees of unionism, outside of which they can find no expression,

The notion of 'two traditions' suits those who want to maintain the *status quo* of an Irish and crypto British state, fiddling only with superficialities. The reality is far more complex. Like all countries with a history of colonialism, 'tradition' in Ireland is composed of many strands, of successive waves of immigration, of a blending of traditions and the creation of new syntheses, of battles between classes and groups in which religion was forced into the background, of intermarriage and shared experiences between new and old immigrants.

No one thinks this extraordinary when considering countries other than Ireland. Are the coloured and Indian populations of South Africa any less African than the black? Are the Spanish-derived or black people of Latin American countries any less Latin American than the native Indian peoples?

If we return to the rape image as appropriate to colonialism, the immigrants who came as colonisers inevitably bore the marks of their parentage. Yet no one would suggest making them pay for the sins of their father. That is, not unless they sought continued adherence to their rapacious parent and claimed special privileges because of his 'superiority', because of their whiter skin—or their religion. Yet the 'two traditions' idea implicitly endorses a pro-British tradition in Ireland as if it were a natural element, an act of nature, despite the fact that those who claimed Britishness also claim special privileges deriving from this status.

Beyond nationalism

The elements in Irish politics which feminists and socialists rightly identify as inimical to the interests of women and of workers are indeed to be found in the ideology built up around the twenty-six county state. But it is wrong to identify this with Irish nationalism, which has become deformed into twenty-six county pseudo-nationalism.

The search for the transformation of the conditions of the poor, many of them women, is not counterposed to the perspective of a totally free and independent Ireland in accordance with the liberationist message of revolutionary nationalism. On the contrary, the aspirations of workers, the poor and all the downtrodden and marginalised in Ireland can only ultimately be met in a framework other than that of the two states now in place on this island.

The only political tradition on this island which rejects the political institutions is that of the republican movement. However, because the republican movement does not seriously engage in any politics of a campaigning kind, postponing the resolution of all problems until the republican millenium, and has not explained its position in anything other than metaphysical terms, it fails to relate to the real concerns of the majority of the potentially disaffected and remains isolated. Nonetheless, at turning points in political life it has attracted considerable support because, I would argue, its rejection of the whole system struck an echo in the hearts and minds of those who sought a fundamental change in their circumstances.

Radical thinking in Ireland needs to reassess the heritage of the republican movement, whose concentration on the military campaign in the north and utter failure to respond to the social and economic problems of the population of the south, has obscured the potentially liberationist kernel of its message—that the political settlement of 1921 established a framework totally resistant to fundamental change, and that this settlement needs to be undone and a fresh start made.

This is not an argument for support for any wing of the republican movement as it exists today, but rather for the content of that tradition to be reintegrated into political debate, rather than excluded on the spurious basis that anyone engaging in that debate must first pass the litmus test of a McCarthyite declaration of the question of violence.

Apart from reassessing our own revolutionary heritage, which differs markedly from the political heritage of other European countries, we could learn from the other post-colonial societies which have also created political systems dedicated to preserving the essence of the social relations of the old society. The traditional parties of the left, while they exist, have singularly failed to challenge the established and governing parties in this country. But what has emerged more recently is a range of extra-parliamentary groups and movements, based on popular initiatives in local areas and specific campaigns on issues like the rights of minorities or in defence of the environment, which have generated widespread support and threaten the status quo. In Brazil (once one of the wealthiest countries in the world) this has led to the foundation of a new political party, the Workers Party, drawing all these movements together. In a few short years this party has succeeded in challenging, not only its rivals on the left, but the main representatives of the right.

So a sense of frustration with and alienation from political institutions need not be a cause for despair among people seeking change. On the contrary, it is to be welcomed as a basis for fresh and creative thinking and the organisation of the disaffected into movements and outlets not tied into these institutions. For almost seventy years the attempts to change Ireland through the political framework established out of the struggle for independence have failed and led people into false hopes. There are now multiple examples word-wide of alternatives to such a perspective.

Far from being ashamed of our colonial past, we should be happy to acknowledge and even embrace Ireland's status as a post-colonial society. Not only are fellow former colonies the centre of fresh thinking about politics in the world today, they are also the powerhouse of the most innovative art and culture, especially in the fields of literature and popular music. This is a far more exciting club to want to belong to than the complacent and paralysed world of the former colonialist and present-day imperialist powers.

In Europe, the countries of Eastern Europe are not as distant from our experience as we are led to believe. They too have similarities with our history (apart from the major difference of the second world war and its aftermath); they experienced a violation of democracy in the foundation and

114

consolidation of their regimes, with a resulting question mark over their legitimacy which remained in the consciousness of the population. Intellectual activity tends to operate outside of, and in implicit opposition to, the established institutions. Nationalism, even though pushed into the background for decades, remains a powerful force in people's consciousness.

Then when eventually popular organisations break through the strait-jacket of repressive mechanisms and force conformism (as in Poland in 1981) they take totally new forms. Solidarity developed as much more than a trade union as this is traditionally understood, and more like an umbrella for a plethora of trade union, political, social and cultural movements, all more deeply rooted and more original than traditional parties or organisations. The resurgence of popular movements in East Germany and Czechoslovakia reveals people's capacity for political creativity outside of established institutions.

So a suspicion of illegitimacy is no bad thing for a state to have. The lack of faith in established institutions it engenders leaves great scope for the development of radical alternatives, movements which allow for people's self-expression in a way which established political parties and trade unions, dominated as they are by fossilised habits and entrenched bureaucracies, cannot do.

In the Irish context the fusion of such movements with a critique of the very basis of the southern state, and therefore of its twin in the north, could allow for the development of an alternative political vision which would go beyond the endless futile tinkering with the existing system and offer the hope of real emancipation to all the impoverished, disillusioned and marginalised in this country.

References and further reading
Andrews, AS. *Dublin Made Me* and *Man of No Property*. Cork: Mercier Press, 1982.

Boland, Kevin. *The Rise and Decline of Fianna Fáil*. Cork: Mercier Press, 1982.

Fanning, Ronan. 'The British Dimension in Ireland: Dependence and Independence'. Dublin: *The Crane Bag* Vol 8 No 1, 1984.

Ferns, HS. *The Argentine Republic*. Newton Abbot: David and Charles. New York: Barnes and Noble, 1973.

Galeano, Eduardo. *Open Veins of Latin America*. New York: Monthly Review Press, 1973.

Rupnik, Jacques. *The Other Europe*. London: Weidenfeld and Nicholson, 1988.
Said, Edward. *Yeats and Decolonisation*. Derry: Field Day Pamphlet No 15, 1988.
Ward, Margaret. *Unmanageable Revolutionaries*. Dingle: Brandon Press; London: Pluto Press, 1983.

Acknowledgements
Thanks to John Daly, Declan Kiberd and Harry Vince for their comments and suggestions.

A note on the author
Carol Coulter was born and spent her childhood in County Sligo, leaving to attend school in Dublin at the age of eleven. She studied English at Trinity College Dublin where she was active in student and left-wing politics. She has been a committed trade unionist and a socialist since then. In 1977 she started working as a freelance journalist and joined *The Irish Times* in 1986. She is interested in both Irish and world politics, and has visited Latin America and Eastern Europe in the course of her work.

6

THE POLITICS OF SEDUCTION

Trudy Hayes, 1990

Introduction

The politics of seduction is about the disparity between the sexes where it is traditional for the male to make the first move in initiating a relationship or a seduction. It is about male sexual conditioning; it is about male expectations; it is about male power and privilege.

If we look at literature, romantic fiction, pornography, popular culture or twentieth century sexology it becomes clear that a large part of male sexuality is intrinsically bound up with power and domination. The fact that men traditionally take a sexual initiative is just one aspect of the whole spectrum of male power. The fact that women rarely take the initiative is just one aspect of female powerlessness. 'The Politics of Seduction' explores male sexual dominance and female sexual passivity, and the political and sexual consequences of this imbalance in the relationship between the sexes.

I was at a party recently with a group of women and we were all having a wonderful time when a fat, drunken man with a monstrous beer belly, his eyes bloated and bloodshot with drink, joined us at a table with a friend. 'Hey Joe—I've found a table full of women for you,' he said, sitting down. He then propositioned every woman at the table, stood up and performed a sort of primitive mating dance around the table and fell over. We left him finally, a drunken, pathetic figure huddled over a bottle of vodka.

Was this the archetypal predatory male, fuelled by alcohol, stalking his territory among the female sex? It is quite inconceivable that a drunken woman would approach a table full of men in such a manner. Women are at the opposite end of the spectrum—they must wait, like quivering violets, for the man to approach them, rather than take the initiative, because it is traditional for the man to make the first move.

Some Seduction Scenes

It is taken for granted in almost all literature that the sexual

117

protagonist is the male. The following is an extract from 'Durling, Or The Faithless Wife' by Sean O'Faolain:

> He had been stalking the beautiful Mlle O'Murphy whose real name was Mrs Meehawl O'Sullivan for some weeks, and she had appeared to be so amused at every stage of the hunt, so responsive, séduisante, even entrainante, that he could already foresee the kill over the next horizon.

This passage quite clearly projects the ritual of seduction as a 'conquest', and maybe men like to see themselves as the aggressor in order to affirm their sense of masculine superiority. The passage reflects the mentality of a caveman and perhaps civilisation hasn't really progressed beyond the pursuit by the beast of his prey. Cavemen armed with clubs no longer roam the forest but smooth young men armed with credit cards can 'score' a conquest in nightclubs with similar gratification.

It is not quite acceptable for the woman to make the first move in initiating a relationship or a seduction, nor even to declare her love first. The following is an extract from *Long Walk To Forever* by Kurt Vonnegut:

> 'If I'd loved you,' she said, 'I would have let you know before now.'
> 'You would?' he said.
> 'Yes' she said. She faced him, looking at him, her face quite red. 'You would have known' she said.
> 'How?' he said.
> 'You would have seen it' she said. 'Women aren't very clever at hiding it.'

So the man is supposed to know by some subtle flutter of the eyelash that the woman loves him. Poor Bridie in 'The Ballroom of Romance' loses Patrick O'Grady because she never told him she loved him, while Judith Hearne in Brian Moore's novel deludes herself that a man loves her because she is not at liberty to make her own intentions clear.

All that was in a bygone era but times have not changed to the point where a woman is free to take the initiative. Even an avowedly feminist novel like *How To Save Your Own Life* by Erica Jong, which champions a woman's right to sexual and emotional fulfilment has the following scene where the sexually liberated heroine invites a young man back to her hotel bedroom for a drink:

> 'I can't let him out of my life,' I thought. I looked up, asking

to be kissed. And when our tongues touched, it was somehow all decided.

'Please stay the night,' I said. I shocked myself by saying this. So brazen. So woman-the-aggressor.

If the heroines of feminist literature cannot challenge the conventions of male sexual domination, what chance has the woman in the street? Jane Eyre is one of the very few romantic heroines to break the mould—she bravely declares her love for Rochester but she has had few successors.

Stephanie Calman's book, *Dressing For Breakfast*, billed as 'the hilarious truth about romance and real life', contains an essay, 'Party Lines', which aptly illustrates the passive role of women in society. It describes, very wittily, the paranoia a woman feels at a party on her own. The heroine stands around feeling conspicuous, in a dress that would look better on a bookcase and a pair of earrings like chandeliers. Suddenly she notices a man who has just arrived. He wears white tennis shoes and a shirt open to the waist and the following conversation occurs:

'If I had a gorgeous girl-fiend like you, I wouldn't let her go to parties on her own.' he remarks.
'Really? I find I can make these decisions on my own.'
'Ooh, you're obviously the independent type.'
'Yes, I can tie my own shoelaces and everything.'
'Ouch. I felt that. You're not one of those women's libbers are you? Oh save me!'
'Well...'
'Nah. You're too good-looking.'

Our heroine escapes from the party idiot and goes over to talk to an old school friend. Suddenly she sees a man, and thinks:

'Who is that gorgeous man over there? I wouldn't mind getting him to nibble the back of my neck. He's looking at me. No, he isn't. Yes he is! Oh, I can't tell anything in here, it's so dark. How can I get to talk to him? I can't just march over and start in!'

But why not? Tennis-shoes has no problem marching over to her but this sharp-tongued young woman does not allow herself the same liberty. She eventually meets Mr Gorgeous in the kitchen while hiding from Tennis shoes. All things being equal, the heroine would have approached the man.

These examples indicate how pervasive male sexual

dominance is both in literature, which mirrors social convention, and real life. Women rarely take a sexual initiative, for fear of compromising their femininity and thereby becoming undesirable to a potential lover. Women's passivity is really a reflection of male expectations, and men expect to be in control. In the same way a woman may not fulfil her true potential for fear of antagonising men by being too strident, too aggressive, too successful. Our whole sexual culture pressurises women into accepting a passive, sexy role. It is essential to throw off this conditioning and confront the insidious pressures defining women's sexuality.

The fetishisation of female bodies

The extent to which the female body is fetishised in our society, unlike the male body, is quite incredible, and there is tremendous pressure on women to live up to an idealised image of female beauty. Down through the ages women's bodies have been pulled, pummelled, tucked and bound into the mythical embodiment of perfection. Endless diets and exercise regimes advise women how to tighten tummies, tauten thighs and firm up bottoms. Advertisements show women how to bolster breasts, and lengthen legs with stiletto heels. The cosmetics industry produces endless creams, lotions and potions and slim, perfect women stare out at us from advertising bill-boards, newspapers and magazines. The Miss World Competition is a powerful symbol of women's preoccupation with appearance and beauty.

This fetishisation of women's bodies places an abominable pressure on women to live up to an image of idealised beauty which is a pressure men simply do not experience as they see themselves in the role of sexual aggressors or 'seducers'. Women, however, may feel they must conform to a stereotyped female image in order to be attractive to men, which is a very unhappy burden for any woman to have to carry around.

The objectification of female bodies is reflected in the huge market for erotic female underwear. One Christmas I went in search of an interesting pair of men's pyjamas. As I wandered from shop to shop I was treated as a pervert because I was looking for a pair of black silk pyjamas. I had a vision of my boyfriend stretched out provocatively in such garb, but after making numerous enquiries of sniggering salesmen, I began to despair.

Finally I came upon a pair of pyjamas which I thought might suit my purpose. The salesman, who was short, fat and balding, could scarcely conceal a lewd grin. 'What size is your boyfriend, Miss?' he asked. I explained to him that the object of my desires was a bit taller than him, a bit slimmer and had more hair. On examination however, I decided against the pyjamas. My quest had proved fruitless—paisley patterns, stripes and spots seemed to be the height of male erotica.

The Page 3 girl is another example of the fetishisation of women's bodies and the ultimate incarnation of female degradation. Surely it is obvious that men who are reared in a society where degrading images of women are part of our everyday culture cannot help but have an insulting attitude towards women? The Page 3 girl phenomenon really reflects the true attitude of males towards females—women's real function is the gratification of male sexuality. Why isn't there a Page 3 boy? Not a chance! The role of sex object is exclusively female.

The society we live in treats women as inferior and this is hardly surprising given the sexual imagery of women which is prevalent. Men who are exposed to insulting and demeaning images of women can hardly respect the flesh and blood embodiment of these images—hence women have to deal with sexism, sex discrimination and sexual crime.

Female Sexuality

Men are commonly perceived as having a stronger sex drive than women, but are men naturally more predatory than women? One thinks of the scene in *Annie Hall* where Woody Allen and Diane Keaton are speaking to a psychiatrist about their relationship difficulties. The psychiatrist asks Diane does she have sex often, and she replies 'All the time—about three times a week.' He puts the same question to Woody who replies—'About three times a week, hardly ever.'

However, there is not much evidence to support the theory that the male sex drive is stronger than the female sex drive. According to the Hite report, it takes women four minutes on average to achieve orgasm while masturbating, but only 30% of the women interviewed achieved orgasm from sexual intercourse. In her book, *More about the Sex Factor and Marriage*, Dr Helena Wright acknowledged that many of her patients would complain that 'Try as we might, my wife can't attain an orgasm from intercourse.' Thus, she writes:

I began to criticise this universal demand...As soon as I began to shake myself free of the current ideal of expectations, and to doubt the efficacy of the penis-vagina combination for producing an orgasm for a woman, the path was cleared and progress began to be made.

A report from the 1930s, 'A Thousand Marriages' by Dickenson and Brean, concluded that sexual intercourse was unsatisfactory for two in three of the 1,000 women they had interviewed. Seymour Fisher's study, *The Female Orgasm*, estimated that only 39 per cent of women reached orgasm through intercourse. *The Women's Book of Love and Sex* reports only 24 per cent of unmarried women reaching orgasm through intercourse. Over half a century, the figures have been pretty consistent.

Malcolm Muggeridge once joked that, 'To the self-evident rights of the Declaration of Independence must be added another—the right to orgasm.' Yet a large number of women are not claiming this right. Even though the centre of gravity has shifted to the clitoris, the quintessential moment of heterosexual sex is still supposed to be penetration.

Sex, however, is not just about procreation. It is intrinsically bound up with love, desire and affection and a woman can often be best aroused by techniques that do not lead to conception. Despite the fact that such a small number of women achieve orgasm from sexual intercourse, it appears that women enjoy sexual intercourse for the emotional 'closeness' it affords, as most women stated in the Hite report. Yet our society revolves around the notion of sexual intercourse as the ultimate sexual experience. In fact, this pressure on women to orgasm during intercourse has been detrimental, and women have always, and still are, resorting to faking orgasms.

'The Performance' (Katy Hayes) is a short story published in *The Sunday Tribune* in 1989. It portrays two characters obsessed with their own image. Initially, both are equally concerned with their appearance:

She stared at herself in the mirror, examining every inch of the carefully applied cosmetics, tilting her head at every angle imaginable, sulking, smiling, pouting at herself. 'You're perfectly beautiful' she told the mirror.

The male is equally narcissistic:

He paused for a moment, held the razor aloft and looked

lovingly at the strong contours of his half-shaven face before
he carefully continued...He took a gilt-edged card from the
book-case, and with a final hard stare in the mirror, he left.

Maintaining the 'performance' metaphor, when the heroine
arrives at the party, 'she paused for a moment in the doorway and the audience turned to look at her figure'. The male
is 'conscious of the desiring eyes of the many women in the
room'. He 'stalks the party', and eventually approaches the
female and 'closes in on her', then brings her home.

And when they go to bed:

> She closed her eyes and saw herself from above. His dark hair
> contrasted beautifully with her blonde curls, his tanned body
> emphasising her pale skin, set off against the background of
> the crisp white linen bed. Panting lightly, he fulfilled an age-
> old need. 'What a performance' he thought to himself as she
> clawed his back and tossed her flaxen curls across the pillow.

> To the thunderous applause of a rapturous audience, she
> threw her arms above her head and quietly feigned a delicate
> orgasm. Exhausted, oblivious, he rolled over and she nestled
> against his under-arm hair.

The male's performance is a true performance—he is
performing sexually, while the female performs in the sense
of playing a role. Despite the fact that both characters are
equally narcissistic, the male is very definitely the 'subject'
and the woman is the 'object'. The man has used her body for
sexual gratification but the woman's gratification comes from
being 'sexy' and desirable—she doesn't have an orgasm.

There are many reasons why a woman might fake an
orgasm. The pressure is so great that an enormous number of
women do so—in the Hite study, out of 3,019 women
interviewed, a staggering 1,664 women confessed to having
faked orgasms. Here are some of their reasons:

- 'I fake it during clitoral stimulation and during intercourse
  when I'm not in the mood. It's quicker and faster than
  saying 'no' and then worry about my husband's feelings
  for me etc.'
- 'When I do it now it's because I know I'm not going to have
  an orgasm but my man is working hard for me.'
- 'I used to do it to please men and get their approval, and
  make them believe I was a sexy chick.'

The fact that women fake orgasms reflects the whole sexual

oppression of women, where a woman is expected to find true sexual fulfilment in being 'desirable', rather than in making sexual demands.

Women are the ultimate victims of a sexual culture which conditions women to be 'sexy' rather than sexual. Against this background masturbation has a great deal to recommend it. As one woman put it:

> I am entitled to orgasms. If I have to masturbate to get them, then my man should have to masturbate for his and that does not mean masturbating in my vagina—ie intercourse when he's the one who has orgasms.

Women feel they 'must' have an orgasm more to please the man than to please themselves. The following are sample remarks from the Hite Report:

> Yes, I like to have orgasms. It is only fair to him, and makes him feel more 'as a man' and successful. I 'perform' to boost his ego.

> Yes, alas, I still feel I must have an orgasm to make him feel, er, macho.

Another pressure is the pressure to be a 'real' woman.

> I can enjoy sex without orgasms, but psychologically I feel like I'm a failure, like a not totally functioning woman.

Women can feel very cheated if they don't have an orgasm. Also, almost unanimous evidence suggests that clitoral orgasm is more intense for most women even though it is basically established that both orgasms result from direct or indirect stimulation of the clitoris. The Hite Report is a validation of the earlier Kinsey Report: 'regardless of the joys of coitus, it is less likely than masturbation to terminate in orgasms—and for some women, it always or almost always terminates without orgasm'.

Despite women's reluctance to demand sexual fulfilment, it is conclusively proven by Masters and Johnston that women have an equal sex-drive to that of men so there is no reason why the male should naturally be more predatory than the female. However, women see themselves as sex objects rather than sex subjects and consequently may not demand sexual fulfilment. This is a very complex phenomenon—it reflects women's cultural conditioning and the conflicting messages women receive. Christianity glorifies virginity and denies sexuality. The sixties revolution liberated women sexually, but men still regard sexually active women as 'sluts'. Men are still expected to take the initiatives sexually so women may not like to make demands, and the endless bombardment of sexual imagery that deeply affects women projects an image of sexual desirability as sexual passivity; so these statistics are not surprising. Women's sexuality cannot be liberated until these conflicting cultural messages have been destroyed.

A further oppressive aspect of our sexual culture is the emphasis on heterosexuality as 'normal' sex when reliable statistics indicate that between ten and twelve per cent of women are lesbians. Sex between women often involves increased affection and sensitivity as well as increased frequency of orgasm. A lesbian relationship may be a more sexually, erotically and politically pleasing prospect than a heterosexual one, in a culture where all heterosexual relations are distorted by the political relationship between women and men.

It is important for women to realise their potential for experiencing sexual desire for another woman without the constraints of an aggressively heterosexual culture. However, one of the consequences of the 'passive' aspect of the female sexual tradition is that women may be slow to initiate a sexual encounter with another woman (outside explicitly gay and lesbian venues), especially as women have been conditioned to eroticise 'being desired' rather than 'desiring'. So for most women, it may be only when women are free from this oppressive conditioning that they will be free to fully express their sexuality, whether heterosexual or lesbian.

Virgin/whore

The ambiguity of male attitudes towards female sexuality is a cause for concern as it may discourage women from carrying condoms as a safeguard against AIDS. The AIDS problem is particularly dangerous for women as it is easier to transmit the disease from a man to a woman than the other way around. But as author and AIDS victim John Mordant said in an interview:

> People find AIDS and the topic of safe sex embarrassing. As one girl interviewed put it—'It's the last thing you'd want to say in the heat of the moment—"Jesus, let's get the johnny

out."' I do a lot of safe sex workshops with nurses and they always say, 'if you take out condoms he'll think we're slags or sluts'.

The ambiguous attitude of men toward women is best reflected in the virgin/whore dichotomy. As a twenty-one year old college student put it in an article in *Ms Magazine*:

> I sometimes think that what men want is a sexually experienced virgin. They want you to know all the tricks, but they don't like to think you did those things with anyone else.

Obviously, men no longer expect to go to bed with virgins but they still have sexually ambiguous attitudes towards women which make it difficult for women. In order to facilitate a man's need to 'seduce' or 'overcome' a woman, a lot of women play hard-to-get. As another American woman put it in the same article:

> At mid-century, it still took an elaborate seduction scenario to get a 'good girl' into bed that operated on the assumption that she didn't really want to, but could be swept away by forces outside her control.

After the sexual revolution of the sixties women discovered sexual freedom but it wasn't long before feminists began to question the more exploitative aspects of the sexual revolution which, in effect, took away a woman's right to say 'no'.

Ideally women would find true fulfilment in a society where they were free to explore their sexuality without pressure to conform to a male model and could choose to conduct their relationships on their own terms without encountering male prejudice or oppressive male expectations.

Male hostility towards women

'Women have very little idea of how much men hate them' wrote Germaine Greer in *The Female Eunuch*. Some men subconsciously hate and fear sex, and therefore women, because sex threatens their sense of rationality and self-control. Do men really hate women, as the whole desecration of women in pornography, misogyny and male sexual violence would seem to indicate? Is this a consequence of the Judaeo-Christian hatred of the flesh? Or are men in awe of women's power over life and death?

Norman Mailer refers to 'Man's sense of awe before a woman, his dread of her position as one step closer to eternity...which made men detest women, revile them, humiliate them, defecate symbolically upon them, do everything to reduce them...So do men look to destroy every quality (in a woman) which will give her the power of a male, for she is already in their eyes armed with the power that she brought them forth...'

There is plenty of evidence that men have always seen the body and soul as being divided. 'A woman's body, by inspiring desire in a man, reminds him of his own animal nature.' The poet Baudelaire wrote: 'Woman is natural, therefore abominable.' St Bernard said of women: 'Their face is a burning wind, and their voice the hissing of serpents but they also cast wicked spells on countless men and animals ... To conclude, all witchcraft comes from carnal lust, which is in woman insatiable.' St Paul was notoriously insulting:

A man should certainly not cover his head since he is the image of God and reflects God's glory, but woman is the reflection of man's glory. For man did not come from woman, no, woman came from man, and man was not created for the sake of woman, but woman was created for the sake of man.

A Dominican inquisitor said in the fifteenth century: 'Woman is more carnal than a man. There was a defect in the formation of the first woman since she was formed from a bent rib and since through this defect she is an imperfect animal—she always deceives.' St Augustine's view was that 'Nothing brings the manly soul down from the heights more quickly than a woman's caresses.' These and many other writers and thinkers provide an insight into the neurotic hostility men feel towards women and their consequent desire to abuse them.

Christianity involves, historically, a hatred of sex which manifests itself as a hatred of women. What emerges from the witch-hunts where thousands of women were burned at the stake is a widespread sexual fear and neurosis—witches were supposed to have sex with the devil and they were held responsible for the nocturnal emissions of sleeping males. The anti-sex propaganda of the church finally resulted in the deaths of thousand of women.

Christianity has always perceived sexuality as an uncontrollable force, as illustrated by the following story:

St Helias was an early Christian ascetic who ruled a convent of nuns. Being overcome by sexual temptation, he found he had to flee. However he was saved by divine intervention. Angels appeared to him—one held his hands, another his feet and the third cut off his testicles with a knife, although this did not happen in reality. Cured of his rampant sexual urges, he was able to go back to the convent.

The Talmud prescribes the following prayer of thanksgiving for a man: 'Blessed art thou, O Lord our God, King of the Universe, who hast not made me a woman.' 'To embrace a woman' wrote Odo of Cluny in the twelfth century 'is to embrace a sack of manure.' Aristotle remarked that 'We should look upon the female state as being, as it were, a deformity—though one which occurs in the ordinary course of nature.' And it was Dean Swift who said 'A little wit is attractive in a woman, as one is pleased when a parrot speaks a few words', not to mind Dr Johnston, who said 'A woman should be struck regularly, like a gong!'

Perhaps there is a deeply embedded hatred of women built into the male psyche. American psychologist Dorothy Dinnerstein argues that because of their experience in infancy, some men experience an overwhelming need to control women in later life: 'The particular power of the Mother over the child is a blend of intimacy and frustration as well as humiliation at the inevitable thwarting of the child's will.' So men's anger at women may be the consequence of a child's rage over his infantile experience of capricious female power with men constantly taking revenge on an unreliable Mother figure.

Or we can go back to Freud to try and explain the male desire to degrade women through violence and pornography. Freud argued that some men repress an incestuous attachment to the Mother, the child's first love-object. In normal development, the boy transfers his desire to another woman but some men, Freud believed, remain maternally fixed. Unable to acknowledge their incestuous desires, they separate sex from affection. Consequently they cannot feel sexual desire for a woman they love, and can only do so for women whom they despise. As Freud put it—'Where such men love, they have no desire and where they desire they cannot love.'

The evidence that some men subconsciously hate women is overwhelming, particularly given the extent of male violence against women. The ultimate consequence of men's 'hatred' of women is the sexual violence against women endemic in our society. All the messages about women which contribute towards a society which produces rapists, child molesters and murderers must be destroyed. Only then can we create a society free from sexual crime and sexual discrimination.

Pornography

Pornography is a crucial issue in the feminist debate. Andrea Dworkin argues that some men are physiologically conditioned to respond sexually to women's inferiority and this manifests itself in the violence in pornography where degrading images of women stimulate men sexually.

In pornography women are raped, chained, beaten and bound—it is a form of psychological, sexual and actual sadism which reduces women to the role of victims and whores.

Even the most banal pornography, which Martin Amis aptly described as 'pictures of women's vaginas and the insides of their anuses', objectifies and degrades women and encourages men to view women as objects. Pornography operates as the propaganda of a patriarchal political system where a woman's function is the gratification of male sexuality; she has no business challenging the male monopoly of power in our society.

Pornography is terrifying because if men can view women as images to feed their sadistic fantasies, how can they relate to them in any 'normal' way in society? A culture that condones the sadistic exploitation of women does not value women very highly and inevitably men learn to regard women as 'filth'. Essentially pornography reduces all women to victims—victims of misogyny, sexism, sexual crime or snuff movies and any attempt to defend pornography denies women the very liberty to live their lives free from the threat of violence. Men's sexism, misogyny, and violence is inextricably connected with the pornographic representation of women.

Martin Amis's sharp, unpleasant novels provide a useful insight into male pornographic sexuality. *Money*, which recounts the sex life of a sixteen-stone slob is a savagely funny novel that reflects the male obsession with money, sex and power. The hero, John Self, is making a film and his obsession with money is only equalled by his obsession with sex. He spends his time drinking, going to go-go bars and screwing his girl-friend Selina. He is well aware that the only reason she sleeps with him is money:

> I had fever. And I had Selina-fever too. Lying in that slipped zone where there is neither sleep nor wakefulness and yet the mind is forever solving, solving, Selina comes at me in clouds of pink smoke. I saw her performing flesh in fantastic eddies and convulsions, the face with the smile of assent and the compliant look in the flattered eyes, the demonology of her underwear suggesting spiders and silk, her sharp shoulders, her fiery hair, the arched creature doing what that creature does best and the thrilling proof—so rich in pornography that she does all this not for passion, not for comfort, far less for love, the proof that she does all this for money. I woke babbling in the night—yes, I heard myself say it, solve it through the dream mumble—and I said it, I love it, I love it, I love her ... I love her corruption.

This passage eroticises power, and particularly the power of money. John Self has nothing to recommend himself to women except his money and he exploits this gleefully. Selina is a live Page 3 girl, and he revels in her pornographic sexual appeal. He has power over her because she depends on him for money and this power is the chief source of his excitement. He acknowledges this time and time again with corrupt glee:

> All set. I'm back at my flat now. The sheets have been changed, the socks corralled, the mags stashed. I myself am scrubbed and primped. Soon the bell will ring and Selina will be here with Persian eyes, overnight bag, hot throat, omniscient underwear...Tonight I will get the lot. I can't say I'm too much bothered, now that pornography is on its way in a cab.

But when John Self meets a woman who doesn't want money for sex he can't get it up. He becomes involved with the wife of a friend and they become friends before attempting to consummate the relationship—and he fails to perform,

> I could raise my rope for Selina Street and a snob of a whore on Third Avenue. This old rope of mine has seen action with all shapes and sizes, with the good and the bad and the ugly. But I can't raise my rope for Martina Twain, no sir.

So without the aphrodisiac of power and money, John Self is impotent.

Money reflects the connection between sex and power in male sexuality, and John Self is all too credible. His sexuality is pornographic in the sense that it depends on the degradation of the female, which is what pornography is all about. The man needs to feel powerful, dominant, superior and therefore he must see the female as powerless, submissive and inferior in order to be sexually aroused. It is not surprising, in this cultural context, that some men derive pleasure from degrading women or inflicting pain on them. Male sexuality is pornographic because of the sexual culture that shapes it and the degrading images that stimulate it.

The violence in male sexuality is not limited to physical acts of rape, pornographic images and literature but manifests itself as a recurring motif in popular culture.

'Let me see your beauty broken down' says Leonard Cohen in 'Take the Longing'. The following is a song, 'Love-Eyes by Louis Mahl, which contains more than a hint of violence:

> Hey love-eyes!
> I mean you!
> Your lipstick's wet and waitin' for my smear.
> Love-eyes stop your starin' and come here.

'Your lipstick's wet and waitin' for my smear' is a distinctly violent image—suggesting a gash or a wound. 'I mean you!' brooks no refusal—it is a command. Contrast this with so many women's longing for a gentle touch and soft caresses in popular songs.

Rape

The novel *The Doctor's Wife* by Brian Moore contains an ugly rape scene which reflects the power dynamic that operates in rape where power is the real aphrodisiac.

The heroine's husband discovered that she is having an affair and takes the plane to Paris where he rapes her:

> And then, as though realising that she would not put him off, she began to sob, but the sight of her tears only excited him further and now he had her naked, and he kicked free of his trousers, pushing his penis in, beginning to pump and strain, holding back an orgasm which in his terrible new excitement he could barely control: this was not his wife, it was some strange woman in a French hotel, and her weeping, her fear and loathing of him made his excitement greater.

It is clearly the woman's powerlessness that excites the rapist. This passage reflects the ultimate in sexual sadism—rape, the consequence of men's hostility towards women. A woman is raped in America every four minutes. Obviously rapists perceive women as 'things', not human beings at all, of so little consequence that they can be forced to accommodate a man's sexual desire for power and domination. One of the reasons why rape is such a common crime is because of the 'objectification' of women in our society. A man cannot help but regard women as 'things', 'objects', inferior beings. We must bring about a society where women will be free of the fear, and the reality, of rape.

Romantic fiction

Male sexuality is quite clearly bound up with power and domination but to what extent have women internalised a sexually passive role?

A typical example of female romance is Danielle Steele's best-selling *Secrets*. It is a romance where eyes meet across crowded rooms, tell everything, get damp and blaze with passion, where men swell up with desire and women melt into their arms, and where the act of fornication takes place regularly, and romantically, beside swimming pools.

The heroine, actress Sabrina Quarles, is tall and beautiful with a mane of blonde hair. She has the sort of body 'that made men want to hold themselves as they sat staring at her in a darkened theatre.' Also cast in the book is an actress with a mane of red hair and 'the sort of breasts that spill out over bikini tops'. Hollywood producers, actors and directors (with and without manes of hair) charm these ladies into their beds and obviously women identify with these beautiful women. At no stage does a heroine in this—or any other romantic fiction—take the initiative with a man.

There are elements in Mills and Boon romance which reflect clearly the 'powerless' role women identify with. *The Icicle Heart* is a Mills and Boon romance which shows female sexuality as delighting in submission. The heroine, Ivory, is a secretary who is dispatched to Amsterdam to bring some important papers to Lawson Alexander, head of Lawson Alexander Corporation. At first her resistance to his advances is total but eventually Lawson begins to overcome them:

> Ivory didn't like at all the way he was looking at her. She saw the challenge, the determination in his look but was completely unprepared for the way his hands snaked out and pulled her towards him. There was a brief moment when their eyes locked, and she gasped in horror at the realisation

of what he was about to do. Then he had half carried her with him inside his room and she heard the door click; his hard, unrelenting mouth came down on her. She struggled wildly in his arms, but he refused to let her go until he had had his satisfaction.

It is only a kiss by the way—women in Mills and Boon romances do not get raped—but it has reverberations of rape. Later on Lawson makes another attempt on her virtue:

But Lawson's kiss when his mouth reached hers was nothing like the Amsterdam kiss. His mouth rested lightly against her, then as his hands left her shoulders and he pulled her into the circle of his arms, the pressure of his lips increased, seeking and searching. Trying to push him away was useless she found. All she was achieving in her struggle as her fists beat against him, was to give him the very encouragement he needed to remove his lips from his mouth, push the dainty straps down her naked arms, and trace butterfly kisses all over her throat and shoulders. Suddenly something was happening inside her that she had never dreamed would happen—not with Lawson. And as his lips left her shoulder to return to her mouth, she felt an awakening in her that made her want to respond to him.

Romantic fiction indicates the extent to which women have internalised the role of 'sex object' in the same way as men have internalised a view of women as 'sex objects.' There is so much pressure on women to conform to a sexually desirable stereotype that it is not surprising that they fantasise about fulfilling this dream. In a society of truly liberated women, there would be no market for this ideologically oppressive literature.

Some women are obviously driven wild by the thought of a man barely able to help himself kissing them passionately until their resistance subsides, which reflects women's obsession with themselves as sex objects. The men in Mills and Boon romances are generally very handsome but I suspect the real aphrodisiac is the man's power and status— he is always socially and economically superior to the woman. This is reflected in real life where women care less about what a man looks like than men care about women.

This question was put to Norman Mailer in *Pontifications*, a collection of interviews with the great man himself who answers the question honestly from a male chauvinist pig perspective:

Q Why do you think physical beauty plays such an important part in men's attraction to women, and why does it play such a lesser part in women's attraction to men?

A Well, because, beauty, finally, is a scalp, no getting around it. When a man goes out with a beautiful woman, he's more respected in the world. I can remember a few ugly women who were attractive to me. But I will say I wasn't happy to be seen in the world with ugly women. You could say that was demonstrably unfair to them.

'Wonderful Tonight' is a song about a beautiful woman which reflects women's obsession with what they look like and men's gratification in being seen with a beautiful woman (Eric Clapton):

And everyone turns to see
This beautiful lady
Who's walkin' around with me.
And then she asks me—Do I look all right?
And I say darlin', you look wonderful tonight.

An extraordinary discrepancy between the sexes is the fact that a man finds true fulfilment in being 'successful' and a woman finds fulfilment in being 'good-looking'. 'Yer papa's rich, and yer mama's good-lookin' is the basic rule and men cannot cope with being less successful than a woman. The reason for this is because men are obsessed with their egos— as Virginia Woolf put it, 'When a man looks at a woman he is looking into a mirror which reflects his ego at twice its natural proportions', and God forbid that a man should look into a mirror and see his reflection diminished. An intelligent woman is a threat to a man and if she is good-looking, she is referred to as 'the thinking man's crumpet', thus reminding her of her real role—that of sex object.

Twentieth century sexology
If we turn to twentieth century sexology we see that the work of Havelock Ellis claims categorically that sexual practice is based on dominance and submission. In the 1920s Ellis was established as the leading scientific authority on sexual behaviour, and his influence has been considerable, right up to the present day.

According to Ellis: 'The woman who is lacking in fear is lacking also in sexual attraction to the normal male.'

Courtship for him meant the pursuit and conquest of the female. The sexual impulse in women is 'fettered by an inhibition which has to be conquered ... her wooer in every act of courtship has the enjoyment of conquering afresh an oft-won woman.' The male's primary role is to 'arouse in her an emotional condition which leads her to surrender.'

The best-selling marriage manual, *Ideal Marriage*, by Dutch gynaecologist Van de Velde was first published in 1928. Its latest reprint was in 1977 and the blurb claims that it has sold over 1,000,000 copies. He writes:

> What both men and women, driven by obscure primitive urges, wish to feel in the sexual act, is the essential force of maleness and absolute possession of the woman. And so both of them can and do exult in a certain degree of male dominance and aggression—whether actual or apparent—which proclaims this essential force.

Masters and Johnston echo this concept of the chase:

> You see, if we take a girl from a basically traditional background, we can be certain that one of the things that turns her on is being pursued. The chase is delightful, and it has erotic value for her because being pursued intensifies her sense of self as a female person.

Ellis writes about the hymen that 'it is nature's wishing to enforce by a natural obstacle the moral restraint of modesty so that only the most vigorous males would issue their reproduction.'

The most obvious way for a man to prove his strength is through force. To quote Ellis:

> Force is the foundation of virility and its psychic manifestation is courage. In the struggle for life violence is the first virtue. The modesty of women—in its primordial form consisting of physical resistance, active or passive, to the assault of the male—aided selection by putting to the test man's most important quality—force. Thus it is that when choosing among her rivals for her favours a woman attributes value to violence.

The danger in Ellis's argument is its potential as a justification for rape. It is argued that women fantasise about rape and maybe they do but that does not mean they enjoy the actual experience of rape. 'A rape fantasy', says Louis Gould, 'has nothing to do with having a couple of teeth knocked out. It's when Robert Redford won't take "no" for an answer.'

The fact that women may have rape fantasies is taken to indicate that women are masochistic but it is not surprising, given the pressure on women to be sex objects, that they should find gratifying the idea of men finding them so devastatingly attractive that they cannot control themselves. The fact is that the fantasy is not masochistic—it is about being desired.

Ellis's report is so disturbing because it portrays human sexuality as being all about conquest, and furthermore, suggests that this is 'natural' rather than socially 'learned' behaviour. If it is 'natural' and 'inevitable' that men should strive to dominate sexually, then it seems equally inevitable that women should have nothing to do with men, but if this is 'learned' behaviour there is some hope of 'reconditioning' men or changing society so that men do not 'learn' this behaviour.

Andrea Dworkin on heterosexuality

Andrea Dworkin's argument against heterosexual sex uncannily echoes the view of sexuality put forward by twentieth century sexology. She considers that it is specifically through sexuality that the fundamental oppression, that of men over women, is maintained. In her view the oppressor actually invades and colonises the body of the oppressed. According to Dworkin:

> The inferiority of women in society, including the civil inferiority of women, originates in intercourse, the woman is not, cannot be the equal of men...Intercourse is commonly written about and comprehended as a form of possession in which, during which, because of which, a man inhabits a woman, physically covering her and overwhelming her and at the same time penetrating her, and this physical relation to her—over her and inside her—is his possession of her. By thrusting into her, he takes her over. His thrusting into her is taken to be her capitulation to him as a conqueror—it is a physical surrender of herself to him. He occupies and rules her, expresses his elemental dominance over her, by his possession of her in the fuck.

Dworkin's argument substantiates the evidence culled from literature, romantic fiction and pornography that men see themselves as sexual 'conquerors'—therefore a woman who sleeps with a man who regards her as a 'conquest' is indeed a 'conquest', whether or not she feels she is.

One can only conclude that men's sexual dominance is intrinsically bound up with their social and political dominance. So, the politics of seduction is not an isolated issue but part of the whole spectrum of male power, which manifests itself in the male monopoly of power in our society. Women's 'passivity' is the result of subtle conditioning (working to men's advantage) which manifests itself not only sexually, but in the fact that women are still not competing with men for equal power.

The Roles Reversed

Most women have accepted the definition of male sexuality to such an extent that they accept that it is 'natural' that the man should initiate and control what happens. The following is an extract from a poem by Aphra Bhen (written in the seventeenth century) which illustrates what happens when the roles are reversed. It tells of Cloris's seduction by Lysander:

The Disappointment
In a lone thicket made for love,
Silent as yielding maid's consent,
She was a charming languishment
Permits his force but gently strove;
Her hands his bosom softly meet,

But not to put him back design'd,
Rather to draw 'em on inclined:

She does her softest joys dispense,
Offering her Virgin Innocence
A Victim to love's secret flame;
While the o'er ravished shepherd lies
Unable to perform the sacrifice.

He curs'd his birth, his fate, his stars;
But more the shepherdess's charms,
Whose soft bewitching influence
Had damn's him to the Hell of Impotence.

This poem gets off to a conventional start—it is the man, Lysander, who initiates the sexual encounter. But Cloris becomes active—she 'too' gently strove. Her own desire awakens and renders her lover impotent. This poem indicates the way in which a man feels his masculinity is threatened by a sexually assertive woman, and things haven't changed that much.

Conclusion

The evidence, overall, is overwhelming that a large part of male sexuality is dangerously power-orientated as it is written about in literature and sexology, as it expresses itself in sexual violence against women and as it is portrayed in pornography, art and popular culture. It also indicates the extent to which women have internalised a 'passive' role. Our whole sexual culture defines women's sexuality as 'passive' and male sexuality as 'active'.

This cultural conditioning is a product of male fear and hatred of women, as expressed in sexual crime and pornography, sexism and misogyny, and the fact that men expect to dominate sexually and every other way. It is only when the connection between male sexuality and power is broken that we will live in a society free form misogyny, sexism, sexual discrimination and sexual violence.

References and Further Reading

Calman, Stephanie. *Dressing for Breakfast*. London: Fontana, 1988.

Cartledge, Sue and Joanna Ryan. *Sex and Love: New Thoughts on Old Contradictions*. London: The Women's Press, 1983.

Corcoran, Clodagh. *Pornography: The New Terrorism*. Dublin: Attic Press, LIP Pamphlet, 1989.

Coveney, L. et al. *Explorations in Feminism—The Sexuality Papers*. London: Hutchinson, 1984.

Dinnerstein, Dorothy. *The Rocking of the Cradle and the Ruling of the World*. London: The Women's Press, 1987.

Dworkin, Andrea. *Letters from a War Zone*. London: Secker and Warburg, 1987.

Ellis, Havelock. *Erotic Symbolism: Studies in the Psychology of Sex*. Philadelphia: FA Davis, 1926.

Fisher, Semour. *Understanding the Female Orgasm*. New York: Bantam Books, 1973.

Greer, Germaine. *The Female Eunuch*. London: Paladin, 1975.

Hite, Shere. *The Hite Report*. (1976) London: Pandora Press, 1989.

Kinsey, Alfred et al. *Sexual Behaviour in the Human Female*. New York: Pocket Books, 1965.

Masters, William, and Virginia Johnson. *Human Sexual Response*. Boston: Little, Brown and Company, 1966.

'The Heat is on: Sex, Romance, Love and Lust in the '90s,' *MS* Magazine, New York: May 1989.

Rich, Adrienne. *Compulsory Heterosexuality and Lesbian Existence*. London: Onlywomen Press, 1981.

Viney, Ethna. *Ancient Wars: Sex and Sexuality*. Dublin: Attic Press, LIP Pamphlet, 1989.

Wright, Helena. *More About the Sex Factor in Marriage*. London: Williams and Norgate, 1947.

A note on the author
Trudy Hayes studied Arts at Trinity College Dublin and since then has worked as a journalist and book critic, among other things. She lives in Dublin and now works as a writer. Her first collection of short stories, *Dream-Girl*, was published by the new Jonathan Cape 'Vintage' imprint in 1990.

7

THE RIGHT TO CHOOSE
Questions of Feminist Morality

Ruth Riddick, 1990

THIS IS FOR ISABELLE SHAW

Introduction

Some time in the last ten years, I had the experience of counselling a working-class Belfast woman with a crisis pregnancy. We met in the inauspicious surroundings of the Central Railway Station. At twenty-two years of age, she was already the glorious widow of a republican martyr. She was Roman Catholic, abortion is murder and she was not to be permitted in her widowhood to have a sexual relationship, much less to produce incontrovertible evidence of her 'betrayal'. This unlovely story is but one from the largely unwritten and unspoken annals of the Irish abortion reality, north and south.

I was reminded of this incident, one of thousands I've encountered as Director of a non-directive pregnancy counselling service, when I was invited to review the published findings of an international enquiry into abortion in northern Ireland. It occurred to me that there is no such contemporary statement on the situation in the Republic, despite the momentous political and legal developments of the eighties.

A further spur to reopening the right to choose debate came from the experience of being a panel member on RTE's *Questions and Answers* programme during which a self-satisfied Fianna Fáil politician assured me and our viewers that 'these matters' had been dealt with once and for all by the Human Life Amendment of 1983—this in a jurisdiction which daily exports ten abortion cases to England, amendments, court orders and injunctions notwithstanding.

Abortion is an issue on which it is possible to have only one public stand in Ireland—unequivocal opposition. This naturally produces a situation in which individual women's voices are silenced, to be replaced by faceless abortion statistics. In the twenty-three years of the British Abortion Act only three Irish women have publicly named themselves as women who have had abortions. In this silence, in these statistics, real women live—individuals, citizens, decision-makers, moral agents.

I have written this pamphlet as an intervention into that silence. It is not, however, the purpose of this pamphlet to make the case for 'allowing' women to have abortions under certain preconditions, nor will I argue for the introduction of legislation permitting abortion (although many will see this as an inevitable implication). Similarly, I have discussed Irish women's abortion experience elsewhere and will not repeat myself here. My project is rather to argue that women are moral agents, that their abortion decisions may be moral decisions. Abortion, as the ultimate exercise of individual fertility control, is the arena in which women have least social acknowledgment and support; it is, therefore, the context in which women's right to choose, that is, women's right to act as moral agents, must be argued.

Of necessity, the discussion here will be introductory. However, debate on these issues has been too long silenced. It is time to reopen Pandora's Box.

Choice in Contemporary Ireland

We are continuing to ignore the real needs and the real problems of our society and continuing to close down the possibility of access to advice and help. I have no doubt at all that the abortion figures will rise strikingly over the years and it is our direct responsibility and particularly the responsibility of Irish politicians.

Mary Robinson, 1980

In late 1979, a small group of Irish feminists proclaimed themselves the 'Women's Right to Choose Group'. The principal aims of the group were the decriminalisation of abortion, illegal under the 1861 Offences Against the Person Act, and the establishment of a feminist pregnancy counselling service for women in crisis. This latter aim was almost immediately achieved with the opening, in June 1980 and under the group's management, of the Irish Pregnancy Counselling Centre. As early as March of that year, the Women's Right to Choose Group hosted a public meeting in Liberty Hall, Dublin. The platform included journalists Jill Tweedie from Britain and Mary Holland, together with representatives from the Group itself and from the Irish

Pregnancy Counselling Centre. Chairing the meeting was Professor Mary McAleese, then a well-known broadcaster, who later claimed to have misunderstood the nature of the meeting. The attendance was vocally antagonistic and the atmosphere highly charged. As an ordinary member of the public, I addressed the meeting from the back of the hall. *The Evening Herald* (11 March 1981) reported:

> A woman, who admitted having an abortion, spoke out strongly in favour of a woman's right to control her own body last night. Ruth Riddick said that the men of this country are not enlightened enough, or choose not to be, when it comes to the question of taking positive steps to avoid pregnancy. They have a right to choose whether they will take responsibility for their actions or not. So why should the basic right of control of one's body be denied to women, she asked.

This unplanned intervention was to have far-reaching consequences for me. I was offered an administrative position with the Irish Pregnancy Counselling Centre and it was through this involvement that I came to realise just how significant the question of fertility control is to women's everyday lives. I also came to see the political importance of offering woman-to-woman help, a 'self-help' process which the women's movement had developed in the 1970s in such groups and campaigns as the Rape Crisis Centres and Women's Aid. This importance is (if possible) magnified where questions of fertility are at stake—the right of women to reject compulsory motherhood is not popular in our society.

Meanwhile, the backlash against a perceived liberalisation of Irish society was under way. Right-wing moralists, quite independently of the existence of the Women's Right To Choose Group, had already focussed on abortion as the issue around which they would 'halt the permissive tide in other areas' (John O'Reilly, *Need for a Human Life Amendment*, January 1981). The foundations of a right-to-life movement had been laid in the 1970s and it only remained for a highly organised 'Pro-Life' Amendment Campaign to convince the legislature of the urgency of its cause.

The campaign took as its model the American 'Human Life Amendment Campaign', which had been launched in the 1970s and which remains a live issue today. The Eighth Amendment campaign of 1982/3, as it became, was to prove long, bitter and divisive, undermining even friendships of long-standing.

During this campaign, the Women's Right To Choose Group suffered a number of body blows: the group split internally; the official opposition to the amendment, known simply as the 'Anti-Amendment Campaign', distanced itself from 'The Right to Choose'; and, finally, the Irish Pregnancy Counselling Centre collapsed under financial pressure, to be replaced, in July 1983, at the height of the Amendment Campaign, by Open Line Counselling . My decision to establish this service was taken for professional, political and personal reasons; specifically, my colleagues and I would not abandon our (future) clients, nor would we allow our service to be intimidated by the anti-choice lobby.

On 7 September 1983, 53% of the electorate, went to the polls to decide the issue of the Eighth Amendment: 66.45% of those who voted agreed to its adoption. Consequently, this provision became Article 40.3.3 of the Irish Constitution. It reads:

> The State acknowledges the right to life of the unborn and, with due regard to the equal right to life of the mother, guarantees in its laws to respect, and as far as practicable, by its laws to defend and vindicate that right.

The 'right-to-life' victory was to have serious consequences for the women's movement. Not only was a fundamental feminist demand overwhelmingly rejected at the polls but many sections of the women's movement and the Left had already abandoned the campaign for abortion rights. The issue was dropped from the media and both the Women's Right to Choose Group and the break-away Right to Choose Campaign eventually disbanded. The focus of subsequent debate became the practical right of access to information about (lawful) abortion services abroad, as, on foot of the Amendment, the anti-choice movement succeeded through the courts in suspending the formal provision of non-directive pregnancy counselling. The contemporary successor to the Women's Right To Choose Group is known as the 'Women's Information Network' and operates independently of the (former) pregnancy counselling services. A consideration of women's moral right to choose has been virtually abandoned.

Speaking on the first anniversary of the amendment, the President of the Society for the Protection of the Unborn Child

(SPUC) issued the following challenge:

> In order to defend the right to life of the unborn, we must close the *abortion referral agencies* which are operating in Dublin quite openly and underneath the eyes of the law. These clinics must be closed and if the 1861 Act cannot close them, we must have another Act that will. (emphases mine).

The non-directive pregnancy counselling services (Open Line Counselling and the Dublin Well Woman Centre, a women's health facility) were thus targeted as the anti-choice movement succeeded in achieving a High Court order (known colloquially as 'the Hamilton judgement') closing the service. *The Irish Times* of the day commented:

> With just four days to go to closure, Kate says it's been like Heuston Station...I sit in the adjoining waiting room with her client's sister, Elaine. Looking up from her magazine, Elaine says she first heard about Open Line's counselling service through a friend who had been there. So she took her pregnant sister Ann up on the bus from Mayo that morning. They could have come from Tullamore, Tuam, Donegal or Dingle...Elaine says she hasn't heard anything about Open Line closing down on January 12, the day the High Court order comes into effect. Indeed, little did Elaine know that Open Line had already ordered the removal van.
>
> Lorna Siggins, *The Irish Times*, 9 January 1987

Having been, in a colleague's memorable phrase, 'made constitutionally redundant', we established an emergency telephone network, the first of its kind in the country, offering access to (anonymous) professional pregnancy counsellors and to information on lawful abortion services abroad. Callers to the Helpline, coordinated through my personal telephone, increasingly emphasised information, rather than counselling, as their priority—that is, information about reputable abortion services in the UK. While the women and the many men who call do appreciate the opportunity of discussing their crisis pregnancy, the valuable role which counselling can play in the decision-making process has been grievously undermined by the separation of 'information' from 'counselling', the effect of the Supreme Court Order of March 1988 (where our Appeal against the Order of the High Court failed). The Chief Justice, Mr Thomas A Finlay was unambiguous:

There could not be an implied and unenumerated constitutional right to information about the availability of a service of abortion outside the State which, if availed of, would have the direct consequence of destroying the expressly guaranteed right to life of the unborn.
Supreme Court Record 185/87, 16 March 1988

It seems to me that this judgement was indeed the only course of action open to the Courts, in the light of Article 40.3.3, and for the following reasons

• the Court could not ban outright the practice of non-directive counselling without undermining the entire therapeutic services, a situation which would clearly not be in the public interest; therefore
• by disbarring certain organisations and individuals from disseminating information about abortion services legally obtainable abroad, the Court could be seen to uphold the rights guaranteed to the unborn, while being mindful that such an Order would be almost impossible to enforce and that women needing abortion would get the information anyhow. As the Chief Justice remarked: 'nor does the Order… in any way prevent a pregnant woman from becoming aware of the existence of abortion outside the jurisdiction.'
Supreme Court Record 185/87, 16 March 1988

That this judgement, for all its sophistry, fails to address either the social rights of women or the political demands of the anti-choice lobby has been borne out by recent developments, as evidenced by:

• the numbers of Irish women achieving lawful abortion in England remain virtually unchanged (allowing for slight annual variations);
• the number of cases currently and potentially before the Attorney General and the Courts seeking to impose a blanket ban on the dissemination of abortion information, a clearly unrealistic aim, given that this information is already in the public domain.

Just how long this information remains accessible is, however, otherwise uncertain, as the case of the monthly glossy magazine for women, *Cosmopolitan*, which has traditionally been marketed as a 'trendy' or 'quasi feminist' publication, illustrates. Page 171 of the January 1990 edition carries a

Publisher's Note which reads:

> Following complaints from the Office of Censorship of Publications in Dublin, this page, which is usually devoted to advertisements providing abortion advice and help, has been left blank in all editions of this magazine published for distribution in the Republic of Ireland. We deeply regret that we are unable to provide the relevant information, but we are advised that if we continue to publish these advertisements it could result in this magazine being made the subject of a Prohibition Order under the Censorship of Publications Act 1946 as amended by the Health (Family Planning) Act 1979.

Meanwhile, little is known or discussed about the actual experience of individual Irish women. Respondents to a questionnaire compiled in the UK by Open Line Counselling commented:

> It would be so much easier if we could find out more about what goes on in London before we come over here. The decision to have an abortion is not half as difficult as trying to find out about clinics here.
> *Some Characteristics of Irish Women Seeking Abortion Services in Britain,* January 1988

This is the real-life context in which the issues raised in this pamphlet are addressed.

Abortion and the feminist agenda

> The history of abortion forms a continuous and irrefutable record of women's determination to make reproductive choices based on their own perceptions and definitions of their social, sexual and economic needs.
>
> K Kaufmann, 1984

Abortion has been on the feminist agenda from the beginning. In 1967, the first conference of the American National Organisation of Women was held in Washington, DC. The conference marked the formal beginning of the current wave of international feminism. Article VIII of the NOW Bill of Rights proclaims: 'The Right of Women to Control their Reproductive Lives', and includes on its list of demands: 'The right of women to control their own reproductive lives by…repealing penal laws governing abortion.'

Only women have wombs; only women give birth. This single elemental fact assures that pregnancy is a uniquely female experience. For this reason, matters of the womb, questions of reproduction are central concerns of feminism.

146

Throughout much of recorded history and in most observed cultures, women are not only differentiated from men because of their womb and its powers, but are relegated to a private sphere where the privileges and power accorded males in the public world are denied them. This is clearly an issue for feminism.

Women, almost universally, are deemed to be at the mercy of their biology, that is, of the womb. Thus, the proposition that biology is destiny, a proposition which is refuted by feminism. So deep is the identification of woman and womb that psychoanalyst Eric Erikson can claim that, as Susan Moller Okin reports in her critique:

> The little girl develops around the possession of an 'inner space' with great potential—the womb. Woman's capacity to bear and nurse children is therefore not just one aspect of her nature; her entire identity and the life she lives must revolve around her 'inner space' and its desire to be filled.

Women in Western Political Thought, 1979

Erikson himself is further quoted as saying, 'Woman is nurturance...anatomy decrees the life of a woman', an almost mythic siting of woman's very essence in the womb. Schools of medicine prescribe ever more radical invasions of the womb—caesarian sections, ovariectomy, hysterectomy—as a panacea for perceived manifestations of female pathology: ie vaginal birthing, the onset of menopause, even psychological/psychiatric disturbances. Even women's expression of rage and frustration, essentially intellectual responses to an objectively hostile world, are dismissed after the womb as hysteria.

A further question for feminists concerns the status of women in the social reality in which we live; are we 'girls', 'wives', 'mothers', 'citizens', 'persons', or none of these?

Under patriarchy, 'the rule of the fathers' in Mary Daly's phrase, the world is defined by, for and about men. Insofar as women are acknowledged in this world-view, it is as relatives—in our roles relative to men, as, for example, sex objects, the mother of 'my' children, 'my' wife etc. The family is a patriarchal unit with 'father' at its pinnacle and other family members defined by their relation to him—as wife, daughter, son. (The death of an individual father doesn't change these relations; we casually refer to 'his widow'.)

This proprietorial patriarchal relationship is clearly

signalled in our society where women adopt by way of identification the surnames of their husbands and fathers.The primary social identification of women, then, is not in ourselves, nor as 'persons' or 'citizens', but in our relation to the patriarch. This means that the first right we must assert for ourselves is the identity of personhood, not simply in a spurious equality with men but as an elemental involvement in the world of morality, decision-making, responsibility, social accountability.

The degree of moral autonomy, personal choice and social responsibility afforded individuals will depend on whether they are considered to be 'persons' or 'relatives'. Women, as we have seen, are more generally assigned to relative status, a position clearly endorsed in Bunreacht na hEireann (the Constitution of the Republic of Ireland), the fundamental code of Irish law and social aspiration, adopted as recently as 1937. The Constitution makes only three specific references to women:

> The State acknowledges the right to life of the unborn and, with due regard to the equal right to life of the mother, guarantees in its laws to respect, and, as far as practicable, by its laws to defend and vindicate that right. (Article 40.3.3, 8th Amendment, adopted 7 September 1983)

> In particular, the State recognises that by her life within the home, woman gives to the State a support without which the common good cannot be achieved. (Article 41.2.1)

> The State shall, therefore, endeavour to ensure that mothers shall not be obliged by economic necessity to engage in labour to the neglect of their *duties in the home*. (Article 41.2.2) (italics mine)

Women in the Irish Constitution are 'mothers' with 'lives' and 'duties in the home'.

Article 40.3.3, the Eighth Amendment to the Constitution, was achieved in part through the exploitative use of pictures of babies to visually represent foetal life in utero. During the amendment campaign, and subsequently, it was claimed that the womb, that most precious signifier of a woman, was no less than 'the most dangerous place in the world to be'—this in a world with the nuclear capacity to annihilate all life many times over.

These issues are of crucial concern to feminists in the light of an extraordinary late 20th century development—the legal idea of personhood of the foetus, the inhabitor and potential product of the womb. This new 'person', the foetus, qualifies for constitutional guarantees not necessarily extended to adult women and may constitute a litigant against women in matters of pre-natal care and birthing procedures.

Feminists are, then, by definition, concerned about matters of the womb and its powers for the following reasons:

• while the womb and its powers are elementally female (at once a site of deep pleasure and satisfaction for women, and a means and justification for exploitation and subjugation), women are more than the sum of womb and reproduction in the same way that men are more than the sum of penis and scrotum

• for women, the unique privilege of being female is perversely a means of reduction to the status of the womb's potential; of subjection to a reproductive capacity beyond our effective control—psychically, socially, philosophically, that is, of subjection to compulsory motherhood.

In short, biology is, or it is not, destiny; the question is ultimately not behavioural, nor technological, but moral.

In the light of these developments, and given the failure of the law, the medical profession, of moral philosophy itself, to clarify the procedure in cases of conflict between mother and foetus, the status of women is vital to our very survival (no idle concern, as the fate of Sheila Hodgers, whose post-partum death was caused by a non-uterine cancer aggravated by but 'morally' untreatable because of pregnancy, demonstrates. Ironically, this unnecessary death took place during the 'right to life' campaign in 1983).

If women are to be simply vessels for progeny—and there is clear evidence that the majority of male, mainstream philosophers and moral commentators, not to mention civil law makers, incline toward this view—how are women to prevail and how are we to defend ourselves against the (proposed) superior claims of the foetus in the (natural) womb?

Clearly these matters are of central concern to the feminist agenda.

The concept of individual choice

I would see the failure to provide abortion as a human rights issue.

Mary McAleese, 1980

Modern theories of political liberty and individual rights,

149

evolving through 17th and 18th century social and moral philosophy, became popular through a series of political upheavals which were to have enormous consequences for our way of life—the English, American and French Revolutions, the last now merely two hundred years old, with its famous rallying cry of *'liberté, égalité, fraternité'* (sic). Political debate in the western democracies has since been preoccupied with how individual rights may be justly balanced and incorporated into the larger political framework we call society, the State, or even 'the common good'.

One of the immediate difficulties raised by this political tradition is the question of whether a society committed to political liberty must also embrace women as holders of personal rights. While modern commentators suggest that such an embrace is implicit in codes such as, for example, Bunreacht na hEireann, a closer examination of both theory and practice would suggest to the contrary that the masculine terminology employed means just that—for men only. Political liberty, as envisaged by the founding 'fathers' of democracy, is for men only—women are to continue in their traditional ('natural') roles as relatives/servants. (This restriction on political liberty extends to other 'minorities', as in the case of our travelling people or in racist societies— hence the close identification by generations of white American feminists with the black movement for civil rights.)

One of the fundamental demands of feminism has always been and remains that women be acknowledged as persons with social and political rights; that is, included in and heirs to the tradition of political liberty. The specific rights which feminism claims for women belong firmly to that tradition.

Thus, the proposition that women have the right to choose presupposes that:

• women are heirs to the tradition of political liberty;
• women are persons of moral autonomy.

Western democracy, the political system which developed out of the social revolutions of the Enlightenment, endeavours, albeit with some discomfort, to balance a number of (seemingly) discordant demands, such as:

• the interests of the nation-state
• the interests of international capital
• the demands of the common good

• the rights of minority interests.

Some of these demands may be inherently exclusive; the modern economic trend, for example, favours a monetary internationalism (as in the projected EC single market) over national economies. (This economic philosophy was challenged in Ireland during the referendum to decide ratification of the Single European Act. Opponents of the SEA included not only individualist economists but the Left and the 'right to life' movement, a bizarre coalition.) Similarly the common good is often pitted against the rights of minorities, especially in the arena of 'moral issues'.

At its most extreme, the conviction that differences cannot be reconciled within the larger framework casts the minority as a kind of social outlaw. Thus, the woman seeking to assert her (minority) rights is problematic, a process clearly demonstrated in the alienation of Irish women who have (legal) abortions. So outraged would the 'common good' be by the provision of abortion services in Ireland for the not inconsiderable number of Irish women requiring them, that these women have to travel abroad in secrecy and under legal threat to achieve their purposes.

In practice, personal liberty is predicated on social consensus; that is, we are permitted the limited exercise of personal rights dependent on the given social order. Equally, prevailing notions of the common good are ideologically constructed. The prevailing ideology in contemporary Ireland is composed of a patriarchal mixed-economy capitalism tempered by some social welfare provision.

The social consensus is constructed through a dialectic composed in part of ideas of monetarism mitigated by social justice; of a conservative catholic morality mitigated by pragmatic compassion.

In practise, this means that, while we agree that abortion should be illegal, we are disturbed that women in crisis might be forcibly restrained from seeking (lawful) abortion abroad. While we are unshakeable in our belief that the act of abortion is a grievous sin, we forgive, privately and in religious confession, the woman who has been driven to such an unfortunate action.

Now, any question of moral choice presupposes a number of factors:

• that a choice may be made between viable possibilities;

- that there is a protagonist to make that choice;
- that that protagonist has the authority to make the choice.

Where the issue of choice is raised by a pregnancy, these factors may be formulated thus:

- is there more than a single course of action which may be pursued?
- is the pregnant woman, the protagonist, to make the decision between such actions?
- does she have the moral right to do so?

There are also different kinds of choices which may be considered:

- Pragmatic choice: where the choice is to be made simply for pragmatic, personally identified, reasons;
- Altruistic choice: where the choice is to be made for idealistic or impersonally identified reasons;
- Moral choice: a dialectic where the pragmatic is informed by the altruistic.

Every woman knows, and this knowledge would appear to be universal in time and culture, that any pregnant woman has a pragmatic choice: she may commit herself to the pregnancy or she may terminally interfere with its course. (She may also postpone the issue, hope for a miscarriage or abandon the resulting infant, practices known to continue in Ireland.)

Again pragmatically speaking, we know that pregnant women, as the 'holders of the baby', assume the role of protagonist in choice (although individual women may modify this role with regard to partner, family, friends etc).

The final question is more problematic as it raises the question of whether women may exercise a moral right to act as their own protagonists where issues of choice arise. Feminists proposing a moral agency in women develop this very question.

In her pioneering feminist work *The Second Sex*, published originally in the late 1940s and repeatedly banned in Ireland, Simone de Beauvoir explored the philosophical concept of woman as the 'other', a concept central to any discussion of the moral agency of women. To be 'other' implies exclusion from the norm; it is to be peripheral, marginal. Women, in de Beauvoir's analysis, are peripheral, marginal; the same women who make pragmatic decisions, decisions which surely have moral content and implications. The question now is: how are women, if we are truly 'other' (the condition of being female under patriarchy), to reconcile the pragmatic with the altruistic in a moral exercise? Mary Daly locates the question thus: 'Sexist society maintains its grasp on the psyche by keeping it divided against itself'.

This is simply the central contradiction, even the tragedy, of women's actual lives under patriarchy, and the source of women's overburdening guilt. That women shoulder this burden is the site of their courage, a courage rarely and insufficiently acknowledged in a culture where courage is measured in terms of men at war.

The rule of the fathers, Mary Daly's definition of patriarchy, regards moral exercise in women as not merely inappropriate, but impossible. The philosopher Schopenhauer described the state of women as 'moral infancy', while Otto Weininger wrote in 1906: 'A woman cannot grasp that one must act from principle; as she has no continuity she does not experience the necessity for logical support of her mental processes...she may be regarded as "logically insane".'

Women may be regarded as ordinary participants in society insofar as they possess such civil rights as the right to vote, to work, to own property, to initiate divorce proceedings (and it must be remembered that where women enjoy such rights, they have been achieved through the efforts of generations of feminist activism). These civil rights are, of course, the ordinary rights of citizens in western democracies, but they do not, alas, necessarily presuppose a moral agency or its exercise.

It may well be that these questions will be the divider between mainstream (civil rights) and radical (moral agency) feminism, with abortion as the focussing issue.

Women's morality in society

> [My] main object, the desire of exhibiting the misery of oppression, peculiar to women, that arises out of the partial laws and customs of society.
> Mary Wollstonecraft, *The Wrongs of Woman*, 1798

Because the reproductive experience of individuals is such a private affair, we tend to think of such activity as being outside of the realm of law or social policy. However, population questions have, in the last two hundred years, become matters of public debate and government action. The decision to permit or prohibit the manufacture, distribution and advertising of contraceptive devices is, for example, a clear demonstration of public law involvement in citizens' private behaviour.

Equally, the existence and nature of abortion laws differ according to prevailing social policy—in China, for example, abortion is an integral part of the state reproductive policy; elsewhere, restricted access to abortion reflects a social commitment to population expansion. In Ireland, the existence of an anti-abortion law, bolstered by a constitutional guarantee of the right to life of the unborn, is an unambiguous statement of public policy, irrespective of the private practice of silent thousands of our 'criminal' citizens (women).

Such questions of social policy very often also raise the spectre of race survival. Dreadful experiments into human reproduction were carried out on persons of expendable race in Nazi concentration camps while abortion was denied to Aryan women, who were encouraged to breed a 'pure' race. Some black male activists in the USA have argued against women's reproductive freedom, seeing contraception and abortion as tools of genocide. Similar fears have been expressed in regard to family planning programmes in the Third World. Meanwhile, wealthy right-wing organisations exhort white, middle-class Frenchwomen to increase the size of their families; educated, middle-class women in Hong Kong are offered financial advantages to the family if they have children. In Ireland, the 'right to life' movement lobbies for subsidies for nuclear families (usually middle-class) at the expense of the single-parent unit (often working-class, certainly financially and socially disadvantaged).

Behind all of these initiatives lies a single, shared, premise: only certain people have the right to breed. And who decides? Not the individual woman—this is patriarchy, after all—but an assortment of outside agencies: the racist ideology, the right-wing pressure group, the authoritarian state. Behind the premise lies the same fear: if we don't breed enough, the hated others ('the yellow peril') will take us over. The American anti-abortionist, Fr Paul Marx, whose speciality is a pickled-foetus roadshow, neatly summarises this viewpoint thus: 'The white Western world is committing suicide through contraception and abortion' (Human Life Centre, Minneapolis, USA).

'[The] preservation of life seems to be rather a slogan than a genuine goal of the anti-abortion force' writes Ursula K LeGuin. 'Control over behaviour; power over women. Women in the anti-choice movement want to share in male power over women and do so by denying their own womanhood, their own rights and responsibilities.' (*Dancing at the Edge of the World*, 1989)

If, as we have seen, individual actions take place within society, within ideology, the question of moral agency comes into focus when we encounter fundamental conflicts in the moral arena, as in the problematic area of maternal versus (proposed) foetal rights, where the social imperative is weighted against the woman. The greater the claim of the foetus (an entity which clearly cannot enter moral debate on its own behalf, a not inconsequential factor when personhood has been traditionally linked to the capacity for consciousness and decision), the more important the recognition of women's moral agency, of she who must bear the moral responsibility of her actions.

The so-called 'right to life' movement argues unambiguously that, while women may have a pragmatic choice of action in pregnancy, they have no right to moral agency; that is, that the foetus's claim self-evidently overwhelms any proposed moral agency in women. (Mary Daly adds that, according to this view, aborted foetuses are to be more mourned than adult human beings killed in war.)

In pregnancy, this struggle for control and responsibility is manifest in the issues which women confront, the 'hard' questions raised in non-directive pregnancy counselling:

- what are the viable options in your situation?
- how will you cope with your grief/anger/guilt?— whatever your decision
- how will you reconcile your decision with your conscience/god/religion?
- how would you feel after an abortion?

Social services correspondent Mary Maher writes:

> The phrase 'non-directive' has become fairly familiar as a description of that kind of therapeutic help which offers a client neither advice nor judgement, but a sympathetic ear...[The] conviction is that people can make choices, good choices, for themselves, and have the right to do so, and that the therapist is there only to facilitate that process...Basic assumptions from which client-centred therapy springs

[are]...that the individual is basically trustworthy, has the capacity and the right to make decisions about life, and the ability to establish a set of values...Most important, they take responsibility for those choices, a necessary part of the growth process.

The Irish Times, 20 November 1986

For Irish women choosing termination, and given our particular cultural heritage, moral exercise is located in the recognition of a prima facie right to life of the unborn which may only be overridden with justification, or good reason, to be provided by the pregnant woman herself.

Apart from surveys undertaken by Open Line Counselling, there has been little study of the abortion experience of Irish women, or of the reasons why Irish women choose abortion as an option in crisis pregnancy. Commenting on her decision to terminate her pregnancy, one Irish woman wrote: 'I would still like to think I can have a good life. I intend to go back and start anew and I don't regret my decision.' A common theme running through women's decision-making process concerning a crisis pregnancy is worry about how the pregnancy, if brought to term, would affect others, principally parents and existing children. Summarising the reasons given for considering abortion, Open Line Counselling reported as follows:

Many younger women feel unprepared for a child, particularly where family and social support is unlikely or insufficient. Many women are also anxious to avoid causing hurt to their parents, especially where a parent has health problems. Older women are worried about the effects of another pregnancy on a grown family, and also about the possibility of a sub-normal child. Instability in the relationship with the putative father, whether casual acquaintance, ex-boyfriend, or where a marriage is under stress, is another common factor.

Separated women with an extra-marital pregnancy are concerned about the irregular status of their relationship with the putative father and also about the threat to their separation agreements if the husband is unsympathetic to the pregnancy. Professional women are increasingly concerned about their future training and employment prospects, particularly in nursing and teaching. Most women decide to seek termination of pregnancy because of a multiplicity of these pressures. (October 1983)

While children born out of wedlock are no longer stigmatised in law as 'illegitimate', post-referendum Ireland has not been notable for its regard for its mothers. A number of tragic cases, from the death in childbirth of a fifteen year old girl to the sacking of a teacher for giving birth to the child of a separated man, have come to light since the human life amendment of 1983. The lessons of these cases, and the social attitudes they reveal, are not lost on other women with unplanned pregnancies.

Although not all of these considerations will be foremost in a woman's mind when she is exploring her options in a crisis pregnancy, they help form the context in which her decisions must be made.

Furthermore, in a patriarchal society, there is the problem of the role of men in women's lives which is at best ambiguous, at worst, fatal.

In the social arena and mirroring women's domestic responsibilities, the so-called 'caring' professions are, at the helping level, almost exclusively staffed by women. Primary care is given by women; status and authority is male.

On a more sinister level, the European witchcraze of 1450-1750, described by Matilda Joslyn Gage in 1893 as 'the age of supreme despair for women', saw the slaughter by men of a minimum of 200,000 women. In the 1970s a new genre of pornography, depicting the real-life murder of women by men, 'snuff movies', brought the witchcraze to the domestic video screen. Men rape, murder, abandon, dominate, disenfranchise women.

Successful women, riding on the achievements of feminism, boast that they are 'just one of the boys', that women 'make dreadful bosses', that as a woman you have to be twice as good but so what? When was the last time a patently high achieving male boasted that he was 'just one of the girls'?

For all our delirious need to believe that men like us, respect us, treasure us, the evidence suggests to the contrary. 'He's just a woman', is a term of abuse, not of respect. And where there is no liking, no respect, there is instead fear and loathing; there is unlikely to be any acknowledgement of rights, of agency, certainly no espousal, no guarantee.

These considerations become acute when women are faced with a crisis pregnancy. By definition, women become pregnant only through congress with men (messenger doves notwithstanding). Men are present in pregnancy, even though one of the common factors in crisis pregnancy is the absence of a man. At its crudest level, this absence is manifest in the man who denies his contribution to the pregnancy: 'It's not mine'. On a manipulative level, it's the man who decides what is to be done: 'the obvious thing is for you to have an abortion (lover/husband); 'I've decided she's to have an abortion' (father).

At its most compassionate, it's the man who withdraws completely from the situation: 'It's her decision'. The problem with this last is that it may, although by no means always, mask a retreat from involvement, it may be a refusal to commit. It is often a position taken by men who are not married to the pregnant woman; husbands tend to have more emphatic opinions (as befits their role as patriarchs) and expect their opinion to prevail, even where these opinions are in conflict with their wives' convictions.

How a man reacts to a crisis pregnancy will have a direct effect on the woman's experience of the pregnancy as the circumstances from which the pregnancy arises are crucial to the woman's moral classification of it; women are most reluctant to carry to term the product of a rape and equally reluctant to abort the product of a loving relationship.

Even in their absence, men are present. Even in this most elemental of female spheres, men are still an inescapable consideration.

For this reason, and by way of the generosity of women in their moral inclusion of men, women are acutely vulnerable to exploitation and manipulation. Consider this exhortation from Fr Bernard Haring concerning women pregnant from rape:

> We must, however, try to motivate her to consider the child with love because of its subjective innocence, and to bear it in suffering through to birth, whereupon she may consider her enforced maternal obligation fulfilled, after which she would try to resume her life with the sanctity that she will undoubtedly have achieved through the great sacrifice and suffering.

This is most sophisticated cruelty. Compare it with this account from the life of the Irish saint, Brigid:

> A certain woman who had taken the vow of chastity fell, through youthful desire of pleasure, and her womb swelled with child. Brigid, exercising the most strength of her ineffable faith, blessed her, caused the foetus to disappear, without coming to birth, and without pain. She faithfully returned the woman to health and to penance.
>
> Liam de Paor, *The Life of St. Brigid* by Cogitatus c. 650, (trans.) (unpub.)

Fathers of foetuses are now legally permitted (to at least attempt) to stop women from having abortions, or to insist on caesarian deliveries. Men are in a position to threaten women with withdrawal of material and emotional support if the woman does not abort a pregnancy which is unwanted by the man. These are positions of great power: personal, social, political. In the patriarchy, these positions are continually open to unchecked abuse.

Towards a feminist morality of choice

> She knows that masculine morality as it concerns her, is a vast hoax.
>
> Simone de Beauvoir, *The Second Sex*, 1949

> Feminism is not merely an issue but rather a mode of being.
> Mary Daly, *Beyond God the Father*, 1973

Feminist philosophy proceeds from the proposition that women are valuable in and of ourselves, a proposition not found in patriarchal philosophy, religion or morality, which teach of the role and duty of women as relative to the absolute value of the man, the patriarch. 'Morally insane' (Weininger), women may be permitted certain courses of action, even in fertility, but only under the direction of male authority; thus, abortion laws, liberal or prohibitive, which remove the moral imperative from women.

Feminist morality restores this imperative. Where liberal philosophers and theologians argue for abortion within the patriarchal framework, feminism resists the scapegoating of women as victims (victims are not authors of moral behaviour). Women's experience, we argue, has an objective moral value.

Patriarchal 'morality' is hierarchical; only the dominant are valid originators of moral claims. Feminism is about no less than the de-structuring of this moral imperialism.

> That I can think more clearly about [my abortion] now, and talk, and write about it, is entirely due to the moral courage and strength of women and men who have been working these thirty years for the rights and dignity and freedom of women, including the right to abortion.
>
> *Ursula K Le Guin, 1989*

Contemporary feminism, as we have seen, has developed a unique system of 'self-help' networks and whereas 'self-help' is a process common to oppressed peoples, for feminism, the personal is political and 'self-help' is no less than the conscious response to women's perceived and stated needs; that is, a political intervention into patriarchal society on behalf of women, not only as individuals, but as a class. This response is possible only when based on listening—to ourselves and to other women. For feminism, this intervention is more than political—it is a moral commitment. Respect for women is a central dimension of this commitment; that is, a respect which acknowledges and celebrates moral agency in women.

The opposition to non-directive pregnancy counselling and the threats to other woman-centred services and activities are ideological and rooted in patriarchal philosophy. Evidence suggests they will become even more violent.

Ireland is unusual, although the present legal climate is certainly volatile, in that Irish women have not, in recent times, been jailed for seeking abortions or for helping women to procure abortions (potentially criminal activities under the law). Not that we congratulate ourselves on this record. Women all over the world have been brave enough to risk jail and worse on behalf of their sisters. And, where feminists in the 1970s provided humorous media fodder, proponents of choice in the 1980s are unemployable. Where students in the 1960s were 'revolting', contemporary student publications are the subject of protracted litigation.

The proposition that women have the right to choose does not enjoy favour as Ireland prepares for the federal Europe of the 1990s (where, to the embarrassment of the State, a Court of Human Rights application on these issues will have to be answered, together with a European Court of Justice reference). Equally, a campaign for abortion rights would certainly encounter opposition even from those women who currently seek (lawful) abortion services in Britain. Ten years ago, feminists had the opportunity to campaign—and a gallant bunch did—for the decriminalisation of abortion. Today, a referendum to remove Article 40.3.3 would have to be successful before the issue could be meaningfully raised.

If, as veteran Irish campaigner Mary Gordon contends: 'A measure of the strength of the feminist movement in any country is the strength and confidence of its abortion rights lobby', a challenge has been issued to the Irish Women's Movement. Now that we have a clearer idea, albeit with the wisdom of hindsight, where the ideological lines are drawn, it is a challenge which we will confront with the greatest urgency.

References and further reading

Arditti, Rita. Renate Duelli Klein and Shelley Minden (eds.). *Test-tube Women: What Future for Motherhood?* London: Pandora Press, 1984.

Caputi, Jane. *The Age Of The Sex Crime.* London: The Women's Press, 1988.

Daly, Mary. *Beyond God The Father.* London: The Women's Press, 1986.

Greer, Germaine. *The Madwoman's Underclothes.* London: Picador, 1986.

Greer, Germaine. *Sex and Destiny: The Politics of Human Fertility.* London: Secker and Warburg, 1984.

Greer, Germaine. *The Female Eunuch.* London: Paladin, 1975.

Le Guin, Ursula. *Dancing on the Edge of the World.* New York: Grove Press, 1989

Moller Okin, Susan. *Women in Western Political Thought.* London: Virago, 1980

Purcell, Betty. Interview with Mary Robinson and Mary McAleese. *The Crane Bag* ,Vol 4 no 1, 1980.

Riddick, Ruth. *Making Choices: The Abortion Experience of Irish Women.* Dublin: Open Line Counselling, 1988.

Spender, Dale. *Mothers of the Novel.* London: Pandora Press, 1986.

Acknowledgements

I would like to thank the following friends and colleagues for their ideas, support and companionship throughout the development of this pamphlet: Sherie de Burgh, Clodagh Corcoran, Christine Donaghy, Brendan Ellis, Christine Falls, Colin Francome, Paul de Grae, Germaine Greer, Susan Himmelweit, Attracta Ingram, Frances Kissling, Diane Munday, Anne O'Neill, Rosalind Pollack Petchesky, Kevin Rockett, Corrina Reynolds, Madeleine Simms, Ailbhe Smyth, Dee Sullivan, clients and staff of the Irish Pregnancy Counselling Centre and Open Line Counselling, and especially Fiacc O Brolchain.

A note on the author

Ruth Riddick has worked with the Irish Family Planning Association, the Dublin Well Woman Centre and the Irish Pregnancy Counselling Centre. In 1983, at the height of the Eighth Amendment Referendum campaign, she set up Open Line Counselling, a non-directive pregnancy counselling service. She administered Open Line until its closure in 1987, following a High Court injunction which is currently under consideration by the European Court of Human Rights. Most recently, she has worked as Administrator of Foyle Film Projects and as a freelance journalist.

8

FROM CATHLEEN TO ANOREXIA
The Breakdown of Irelands

Edna Longley, 1990

Northern Ireland has been called a 'failed political entity'. I think it's time to admit that both parts of Ireland are failed conceptual entities. That is, the ideas which created them and the ideologies which sustained them have withered at the root. If 'Northern Ireland' has visibly broken down, the 'Republic' as once conceived has invisibly broken down. And since 1968 each has helped to expose the inner contradictions of the other.

In his poem 'Aisling', written near the time of the hunger strike, Paul Muldoon asks whether Ireland should be symbolised, not by a radiant and abundant goddess, but by the disease anorexia:

> Was she Aurora or the goddess Flora,
> Artemidora or Venus bright,
> Or Anorexia, who left
> A lemon stain on my flannel sheet?

In blaming the hunger-strikers' emaciation on their idealised cause, the poem equates that cause with a form of physical and psychic breakdown. 'Anorexia' is thus Cathleen Ni Houlihan in a terminal condition. Anorexic patients pursue an unreal self-image—in practice, a death-wish. Similarly, the nationalist dream may have declined into a destructive neurosis.

Feminists question any exploitation of the female body for symbolic or abstract purposes. So perhaps Anorexia should, rather, personify Irish women themselves: starved and repressed by patriarchies like unionism, Catholicism, Protestantism, nationalism. But here we come up against a difficulty. Not all Irish women resist these patriarchies. And for some, mainly from the North, Cathleen flourishes abundantly still. The northern women's movement has been divided and retarded; while the southern movement, preoccupied with church-and-state, has largely avoided 'nation'. Eavan Boland's feminist poem *Mise Éire* (I am

162

Ireland) destabilises Mise but not Éire. There is some reluctance, partly for fear of further division, to reopen the ever-problematic, ever-central issue of 'nationalism and feminism'. Later I will ask whether they are compatible. For the moment, I offer the reluctance as symptomatic.

This pamphlet will mainly focus on the ideological breakdown of nationalism because its breakdown is more complex and less obvious. nationalism and unionism are not in fact the same kind of ideology, nor do they function in the same manner. So they differ in their modes of collapse as in their modes of construction. Unionism since the first Home Rule Bill has always been reactive: a coalition of sects, interests, loyalties and incoherent hatreds in the face of a perceived common emergency. No totalising philosophy covers the whole coalition, even if religious and secular alarm fuse on its fundamentalist wing. Orangeism and Paisleyism maintain a select tribal memory-bank of historical persecutions, in which emblematic events (1641, 1690) are reinforced by biblical parallels. But this has never developed into a comprehensive symbolic system. You can't personify unionism. 'Orange Lil' is not the whole story.

As a separatist movement, nationalism had to put together a more elaborate ideological package and make more absolute claims. Also, like Polish nationalism, it is informed by Catholic theological habits. When the SDLP and Sinn Féin deny any sectarian component in their politics, these very habits blind them to the seamless join between Catholicism and nationalism, a join which is a matter of form as much as content. Nationalism thinks of unionism as heresy—hence past failures to analyse or understand it. And to come up against the church on *ne temere* or integrated education is to be as chillingly excluded as when one meets the guardians of the republican grail.

Lapsed nationalists are, therefore, more liable than lapsed Unionists to suffer from metaphysical angst. One example is Richard Kearney's compulsion to redefine the platonic Republic. Other southern writers and intellectuals strangely complain that 'Ireland does not exist'. This seems less an empirical judgement than a state of unconscious mourning for a god, a goddess, a symbolic future that failed. Two other post-nationalist reactions are revisionism and cynicism. But there has to be *some* reaction. Nationalism was internalised as God, nature and family. So it can leave painful withdrawal symptoms as it recedes.

Unionism does not linger like bog-mist in unsuspected crannies. For better or worse, you generally know it's there. Unionism exposes its contradictions in public: in the gap between its interior monologues and what it can get the rest of the world to believe. All ideologies work through unconscious assumptions as well as conscious creeds. But the unionist unconscious, in both its secular and religious versions, has never been open to outsiders, whereas the reflexes of the nationalist unconscious have been widely accepted as norms. The situation in the North is not helped by the tendency of nationalist Ireland to swallow or re-import its own dated propaganda. Patrick Kavanagh once said (with regard to the popularity of *The Quiet Man* in Dublin): 'the only place now where phoney ould Oireland is tolerated is in Ireland itself'. Unfortunately, he underestimated an export market which continues to boom. When flattered by Irish-American sentiment or left-wing 'Brit guilt', nationalism becomes less disposed to self-criticism and forgets its inner malaise.

Literature plays a part in all this too. (We import some starry-eyed lit crit from the USA). Now and then I will use contemporary writing as an index of the double ideological breakdown in Ireland. There are good historical reasons why Irish nationalism so often reads like bad poetry and Ulster unionism like bad prose. Cathleen of course has been muse as well as goddess. Eoin MacNeill tried to lower the political temperature before the Rising by sending round a circular which plainly stated: 'What we call our country is not a poetical abstraction ...there is no such person as Cathleen Ni Houlihan ...who is calling upon us to serve her.' Ulster Protestantism, which prides itself on plain statement, has been slow to evolve a self-critical prose tradition, let alone qualifying clauses. Thus from the 1920s most writers had no option but to constitute themselves an opposition to the ideological clamps holding both Irish entities together. In my lifetime, these clamps have distorted ethics, politics, social and personal relations, the lives of women, education, what passes here for religion, and our whole understanding of Irish culture.

Literature remains the primary place where language changes, where anorexic categories are exposed. This is no less the case in Ireland than in Eastern Europe.

Irish, Irisher, Irishest

'Irishness' is the most inclusive category for Irish Nationalist ideology—and also the most insidious. In the last paragraph of *Modern Ireland*, Roy Foster criticises the recurring theme of 'being 'more' or 'less' Irish than one's neighbours; Irishness as a scale or spectrum rather than a simple national or residential qualification; at worst, Irishness as a matter of aggressively displayed credentials'. Last Easter, Cardinal O'Fiaich proved how this theme persists in the collective unconscious. 'Many Protestants', he said, 'love Ireland as devoutly as *any* Catholic does' (my italics). He then recited the litany of patriot Prods (Tone, Emmet etc) usually produced in support of such statements. It sometimes seems as if Protestants have to die for Ireland before being allowed to live here.

The Cardinal meant his remarks kindly. But in so deliberately including Protestants, he excluded them. He fed the belief that Protestants have to work their passage to Irishness. Catholics, on the other hand, are born loving the country, knowing by instinct its entire history and literature, and generally 'kinned by hieroglyphic peat' (Seamus Heaney). This nonsense, out of date in the Republic, is widely swallowed by both sides in the North. But Ulster Irishness, like Ulster Britishness, is a state neither of nature nor of grace. It is enforced and reinforced by socialisation, often by simplifications and stereotypes. In *Ripley Bogle* Robert McLiam Wilson satirises the conditioning processes of the North:

> I learnt a great many things on my first day at school. I discovered that I lived in Belfast and that Belfast lived in Ireland and that this combination meant that I was Irish. The grim young bint we were loaded with was very fervent on this point. She stressed with some vigour that no matter what anyone else were to call us, our names would always be Irish...[she] told us that the occasional Misguided Soul would try to call us British but that of all things to call us—this was the wrongest. No matter how the Misguided Souls cajoled, insisted or pleaded, our names would remain Irish to the core, whatever that meant... in the spirit of compromise (ever with me even then), I dubbed myself 'Ripley Irish British Bogle'.

Roy Foster would replace the competing indoctrinations with 'a more relaxed and inclusive definition of Irishness, and a less constricted view of Irish history'. Who would not agree? Yet when he developed this idea in his lecture 'Varieties of Irishness', the Unionist David Trimble felt political pressures in the very term 'Irishness', however far its elastic might stretch. Of course Unionists can be equally paranoid about being called Irish and not being called Irish (as Jews in pre-war Poland resented the alternatives of assimilation and expulsion). But this seeming paradox is in fact an accurate response to the rhetorical tactics famously admitted by Senator Michael Hayes in 1939: 'We have had a habit, when it suited a particular case, of saying they were Irish, and when it did not suit a particular case of saying they were British'.

One way of circumventing an elaborate quadrille, in which the dancers contrive never to meet on the same ground, might be to accelerate the separation between political Irishness and culture in Ireland. Culture in Ireland is a range of practices, expressions, traditions, by no means homogeneously spread nor purely confined to the island. Political Irishness, on the another hand, is the ideology of identity ('Irish to the core') mainly packaged by the Gaelic League, which, twined with Catholicism, served to bind the new state. In the Republic the strings of this package have got looser and looser, and much of its substance has leaked out. In the North, Sinn Féin still tries to deliver a fossilised and belated version. There, whether embraced or resisted, Irishness endures as an absolute abstract noun. When threatened by that absolute, Unionists reach for the security-blanket of Britain or Ulster. Meanwhile, they are happy enough with relative or adjectival usages: Northern Irish, Irish Protestant, even Irish Unionist. In these usages, Ireland stands for the country, not the nation, and 'Erin's Orange lily' feels at home. The often-put question 'Are you British or Irish?' is strictly meaningless, since 'Irish' does double duty as an allegiance and as an ethno-cultural description. 'British' is only an allegiance, an umbrella for English, Scots, Welsh and some Northern Irish. Allegiance has cultural effects, and culture influences allegiance. Yet 'Britishness' is not opposite to 'Irishness': it is the affiliation whereby Ulster Protestants seek to maintain those aspects of their identity which are threatened by political Irishness.

Perhaps their reactions might seem less paranoid after we have visited the political unconscious of Alban Maginness, SDLP Councillor in Belfast. Here he is replying to an article by John Wilson Foster in which Foster contends that

'Northern Protestants have been excluded by the Nationalist majority in Ireland from being Irish'. Maginness says:

> Curiously, in some non-political situations, the Northern Protestant, which Foster unapologetically claims to be, concedes, asserts or even claims Irishness...the train loads of rugby supporters from Belfast to Lansdowne Road...bear witness to [it]. A tired and over-worked example some might say, but it does raise the question, why can't this 'sporting' patriotism be translated into political patriotism?
>
> My understanding of modern Irish history is that the majority culture was and still is inclusive, not exclusive and has an almost missionary zeal to persuade if not cajole Northern Protestants into realising or owning up to their innate Irishness...why this absurd denial of Irishness?
>
> *Studies*, Winter, 1988

The above manifests a deep confusion between cultural and political Irishness. Maginness's rugby example should indeed be laid to rest since the only group not heading for Lansdowne Road are Ulster Catholics. The culture of sport is heavily politicised in the North, keeping talent from the great games of rugby and hurling. And surely Maginness answers his own questions when he finds Irish Protestants, Irish Unionists relaxed about their affiliations to this country—a different matter from patriotic acceptance of the Republic—when the political heat is turned off. (People constantly generalise about 'Ireland' when they mean the Republic.)

Maginness might also compare his own feelings whenever unionism proposes to 'include' him, or professes 'missionary zeal' about persuading him to own up to his innate Britishness. And what exactly should Foster be *apologising* for?

As unionists shy away from cultural areas that seem appropriated by nationalists, so nationalists assume that cultural 'Irishness', very narrowly defined, functions as a prelude to the political variety. A *cúpla focal* on the lips, a twiddle on the fiddle, and 'from their full and genial hearts/An Irish feeling [will] burst.' Labhrás Ó Murchú actually told the New Ireland Forum that 'any unionist who is exposed to the *Tobar an Dúchais* will come up with a much more legitimate status for himself than the status that was contrived'. (This is the same man who decided that traditional Irish music opposed abortion.) The celebrated dulcimer-player John Rea was an Orangeman who, although always friendly toward Catholic fellow-musicians, called them 'them' to the end of his days. False hopes and fears are invested in 'the convert syndrome'. This encompasses the Protestant Gaeilgeoir as well as the Protestant patriot. Unfortunately, all converts impress the congregation they join a lot more than the one they have left. (They may also be subtly patronised as heretics who have seen the light.) A type of Aran-knit Ulster Protestant is particularly misleading in this respect, and has no battalions at his (or her) back. But even if East Belfast was teeming with potential Douglas Hydes, it doesn't follow that the language leads to the nation. After all, Samuel Ferguson set out to show that Gaelic literature is not the exclusive property of Catholics and nationalists. Mutterings to this effect have even been heard from the vicinity of the UDA.

What about literature in English written by Irish people? Does it belong to the nation, the country, the island, these islands, the world? Patrick Kavanagh knew he was on dangerous ground when he claimed that 'the writers of Ireland [are] no longer Corkery and O'Connor and the others but Auden and George Barker':

> Saying this is liable to make one the worst in the world, for a national literature, being based on a convention, not born of the unpredictable individual and his problems, is a vulnerable racket and is protected by fierce wild men.

John Banville has been able to say more coolly that 'there is no such thing as an Irish national literature, only Irish writers engaged in the practice of writing'. Yet when progressive cultural thinkers in the Republic dwell on the Europeanism or Atlanticism of Irish writing, they sometimes forget that its Irishness has been shelved rather than interrogated. For naive readers some Irish writers and texts are still more Irish than others. And, thanks to the Irish Literary Revival, the canon retains a vaguely nationalist aura, abroad if not always at home.

This is ironical, given that some literary critics have problems with Yeats's English literary connections, and with his latter-day cult of the Anglo-Irish Ascendancy. But if Yeats's Protestant and English affiliations were more sympathetically regarded, it might illuminate the role of the North in Ireland's literary culture. Still quoted is AE's dictum: 'Unionism in Ireland has produced no literature'. This, like Irishness and Britishness, involves a false alternative whereby anything written by Irish people can be turned to the glory of nationalism. Meanwhile, Protestant cultural expression is caricatured as drums and banners (not that the interest of these should be overlooked). Such perceptions reproduce an image foisted by political Irishness on to political Protestantism (and sometimes internalised by it). This image excludes the dual Irish-British context, and what Protestants actually write, paint and perform, whatever their political allegiances.

In 1985 Gerald Dawe and I edited a collection of critical essays entitled *Across a Roaring Hill: The Protestant Imagination in Modern Ireland*. To some, the category appeared sectarian (whereas 'Irish' would have been taken for granted). One reviewer (Declan Kiberd) assumed that we had a hidden unionist agenda; another (Enoch Powell) assumed that we belonged to the nationalist conspiracy. Brendan Kennelly quoted an acquaintance who reacted to the book's title by declaring that 'Protestants have no imagination at all'. This stereotype partly results from the inhibition of artistic expression within Scottish and Ulster Calvinism. But instead of putting down that culture with reference to 'the wonderfully rich Irish literary tradition etc' it should be understood in its own terms. Again, the relation of all Irish writing to Protestantism and Catholicism, an issue masked by homogenising 'Irishness', should be opened up—as should relations between Irish and English literature after 1922.

So I think that 'Irishness' with its totalitarian tinge, ought to be abandoned rather than made more inclusive. To include/exclude the Ulster Prods involves another false alternative (cf Senator Hayes) with underlying nationalist assumptions. 1798 is no more practical use to us than 1916. Charles Haughey may have pragmatically modified his views since he made his opening speech to the Forum. Yet, in his psychic alarm, he identified the real agenda: 'The belief has been canvassed that we would have to jettison almost the entire ethos on which the independence movement was built and that Irish identity has to be sacrificed to facilitate the achievement of Irish unity.' In fact, some such sacrifice may be necessary for the sake of peace let alone unity as once dreamed. But cultural change and changing awareness of culture, in the Republic and even in the North, have already exposed political Irishness (the 'ethos on which the independence movement was built') as now more a prison than a liberation.

Northern nationalists and southern revisionists

When nationalism achieves its object it 'begins to die'. So said Séan O'Faoláin in 1951. This means that the relation between southern and northern Nationalism is one of uneven development. The southern state was gradually born into evolution, while northern nationalism (like unionism) froze in an archaic posture. It stayed bent on realising what revisionism now seems wantonly to discard. But perhaps northern nationalists, nearly as anachronistic in Dublin as the unionists in London, will have to accept that the southern clock cannot be stopped or wound back.

As Clare O'Halloran shows in *Partition and the Limits of Irish Nationalism*, between northern and southern nationalists there lies a distance not only of time but experience, a distance usually disguised by rhetorical togetherness. She quotes John A Costello on the adversarial imperative that gives northern nationalism its distinctive shape: 'they have to fight their fight up there as a minority, and every piece of Protestant bitterness in the North has its counterpart, both politically and in a religious sense, in the hearts and in the actions of a northern Catholic. We in the South have got to recognise that we cannot understand that problem or appreciate it to the full.' That applies whether you are shocked by the atavisms of the North, or whether you don't want the North to rock the (relatively) secure southern boat.

The affair of Conor Cruise O'Brien, Garret FitzGerald, Senator John A Murphy and the SDLP was a tremor produced by the largely unexamined relation between northern and southern nationalist consciousness. This relation rarely reaches the political surface, because there is assumed to be not relation but identity: identity of perception, interest, objective, context, historical moment. In this case tensions surfaced over SDLP attitudes to the RUC. Yet the emotional temperature of the row, particularly the reflex to execrate O'Brien and protect Hume, soared above its occasion. That signalled psychic alarm: the alarm-bells that ring whenever northern nationalism and southern revisionism touch.

In fact to deny any split or breakdown within the Irish nationalist psyche is to deny well-attested trauma. The South's long neglect of northern nationalists (documented by O'Halloran) breeds guilty over-compensation—which does not necessarily heal underlying resentments. (Go back, Austin Currie.) But Senator Murphy's hostilities, like O'Brien's certitudes, may be unwise in trying to break a taboo with a crowbar. Meanwhile slagging the South goes down well in West Belfast, and opinion in the republic swings between indifference and feverish identification. The latter, however, is mostly roused by events which concern 'British justice' (the Gibraltar killings) and thus recall shared experience before 1922. In my view such philosophical and political incoherence serves neither side in the north, and retards the Republic's maturation into being part of the solution rather than central to the problem. It might advance the Hillsborough Accord if psychic separation were promoted not only between Britain and the unionists, but also between the Irish Government and northern nationalists.

Even *Irish Times* editorials can regress towards political infancy when championing the SDLP: 'the SDLP and Provisionals may share, in part, a mistily defined political objective—the unification of Ireland. That is not an illegitimate objective: indeed it is a noble and attractive ideal' (22 April 1989). The last twenty years have seen the nemesis of misty definitions and attractive ideals. As for 'noble' (an adjective generally reserved for the male sex), in a fit of crazed ecumenism Bishop Cahal Daly recently maintained that unionism and nationalism were *both* 'noble aspirations'. It would be preferable to downgrade nationalism to the ignoble status traditionally enjoyed by unionism, rather than cling to the notion that a 'good' or 'real' nationalism exists in some zone uncontaminated by the Provos. We could also give 'aspirations' a rest. Fintan O'Toole has argued (*The Irish Times*, 20 April 1989) that Section 31 permits physical-force Republicanism to function as the id of the body politic. It subsists at an unconscious level where it cannot be interrogated. And if Sinn Féin remains below interrogation, the SDLP (a political party after all) remains above it. Thus southern nationalism cedes control over its own redefinition. The very structure of the New Ireland Forum, in asserting the unity of the nationalist family, excluded agonising reappraisal of other unitary principles. Nevertheless, *de facto* reappraisal takes place all the time: at the level of economic necessity, historical revisionism, cultural change, the cycles of shock and weariness over the northern war.

Literature makes a good barometer of asymmetric consciousness in Ireland. As a literary critic who sometimes notices distinctive elements in northern writing, I have been suspected equally of partisanship and partitionism. This looks like another over-anxious unitary reflex. It is absurd to contend that Northern Ireland and the Republic have had identical socio-political experiences since 1922, or since 1968. And if we believe that literature is (up to a point) conditioned by society, and criticises society, we should not sacrifice any insights it can offer. For instance, I have certainly learned more about the culture of the North from Medbh McGuckian's or Seamus Heaney's poetry (even after his move to Dublin), and that of the Republic from Paul Durcan's or Thomas McCarthy's.

Durcan's visionary radicalism, for instance, criticises a particular *status quo*. Unlike the majority of southern poets, he broaches the North. But he does so from outside the territory, without inhabiting its tensions as do the imaginations of Muldoon or Heaney. And Durcan's special focus is to open up the Republic's implication in the war. Thus long before Enniskillen he wrote the satirical 'National Day of Mourning for Twelve Protestants'. Life slowly catches up with art. Durcan's poetry neither renounces its own cultural roots nor overlooks loyalist terror. But he concentrates on the spiritual failings of the society he knows and for which he feels responsible. So, generally, do other writers North and South. An exception that proves the rule may be recent fiction and drama from the Southern border counties, which contains two-way perspectives from a neglected limbo and source of light. But the republic's writers are distinctively obsessed with secularism, sexuality, socialism, versions of feminism, and other libertarian themes. Literature and theatre seem to be mounting a communal psycho-drama that releases what the official political culture won't admit.

Field Day is often perceived as speaking for Ireland. The company has indeed sometimes sponsored pluralism: in staging Stewart Parker's *Pentecost*, in publishing a pamphlet by Unionist Robert McCartney. But the pamphlet-topics so far chosen give a northern nationalist priority to cultural and political 'decolonisation'. The latest trio was written by foreign literary critics better acquainted with general theories of colonialism than with Ireland after 1922. For Edward Said and Terry Eagleton, all 'the Irish people' are still engaged in a single national struggle. Reviewing the pamphlets (*Fortnight* no 271), Colm Tóibín found a time-warp in Field Day's own perceptions: 'the social and cultural revolution of the 1960s

172

has left the artists in the Field Day group singularly unmoved...They write as though nothing had ever changed: their Ireland is distinctly pre-decimal. Thus England is the problem and the enemy (and the dramatic other).' Field Day's latest production *Saint Oscar* looked out of date in Dublin because it was an instance of the re-imported nationalist propaganda I mentioned earlier. Its author, Eagleton again, used Wilde to present a timeless thesis about imperialist oppression. Field Day's eagerness to collude with the hoary stereotypes of the English hard Left seems significant.

Common to Friel's drama and the critical writings of Seamus Deane is a powerful sense of Palestinian dispossession. The alienation of Friel's Ballybeg is utterly different from the post-nationalist alienation of Tom Murphy's *Bailegangaire*. When speaking of Ireland's literary and political traditions, Deane repeatedly uses the terms 'crisis' and 'discontinuity'. These conditions he generalises to cover the total past and this total island now. But his perceptions cannot be divorced from the recent history of Derry with its lost hinterland. (The other side of this bleak coin is the siege-haunted Derry Protestant.) The same affiliation may show itself in Deane's intellectual resistance to the 'mystique of Irishness' concocted by Yeats on the one hand, Corkery on the other. Perhaps his otherwise rather extreme (and contradictory) desire for 'new writing, new politics, unblemished by Irishness, but securely Irish' (*Heroic Styles*) reflects, and aspires to redress, the exclusion of northern nationalists from the self-images and cultural definitions that became operational in the new state. Certainly, critics associated with Field Day approach the Irish Literary Revival both as a colonial manifestation, and as a present hegemony (not a receding phase in literary history). They question the Revival's cultural power as revisionists question the political power of 1916. As for Corkery, Tom Garvin argues that Munster, remote from *both* Ulster communities, played a disproportionate part in theorising the revolution (see *Nationalist Revolutionaries in Ireland 1858-1928*). Perhaps that explains the tiff between John A Murphy and Nell McCafferty.

Whatever its other purposes and qualities, the Field Day project for 'a comprehensive anthology' of Irish literature ('what writing in this country has been') shows a desire to influence definitions. Within the literary sphere it seeks to piece together a broken past, to go back behind all deforming colonisation, to return to origins (550 AD), and thus to clarify 'Irish reality' so that we can start again. In contrast, revisionism seeks to break down a monolithic idea of the past, to go back behind the revolution's ideology, to return to origins in 1922 and understand them more empirically. In my view the former project risks the dangerous fantasy that loss and breakdown can be retrieved. Rather than start a new literary and political clock, I think we should try to tell the time accurately.

John Hume and 'An Island Once Again'
Political language goes out of date when its objective basis shrinks. It's easy to see that Sinn Féin inhabits a rhetorical dead-end—though their terminology should be directly challenged in the Republic, *the only place where it can be*. But what about the political language of John Hume? Does he breathe new life into nationalist ideology? Or (like Field Day at times) does he simply translate traditional concepts into an updated idiom?

Hume keeps his political unconscious under better control than do Haughey, Maginness and O'Fiaich. He thus seems a model of eloquent flexibility as compared with the monotonous negatives of Unionism. But unionism may be a better critic than author—or at least a close reader of the subtexts that concern it. And on closer inspection Hume's language has much in common with George Orwell's metaphor for Marxist jargon: 'prefabricated phrases bolted together like the pieces of a child's Meccano set'.

Hume likes to stress that he has moved beyond the old definitions. So let us test him on the questions of 'Irishness' and 'revisionism'. On the former topic he has criticised 'those who are so unsure of their Irishness that they need to remind us of it constantly' (thus acknowledging competition between the SDLP and Sinn Féin over degrees of Irishness). And he has rejected the Republican category of 'the Irish people', favouring instead: 'Protestant fellow Irishmen', 'the people of this island', 'the Unionist people and the rest of the people of this island' (*London Review of Books*, 2 February 1989). But is this quite as innocent and open as it looks? Or is it the 'particular case' which it suits to say that they are Irish? Hume's article does not call the Unionist people 'British', thus minimising the significance of this self-protective definition in their own consciousness. Again, while Ireland as island is an improvement on Ireland as nation, it omits 'the totality of relations in the archipelago'. Although Hume's vision is larger than that of most northern politicians he too selects the 'whole' on which he desires attention to concentrate. Nobody catches all the snooker-balls in the triangle.

Hume's *cultural* perception of his 'Protestant fellow Irishmen' is remarkably narrow. It excludes most of their affiliations to the other island—and indeed to this one. He characterises their 'long and strong tradition in Ireland' as religious, military, industrial: 'pride in their service to the crown...in their work ethic and in their faith'. Obviously there is truth here, but limited, stereotypical and dated. Meanwhile 'Irishness', so 'sure' as to be given no definition whatsoever, seems another matter entirely. (It also seems, unlike unionism, to have no religious affiliation.) Hume's incomplete, and unconsciously polarised, cultural awareness may reflect the binary geography of Derry.

As for revisionism: Hume contributed an article on 'Europe of the Regions' to Richard Kearney's compilation *Across the Frontiers: Ireland in the 1990s*. The contrast between it and the editor's own contribution illustrates once again the uneven development of Nationalist consciousness. This is the post-nationalist Kearney:

> An Ireland without frontiers is obviously an Ireland without borders. This does not, however, entail a united Ireland in the traditional sense of the term. For the nation-states of Britain and Ireland, which constitute the very basis for the opposing claims of Nationalist and Unionist ideologies would be superseded by a European constellation of regions.

Hume's Europe, in contrast, becomes less and less regional the closer it gets to home. He does not advocate Ulster regionalism, or any other form of Irish Balkanisation, but emphasises what 1992 will do for the Gaeltacht. And he falls into Nationalist idiom: 'the real "new republicanism"...rather than being any reversal of the national destiny...will allow us better to fulfil our potential as a people...and to enjoy properly the inchoate European outlook and vision which was lost in our oppressive and obsessive relationship with Britain'. Wearing his SDLP hat, Hume remains interested in a relationship which his Euro-regionalist hat occludes.

When interviewed in *The Irish Times* by Frank Millar (13

January 1989), Hume endlessly repeated the unitary Meccano-phrase 'this island', *not* 'these islands': 'the central relationship being that of the Unionists and the rest of this island and *then* the relationship between Ireland and Britain' (my italics); 'Going to the heart of the problem is the relationship between the Unionist people and the rest of the people of this island'; 'do they want [to] work out with the rest of the people of this island how we share the island?' 'What I want to see is the representatives of the divided people of this island reaching an agreement on how they share the island...'

In a kind of linguistic tug-of-war, Hume first tries to yank the unionists off their UK base, then to pull them across the border. 'Island-sharing' (I wonder how keen they are in Kerry?) is a very different matter from 'power-sharing' within the existing framework. Hume is in fact skilfully playing a political word and map game with specific origins in Northern Irish politics. There, trying to control bounds and definitions has always been part of the territorial battle. But unionists are unlikely to swallow his island-Nationalism unless nationalism equally swallows their archipelagan-Britishness. Britain and the Republic find themselves guarantors of communities more unionist and more Nationalist than themselves, for whose neurotic pathologies their own incoherence is much to blame. Only by rethinking their own relationship, outside existing nationalist and unionist categories, can Ireland and Britain generate new political language for their frontier-region.

Women and nationalism

I have compared Irish nationalism to bad poetry. In bad poems the relations between word, image and life break down. Political images, like political language (from which they are never quite distinct), eventually exhaust themselves or prove incapable of renewal. I think this happens at the juncture where the image women-Ireland-muse meets contemporary Irish women. There, I believe, the breakdown of nationalist ideology becomes particularly clear.

In the film *Mother Ireland* (Derry Film and Video) Nell McCafferty regrets that the Committee for the Liberation of Irish Women, to avert a potential split, decided not to talk about the north. She would now welcome general debate on topics like 'Feminism and physical force'. While I might hope for a different outcome than she does, I agree that the issue of women and nationalism cannot be dodged for ever. Southern women too are implicated in this issue, although they may neither know it nor wish it. Even on her death-bed Cathleen-Anorexia exerts a residual power over the image and self-images of all Irish women. Both at home and abroad, she still confers status on selected kinds of Irish woman-ness (not, for instance, the Rhonda Paisley kind). The absurd 'Irish' edition of *Spare Rib* (August 1989), of which more anon, is a case in point.

Of course the Ulster Protestant community, though dragged forward faster by Westminster legislation, is as traditionally patriarchal as Catholic nationalism. This tribe too has its cult of male chieftains: Carson, Moses, the Big Man (compare Dev, the Pope, the Boss). And the whole country abounds in Ancient Orders of Hibernian Male-Bonding: lodges, brotherhoods, priesthoods, hierarchies, sodalities, knights, Fitzwilliam Tennis Club, Field Day Theatre Company. But at least unionism does not appropriate the image of woman or hide its aggressions behind our skirts. Nor does it—as a reactive ideology—seek ideological mergers. A unionist feminist might be these things separately, though genuine feminism would erode her Unionism. A nationalist/republican feminist, less readily regarded as a contradiction in terms, claims that her ideologies coincide. And in so doing she tries to hijack Irish feminism.

Terry Eagleton (in *Nationalism: Irony and Commitment*) develops an analogy between nationalism and feminism as responses to 'oppression'. He argues that nationalism must not prematurely sell its soul to revisionism and pluralism, just as feminism—until women have been truly liberated—must not sell its soul to 'a troubling and subverting of all sexual strait-jacketing'. As I will indicate later, with respect to the history of women and nationalism, strait-jackets tend to remain in place after the revolution unless their removal has been intrinsic to the revolution. Eagleton does not recognise that Catholic nationalism has often been as great an oppressor of Irish people, Irish women, as British imperialism or Ulster unionism. Perhaps the equivalent of advanced feminist 'troubling and subverting' is precisely what our nationalist and unionist patriarchal strait-jackets need.

Subversions occur wherever Protestants and Catholics in Ulster evade the binary ideological trap. But we need help

177

from the Republic. I was surprised that Eavan Boland's LIP pamphlet, *A Kind of Scar: The Woman Poet in a National Tradition*, ignored the extent to which the North has destabilised the 'nation'. Boland holds to unitary assumptions about 'a society, a nation, a literary heritage'. Troubled about 'the woman poet', she takes the 'national tradition' for granted—and perhaps thereby misses a source of her trouble. Because *A Kind of Scar* activates only one pole of its dialectic, it does not evolve the radical aesthetic it promises. By not asking why 'as a poet I could not easily do without the idea of a nation', Boland fails to challenge an idea of Irish poetry which is narrow as well as patriarchal. She refers to 'marginality *within* a tradition' (my italics) and regrets that 'the Irish nation as an existing construct in Irish poetry was not available to me', without considering how that construct itself, both inside and outside poetry, has marginalised and scarred many Irish women and men.

Earlier I suggested that to over-stress the independence of Irish literature from English literature (and vice versa) distorts literary history and does not help contemporary politics. Boland, it seems to me, feels unnecessarily guilty for (as an apprentice poet) having read 'English court poetry' on Achill, and having imitated the English 'Movement' mode of the early sixties. To whom, to what avatar, to what icon is she apologising?

In fact, it is to Mother Ireland herself. Although Boland criticises male poets for having made woman a silent object in their visionary odes (to 'Dark Rosaleen. Cathleen Ni Houlihan. The nation as woman: the woman as national muse'), she insists: 'in all this I did not blame nationalism'. Because she does not blame nationalism, her alternative Muse turns out to be the twin sister of Dark Rosaleen etc: 'the truths of womanhood and the defeats of a nation. An improbable intersection?' No, as Conor Cruise O'Brien said in a similar context, 'a dangerous intersection'. Boland's new muse, supposedly based on the varied historical experience of Irish women, looks remarkably like the sean bhean bhocht. Her pamphlet begins by invoking an old Achill woman who speaks of the Famine. The 'real women of an actual past' are subsumed into a single emblematic victim-figure: 'the women of a long struggle and a terrible survival', 'the wrath and grief of Irish history'. By not questioning the nation, Boland recycles the literary cliche from which she desires to escape.

Boland notes that 'the later Yeats' is a rare exception among poets who 'have feminised the national and nationalised the feminine'. There are good reasons why this should be so. Yeats's early play *Cathleen Ni Houlihan* helped to propagate the feminine mystique of Irish nationalism. During the three years after 1916, in such poems as 'On a Political Prisoner' and the much misunderstood 'A Prayer for my Daughter', he broke the icon his poetry had gilded. That is, he questioned Cathleen as then incarnated by Constance Markievicz and Maud Gonne MacBride.

In 'A Prayer for my Daughter' Yeats criticises Ireland/Gonne for her 'opinionated mind'. By 'opinion' he always means dogmatic nationalism. So he is revising his image of woman-Ireland-muse, and divining Anorexia in Gonne 'choked with hate':

Have I not seen the loveliest woman born
Out of the mouth of plenty's horn
Because of her opinionated mind
Barter that horn and every *good*
By quiet natures understood
For an old bellows full of angry wind?

That 'old bellows' is already full of destructive cliches. Yeats may be patriarchal in the female qualities he values above ideological rigidity: 'natural kindness', 'heart-revealing intimacy', 'courtesy', rootedness'. But it might be argued that at least he replaces the aisling of nationalist male fantasy with a model for the Irish future that draws on (some of) women's own qualities—the 'womanly times' for which Ian McEwan has called.

However, Gonne, Markievicz and Maeve the warrior-queen have enjoyed a new lease of life in northern republican ideology. Perhaps Feminists too readily assume that it's *always* a good thing when passive versions of women are transformed into active ones. Both have political uses.

Two passive images are the vulnerable virgin and the mourning mother: images that link Cathleen with Mary. They project the self-image of Catholic nationalism as innocent victim, equally oppressed at all historical periods. (Is there a subconscious admission that Irish men victimise women?) This assigns to Britain the perpetual role of male bully and rapist. In Seamus Heaney's 'Ocean's Love to Ireland': 'The ruined maid complains in Irish'. In the mid-1970s Heaney could still symbolise the northern conflict as 'a struggle between the cults and devotees of a god and a goddess'; between 'an indigenous territorial numen, a tutelar of the whole island, call her Mother Ireland, Cathleen Ni Houlihan...the Shan Van Vocht, whatever' and 'a new male cult whose founding fathers were Cromwell, William of Orange and Edward Carson'. To characterise Irish nationalism (only constructed in the nineteenth century) as archetypally female both gives it mythic pedigree and exonerates it from aggressive and oppressive intent. Its patriarchal elements also disappear. Here, perhaps, we glimpse the poetic unconscious of northern nationalism. At the same time, Heaney's mouldering 'Bog Queen' in *North* may indirectly represent the cult of Cathleen as a death-cult. The book contains an unresolved tension between two Muses: a symbolic mummified or mummifying woman (not yet Anorexia) and the warmly creative, life-giving aunt who bakes scones in the poem 'Sunlight'.

While Virgin-Ireland gets raped and pitied, Mother Ireland translates pity into a call to arms and vengeance. She resembles the white-feather-bestowing 'Little Mother' in First-World War recruiting. Traditionally, it is *her* sons whom Mother Ireland recruits and whose *manhood* she tests. More recently, some of her daughters have also become 'freedom-fighters'. In *Mother Ireland* Bernadette Devlin and Mairead Farrell differed in their attitudes to the personification. Devlin felt that Mother Ireland had empowered her as a strong woman; Farrell said: 'Mother Ireland, get off our backs'. But did she? Is there not collusion between all feminine nationalist images, between Queen Maeve and Mother Ireland, between the feminine-pathetic and the feminine-heroic? The latter too disguises or softens aggression: the looks and dress of Gonne and Markievicz were propaganda-assets. On the cover of the biased *Only The Rivers Run Free: Northern Ireland: The Women's War* a glamorous young paramilitary woman fronts a desperate-looking Sean Bhean.

Such images of Irish women are among those selectively approved by Anorexia. The cover of *Spare Rib* (August 1989) features another: a West Belfast Mother Courage with child in pram, smoke and flames behind her, and insets of a British soldier and 'Stop Strip Searches'. Of course there are many courageous working-class mothers on the Falls—ditto on the Shankill. But does it help them if this magazine distorts the profile of Irish women to include no police or UDR widows; no non-aligned social-workers, doctors or teachers; no members of the DUP; no Belfast or Dublin yuppies; no Southern feminists; no TDs? There are also articles with titles like 'Britain's War on Ireland' and 'Irish in Britain—Living in the Belly of the Beast' (an interesting variation on rape-images: cannibalism? Jonah and the whale?). And a literary section, among other poetic sentimentalities, reprints Susan Langstaff Mitchell's 'To the Daughters of Erin': 'Rise from your knees, O daughters rise!/ Our mother still is young and fair...Heroes shall leap from every hill...The red blood burns in Ireland still'. (Feminism, where are you?) *Spare Rib* has certainly provided the most ludicrous instance yet of the British Left's anachronistic and self-righteous pieties on Ireland. But it's up to Irish women themselves to expose the loaded terms in a statement like: 'In the *Six Counties Irish* women experience *oppression* both as women and as members of a *colonised people*' (my italics). I attended a 'Time To Go' conference in London which offered a seminar on 'Ireland in Feminism'. I think Feminism in Ireland should have something to say about that.

During the Irish revolution nationalist women discovered—though not all acknowledged or cared—that their oppression as women did not end with the Dawning of the Day. The briefly eulogised 'Dáil Girl...wielding a cudgel in one hand and a revolver in the other' soon gave way to Dev's ideal of 'life within the home'. Nor had the Dáil girl necessarily taken up her cudgel for Feminism. As a general rule: the more Republican, the less Feminist. The ultra-nationalism of the six women deputies who opposed the Treaty was, in Margaret Ward's words, governed by the 'ghosts of dead sons, husbands and brothers'. Theirs were 'opinionated minds' with no—female?—capacity for compromise, and they set a pattern for the limited participation of women in the Free State/Republic's political life: almost invariably licensed by male relatives, by dynastic privilege. Rosemary Cullen Owens in *Smashing Times* (less romantic than Ward's *Unmanageable Revolutionaries*) brings out the tension between nationalism and suffragism: 'From 1914 onwards, with Home Rule on the statute book, it was the growing separatist movement which created the greatest obstacle to a united women's movement'.

Sinn Féin women (the only women quoted in *Spare Rib*)

have recently adopted some feminist ideas. But they cling, like their elder sisters, to the prospective goodwill of republican men, and to the fallacy that: 'there can't be women's liberation until there's national liberation'. Devlin in *Spare Rib* seems significantly wary of 'the gospel according to the holy writ of feminism'. What a woman 'needs to know is that we, her sisters, will catch her if she stumbles, help her find the questions—the answers she must find herself'. Who are 'we, her sisters'? And what kind of elitism lurks in Devlin's assertion (in *Mother Ireland*) that 'the best young feminist women today are those who have come through the experience of the Republican movement'?

While admiring the bonding that tough circumstances beget, and perceiving these circumstances as tragic, I do not accept that either the supportiveness of the ghetto or the essential survival-strategy in Armagh Gaol affords a model for Irish women in general. The basis of such bonding is tribal rather than sisterly. It remains true that the vast majority of Republican women come from traditionally Republican families—recruited by and for a patriarchal unit. The Irish women's movement, instead of walking away or vaguely empathising, might examine the role of nationalist conditioning in all this: the ideological forces which played a part in sending out Mairéad Farrell to be shot.

Contrary to Nell McCafferty, I think that 'feminism and physical force' is self-evidently a contradiction in terms. Years ago a member of the Irish Women's Franchise League said: 'It is our conviction feminism and militarism are natural born enemies and cannot flourish in the same soil'. Militarism, that touch of Madame Defarge, gives the Sinn Féin sisterhood its faintly chilling aura. In *The Demon Lover: On the Sexuality of Terrorism*, Robin Morgan argues that revolutionary terrorism inevitably involves a death-cult. It enacts the quest of the male hero who already 'lives as a dead man'. She asks: 'Why is manhood always perceived as the too-high price of peace?' and notes that when men take over any movement: 'what once aimed for a humanistic triumph now aims for a purist defeat. Martyrdom'. The same syndrome can be detected in Protestant anticipations of Armageddon, apocalypse, their last stand (the ghosts of religious wars walk on both sides). Morgan's conclusion mirrors the Irish nationalist historical pattern: 'The rebel woman in a male-defined state-that-would-be is merely acting out another version of the party woman running for office in the state-that-is'. Unionist party-women have been equally acquiescent in militarism.

Cathleen-Anorexia encourages women to join a male death-cult which has a particularly masochistic martyrology. This cult's rituals deny the 'connectivity' which Morgan sees as the 'genius' of feminist thought: 'In its rejection of the static, this capacity is witty and protean, like the dance of nature itself…It is therefore a volatile capacity —dangerous to every imaginable status quo, because of its insistence on *noticing*. Such a noticing involves both attentiveness and recognition, and is in fact a philosophical and activist technique for being in the world, as well as for changing the world'. In 'Easter 1916' Yeats understands that 'Too long a sacrifice / Can make a stone of the heart', and contrasts that stone with 'the living stream'. Surely the chill, the stone, the self-destructiveness at the heart of Irish nationalism shows up in its abuse of women and their gifts of life.

Conclusion: after Anorexia

I have argued that nationalism and unionism in Ireland are dying ideologies, death-cult ideologies. Yet these ideologies are also masks for an intensely local territorial struggle. Ulster's territorial imperative has produced a politics which pivots on male refusal to give an inch. John Hewitt characterises the Protestant people as 'stubborn'; Seamus Heaney characterises the Catholic people as 'obstinate'.

But this polarised macho politics travesties the North's cultural complexity. In the report on *Cultural Traditions in Northern Ireland* Brian Turner emphasises how the thriving local studies movement has 'challenged the "two traditions" terminology'. And Anthony Buckley in 'Collecting Ulster's Culture: Are There Really Two Traditions?', illustrates ways in which culture has been caricatured for the purpose of 'asserting group identities'. A more negative term for this is 'cultural defence'. In fact insecurities underlie the self-assertive rhetorics of both unionism and nationalism. Cultural defence is the reflex of frontier-regions where communities fear extinction or absorption. It explains, for instance, the Catholic Church's not-an-inch attitude to integrated education. And it explains unionism's perennial paranoia about the Irish language (only now to be properly supported and thus depoliticised).

That the Free State's Gaelicisation policy attracted more unionist jeers than did Rome Rule indicates fears of ethnic exclusion (and also the counter-productiveness of nationalist ideology). Yet Gaelicisation, which attempted an *impossible* separation of Irishness from Britishness, was itself a form of cultural defence. Its errors are reproduced today by Sinn Féin's cultural self-ghettoisation. There is a sad element of barren triumphalism in the West Belfast festival.

Locked into dying ideologies, a territorial imperative and cultural defence, Northern Irish people do not immediately hold all the keys to their own salvation. One key is held by the Republic and Britain; another by a slow process of education.

Firstly, only the Republic and Britain together can defuse the mutual fear of their client communities. This should involve the Republic honestly re-examining its own nationalism; making its constitutional claim as inoperative in theory as it is in practice; and adopting the same hands-off stance as the UK government. (John Hume's argument that the British have thereby left matters up to the people of Ireland should be resisted.) Advance depends on an intricately engineered four-wheel drive which engages all parties to the dispute, and which encourages momentum within the North.

Secondly, without education in the broadest sense we cannot loosen the grip of Anorexia, of ideological rigor mortis. Progress will not only stem from official or institutional sources—Education for Mutual Understanding, Co-operation North, putting Cultural Traditions on the curriculum etc—it occurs wherever people work together practically and constructively. Yet, as with the Irish language, we also need more formal means to dismantle the frameworks of cultural defence.

One pilot-model is the local studies movement. This, at the micro-level, breaks down monolithic versions of nationalist and unionist history. It also maximises the strength rather than the weakness of Ulster's territorial imperative: attachment to place. Local studies promote the 'noticing' that Robin Morgan values. Many Unionists (the OUP wing) refuse to notice the ground under their own feet, the very territory they claim. Since 1922 they have often imported an anxious, ersatz and self-mutilating Englishness to stand in for Britishness and fend off Irishness. The Campaign for Equal

Citizenship (for getting British parties to organise in Northern Ireland) is a recent instance of unionists staring across the water and trying to walk on it. Really, they are motivated by political sulks and cultural defence in the wake of the Anglo-Irish Agreement. Unionist attempts to base themselves in London, like the SDLP inclination to identify with Dublin, show the vital importance of the regionalist concept. Some local councils now lead the way in power-sharing, as local studies do in culture-sharing.

Another model—which gives the lie to equations of the regional with the provincial—is northern writing, especially since the early 1960s. At the start of this pamphlet I called literature the primary place where language changes and anorexic categories are exposed (not always a conscious process). Writers born into an over-determined, over-defined environment, into a tension between political simplicities and cultural complexity, have felt impelled to redefine: to explore and criticise language, images, categories, stereotypes, myths. Northern writing does not fit the binary shapes cut out by nationalism and unionism. It trellises the harsh girders with a myriad details. It overspills borders and manifests a web of affiliation that stretches beyond any heartland—to the rest of Ireland, Britain, Europe. But the range of styles, histories, myths and influences perhaps could only enter the imagination in this unique zone of 'problems and cleavages' (John Hewitt's phrase). All the 'cultural traditions' count somewhere; nor are the political divisions discounted.

There is a third model in women's groups whose generally pragmatic priorities have theoretical implications. These groups exemplify how we learn and teach by doing. Recently, when the sectarianism of that male-dominated mayhem, Belfast City Council, blocked a grant to the Falls Road Women's Centre, their indignation was shared by the Women's Centre on the Shankill.

The image of the web is female, feminist, 'connective'—as contrasted with male polarisation. So is the ability to inhabit a range of relations rather than a single allegiance. The term 'identity' has been coarsened in Ulster politics to signify two ideological package-deals immemorially on offer. To admit to more varied, mixed, fluid and relational kinds of identity would advance nobody's territorial claim. It would undermine cultural defences. It would subvert the male pride that keeps up the double frontier-siege. All this would be on the side of life—like noticing, redefining and again redefining, doing.

Bernard Crick argues:

> While nationalisms are real and authentic in these islands, yet none are as self-sufficient as their adepts claim. In Northern Ireland most people are, in fact, torn in two directions: 'torn', that is, while their political leaders will not recognise that people can, with dignity, face in two directions culturally at once, and refuse to invent political institutions to match. In the world before nation-states such dualities and pluralities were common enough, as in some other border-areas today.

Irish Review, 5, Autumn 1988

Both Irish nationalism and Ulster unionism must accept the reality of the North as a frontier-region, a cultural corridor, a zone where Ireland and Britain permeate one another. The Republic should cease to talk about 'accommodating diversity' and face up to duality. This would actually help the North to relax into a less dualistic sense of its own identity: to function, under whatever administrative format, as a shared region of these islands. At which point there will definitely be no such person as Cathleen Ni Houlihan.

References and further reading

Boland, Eavan. *A Kind of Scar: The Woman Poet in A National Tradition.* Dublin: Attic Press (LIP Pamphlet), 1989

Buckley, Anthony. *In The Use of Tradition.* Alan Gailey (ed) Cultra: Ulster Folk and Transport Museum, 1988

Dawe, Gerald and Edna Longley (eds). *Across a Roaring Hill: The Protestant Imagination in Modern Ireland.* Belfast: Blackstaff, 1985

Eagleton, Terry. *Nationalism: Irony and Commitment.* Derry: Field Day Pamphlet No 13, 1988.

Foster, Roy. *Modern Ireland 1600-1972.* London: Allen Lane: The Penguin Press, 1988.

Garvin, Tom. *Nationalist Revolutionaries in Ireland 1858-1928.* Oxford: Clarendon Press, 1987.

Kearney, Richard. *Across the Frontiers: Ireland in the 1990s.* Dublin: Wolfhound Press, 1989.

Morgan, Robin. *The Demon Lover: On the Sexuality of Terrorism.* London: Methuen, 1989.

O'Halloran, Clare. *Partition and the Limits of Irish Nationalism: An Ideology Under Stress.* Dublin: Gill and Macmillan, 1987.

Owens, Rosemary Cullen. *Smashing Times: A History of the Irish Women's Suffrage Movement.* 1889-1992 Dublin: Attic Press, 1984.

Said, Edward. *Yeats and Decolonisation.* Derry: Field Day Pamphlet No 15, 1988.

Turner, Brian. Local Studies Section in *Cultural Traditions in Northern Ireland*. Belfast: Queen's University Institute of Irish Studies, 1989.
Ward, Margaret. *Unmanageable Revolutionaries*. Dingle: Brandon Press/London: Pluto Press, 1983.

A note on the author
Edna Longley is a Reader in English at Queen's University Belfast and well-known as a critic of poetry and as a cultural critic. Author of two books, *Poetry in the Wars* (1986) and *Louis MacNeice: A Study* (1988), she is also an editor of the *Irish Review* and on the editorial board of *Fortnight*. 'From Cathleen to Anorexia' is partly based on her controversial *Irish Times* articles which appeared in Summer 1989.

9

SEX AND NATION
Women in Irish Culture and Politics

Gerardine Meaney, 1991

The aim of this pamphlet is to challenge the assumptions made by and about the women's movement in Ireland. It is to some extent a retrospective exercise, an attempt to analyse and respond to some of the ideas put forward in previous pamphlets in this series. It is, more importantly, an attempt to suggest directions in which Irish feminism can move in the future, an attempt to learn from the reverses and successes of the 1980s and to identify opportunities which will be available to Irish feminism in the 1990s.

Sex and Nation

Many of the previous pamphlets in this series have made the point that, in Ireland, sexual identity and national identity are mutually dependent. The images of suffering Mother Ireland and the self-sacrificing Irish mother are difficult to separate. Both serve to obliterate the reality of women's lives. Both seek to perpetuate an image of Woman far from the experience, expectations and ideals of contemporary women. The extent to which women only exist as a function of their maternity in the dominant ideology of southern Ireland became apparent during the referendum on the eighth amendment to the constitution. The constitutional prohibition on abortion which was the result of that referendum has proved entirely ineffectual. The number of Irish women seeking and obtaining abortions in Britain has continued to increase. One is tempted to speculate that abortion itself was quite incidental to those who campaigned so vociferously for an unworkable constitutional ban. The only real effect of the eighth amendment has been to compromise any general or 'human' constitutional rights which might give precedence to the woman's rights as an individual over her function as a mother. That such a constitutional amendment was felt to be necessary by conservative groups—and that they were able to mobilise an available reservoir of mass hysteria to achieve it— is indicative of the anxiety which changes in women's role and self-concept have induced in Ireland. The assumption that the law needed to intervene in the relationship between woman and foetus—to protect the so-called 'unborn child' from its mother—is indicative of a deep distrust and fear of women. This distrust and fear is paradoxically rooted in the idealisation of the mother in Irish culture as an all-powerful, dehumanised figure. On the one hand, the 1980s saw the Catholic Church and the Right expend very considerable energy in the attempt to contain women within their traditional role. On the other hand, it was that traditional role which excited precisely the fear and anxiety (in men and women) which the Catholic Church and the Right shared and exploited to induce an electorate to endorse a constitutional compromise of the rights of women.

The participation of women in the so-called 'pro-life' movement is indicative of an even more complex and contradictory response. Such women seek to perpetuate the idealised virgin/mother figure of woman so that they can be that figure. Such identification offers women one of the few roles of power available to them in patriarchy. The hard struggle for political and economic power and equality cannot yet compete with those consolations for many women. The attractions of the traditional feminine role, particularly as the Catholic Church defines it, are grounded in a deep loathing of femininity, however, and those women who identify with it are also expressing a form of self-hatred, a revulsion against themselves as women. They are unable to accept themselves as thinking, choosing, sexual, intellectual and complex ordinary mortals and instead cling to a fantasy of women as simple handmaids of the lord.

This inability is the product of centuries of education and socialisation of women into acceptance of restricted lives and poor self-concepts and it is exacerbated in this country by the churches' continuing hold over education. Patriarchy's strongest hold over women is its ability to promote this inner division, which inhibits women's will for change and recruits women damaged by patriarchal ideology to the cause of patriarchy itself and sets them campaigning and voting against their own interests.

The election of Mary Robinson as President of Ireland has been welcomed by many as an indication that this pattern has finally been broken. Certainly the widespread identification by women with a woman who has so consistently opposed the conservative version of Irish womanhood indicates that that version no longer holds the same enchantments, even for the rural women so often seen as its especial adherents. Moreover, the celebration of Robinson's victory as a triumph for Irish women, in which so many women participated, is evidence of a new confidence and spirit of self-assertion. Attempts by political opponents to use Mary Robinson's sex as a weapon against her failed and the knee-jerk response of distrust and loathing of femininity was not forthcoming. The extent of the political fallout from Robinson's election suggests the potential of such a self-conscious and self-confident sense of common cause among women to affect change.

The context in which Mary Robinson's election victory was achieved must be recalled before we become too optimistic about the future, however. The common cause of women obviously benefits when left-wing and progressive groups in general join in alliance. It is difficult to assess the extent to which public disgust at the unedifying spectacle of the Fianna Fáil/Fine Gael campaigns created a protest vote which was not so much for Robinson as against Lenihan and Currie. That such a protest occurred is in itself a hopeful sign, however, and it must be remembered that even prior to the Lenihan debacle Robinson was doing better than anyone would have predicted. Change, then, is on the political agenda, but before it can proceed it is important to assess the reverses of the 1980s, their causes and effects, and to analyse the most pressing issues facing feminism in Ireland in the 1990s.

Constituting Irish Women

The choice of the Constitution as the vehicle for the attack on women's rights in Ireland in the 1980s was, as Ruth Riddick has pointed out in this series, entirely in keeping with the spirit of that document and its original authors. The identification of the family (rather than, for example, the individual) as the basic building block of society is more than pious rhetoric in the Irish Constitution. In post-colonial southern Ireland a particular construction of sexual and familial roles became the very substance of what it meant to be Irish.

The Indian political philosopher, Ashis Nandy, has argued that a history of colonisation is a history of feminisation. Colonial powers identify their subject peoples as passive, in need of guidance, incapable of self-government, romantic, passionate, unruly, barbarous—all of those things for which the Irish and women have been traditionally praised and scorned.

Nandy points out that the subject people, in rebelling and claiming independence and sovereignty, aspire to a traditionally masculine role of power. The result is that colonised peoples, often long after colonisation itself has ended, tend to observe or impose strictly differentiated gender roles in order to assert the masculinity and right to power of the (male) subjects. This has been the case, Nandy argues, in his native India. It is readily identified as a trait of fundamentalist Islam and it is not difficult to trace this process at work in the sexual conservatism and political stagnation of post-independence Ireland. Anxiety about one's fitness for a (masculine) role of authority, deriving from a history of defeat or helplessness, is assuaged by the assumption of sexual dominance.

Women in these conditions become guarantors of their men's status, bearers of national honour and the scapegoats of national identity. They are not merely transformed into symbols of the nation, they become the territory over which power is exercised. The Irish obsession with the control of women's bodies by church, state, boards of ethics and judicial enquiries, has its roots in such anxieties, though it is arguable that any form of national identity must constitute itself as power over a territory defined as feminine.

That the real experience of women is to be specifically excluded from Irish national identity is inscribed in the Constitution in which the Republic of Ireland describes itself to itself. Women's 'duties in the home' are constitutionally reinforced.

The most basic 'civil right', the right to life, is constitutionally compromised in the case of women, a circumstance which provides a grim gloss on an observation by one of the architects of the concept of civil liberties—Rousseau commented (ironically in his Discourse on the Origin of Inequality) that, for citizenship in his ideal Republic, 'it must be men.'

The consequences of the circumscription of one basic 'right' for women has been, as a series of High Court and Supreme Court judgements have made clear, very specific limitations on the right to freedom of information and free speech. Women, in everything which is specific to them as women, are quite obviously not citizens of the republic.

Feminism and Unionism

Irish nationalism may have little to offer Irish women, but what can the relationship be between feminism and unionism? Mary Holland in an 'open letter' in her *Irish Times* column (30 May 1990) to the Unionist MP, John Taylor, articulated, tentatively and sceptically, what has long been a furtive wish of liberal forces in the south—an alliance between those forces and Ulster protestantism. Holland welcomed Taylor's intervention in the dispute over the future of the Adelaide Hospital, the last remaining Protestant hospital in the Republic.

There have been repeated attempts to use Unionist opinion as a lever to put pressure on conservative nationalism to reform. During the divorce referendum the point was unsuccessfully made that a vote against divorce was a vote against pluralism and as a consequence a vote against the unification of Ireland. Since the electorate seems to have responded, not to such abstract principles, but to fear of dispersing family landholdings, it is difficult to make assumptions about the priority of Catholic moral teaching over nationalist aspirations. Nonetheless it is difficult to avoid the conclusion that the majority in the south is unwilling to concede that any form of united, federated or more closely integrated Ireland must also be a more heterogeneous Ireland.

A second referendum on the divorce issue seems likely in the near future and it will be interesting to observe how far the southern electorate has moved towards a more pluralist notion of Irishness. It is unlikely that any such shift in public opinion will be a product of a reconsideration of the northern situation. It is likely, however, that Unionist alienation will be once again invoked by those seeking change as a spectre to ward off the worst excesses of groups such as SPUC (Society for the Protection of the Unborn Child) and Family Solidarity. That invocation has, in the past, created some confusion and misunderstanding of the Unionist position. Part of this confusion stems from a more fundamental confusion in the southern mind between what has become known as 'the protestant ethos' (associated in the public mind with the Adelaide Hospital, compassionate medicine and liberal attitudes to social and sexual matters, in that order) and the perceptions and beliefs of northern unionism. The former is to some extent identifiable with the Church of Ireland, but it really represents the residue of a secular, humanist tradition which was not and is not exclusively of that faith. It is part of a cultural heritage which feminism elsewhere has had to fight, but which in Ireland might be a significant ally if only it were stronger, a little less complacent and a lot less conservative. It added an important leaven to the dreadful dough of the confessional southern state from the 1930s to the 1960s. It is, in many important respects, part of the culture and the self-concept of the Republic.

Northern unionism is a quite distinct entity from this amorphous cultural 'ethos.' It has a different class base and a different denominational orientation. It has no history of aristocratic guilt: politically it has an unrepentant, recent and continuing record of civil rights abuses and intimidation. That record is rooted in a fear of nationalism which glib generalisations about the 'protestant ethos' and reconciliation at best obscure and at worst entrench further. It is not a likely ally of any group in the south and its brand of protestant fundamentalism will not be comfortable with liberalisation. To suggest otherwise is to ignore the facts and to contribute, not to reconciliation, but to further misunderstanding and antagonism. As Mary Holland, in her address to John Taylor, pointed out 'many, many unionists' opposed the decriminalisation of homosexuality. Unionists and nationalists appear to be able to make common cause against the extension of UK abortion legislation to northern Ireland. Whatever other divisions there are, Ireland, north and south, is united in its denial of women's right to choose.

It is not just nationalist Ireland which exhibits the traits of sexual conservatism and social stagnation. Unionism is if anything more insecure and equally prey to the sexualisation of political identity, even if this takes different forms. The fundamentalist streak in northern protestantism is as hostile to feminism as is Catholicism. American feminists have had long and bitter experience of evangelical and fundamentalist protestantism's efforts to combat feminism and to use the concept of the right to life of the 'unborn' to restrict the rights of women. If southern Irish feminism has nothing to say to women in the Unionist community in northern Ireland beyond an assurance that they would be worse off if they were Catholics, then it really will have been defeated by nationalism. Preoccupation with the ill effects of nationalism will have induced a moral and political blindness which obscures other ills.

From Cathleen to revisionism: the hijacking of feminism

Precisely because nationalism has proved so hostile to women, feminism offers a convenient cover for those who wish to attack any attempt to understand Ireland's past and present in terms of colonisation and decolonisation as reactionary and inherently anti-feminist. Edna Longley's recent pamphlet in this series, *From Cathleen to Anorexia: the Breakdown of Irelands*, presents itself as an attempt 'to re-open the ever-problematic, ever-central issue of "Nationalism and Feminism."' Re-opening the issue has become a matter of urgency. Longley's focus is literary and, to a lesser extent, historical, though it diverges into an attack on John Hume, who is found guilty of 'fall(ing) into nationalist idiom.' Edna Longley's interrogation of Hume's rhetoric is indicative of the tone of the whole piece: 'Hume likes to stress that he has moved beyond the old definitions. So let us test him on the questions of "Irishness" and "Revisionism."' A whole series of persons and institutions are similarly tested and similarly found guilty of clinging 'to the notion that a "good" or "real" nationalism exists in some zone uncontaminated by the Provos.' This 'nationalism' is effectively indistinguishable from 'Irishness' in the essay and '"Irishness" with its totalitarian fringe' is always culpable—British feminism and 'foreign literary critics' like Edward Said and Terry Eagleton are tainted by association with it. That use of 'foreign' seems strange from a writer who advocates the abolition of the concept of Irishness and it should alert the reader to the inconsistent assumptions underlying the pamphlet. On the one hand there is a rejection of Irish nationalism: on the other there is vociferous resistance to analogy or comparison of the Irish situation with that of any other country or group.

Reference is made to a recent collection of essays, *Across the*

Frontiers: Ireland in the 1990s. The competing claims of regionalism and European integration framed that collection. Edna Longley knows a good deal about regionalism—but there is no reference in her pamphlet to the European context which has been such a valuable asset to Irish feminism in the last decade. Similarly, attempts to understand Ireland's colonial experience in the context of other countries and cultures marked by a colonial past are derided. (Edward Said would doubtless be amused to find 'Palestinian' used as a generalised term of abuse.)

Edna Longley's campaign against the Field Day group is somewhat jaded and in this essay she tries to revitalise it by using feminism as ideological high ground from which to throw the same old stones at the same old targets. Field Day is by no means the only exclusively male cultural institution in Ireland. It is certainly not the only one to suffer from the masculine myopia which such a composition induces. Neither is it, however, the monolithic, inward-looking, defensive formation Edna Longley describes. Moreover the work of that group has created spaces for the discussion of gender and nationality of which feminism can avail. (The forthcoming Field Day anthology seems likely to be the first non-feminist anthology of Irish literature to give some visibility to the writing of women.) The analogy between feminism and nationalism made by Terry Eagleton in his contribution to the Field Day series has, as Edna Longley points out, the potential to annoy both elements in his equation. Annoyance value is not to be scorned, however, and an analogy which provokes such antagonism must have touched a crucial nerve. Eagleton's comparison of movements which perceive themselves to be mutually incompatible, even mutually exclusive, upsets the too-easy repudiation of nationalism as reactionary by feminism and the too-easy rejection of feminism as alien by nationalism. For many women, particularly in northern Ireland, both feminism and (at least some variants of) nationalism are positive forces for change in their society.

Edna Longley's denial that it is possible to be both feminist and republican is not only an historical absurdity, it runs the risk of making Irish feminism no more than a middle class movement directed towards equal partic-ipation by privileged women in the status quo. Indeed, a feminism which refuses to engage with the hard realities of Ireland can be no more than that. A feminism based on exclusion will continue to be itself excluded. A feminism which participates in the translation of political into moral categories which bedevils discussions of Ireland, north and south, will itself continue to fall prey to such translations. Feminism must interrogate nationalism, must maintain its own interests and women's interests against any monolithic national identity which perpetuates patriarchy. In engaging with nationalist women, it must point out how little nationalism and republicanism have promoted or protected women's interests, how much they have done to denigrate and oppress women. Nonetheless, if feminism in the south continues to regard nationalism and republicanism as contagious diseases and to protect itself from contagion by a refusal to engage with either it will also continue to occupy the political margins and to lose referenda. Instead of increasing the isolation of republican women and pushing them further into a ghetto where violence is the only form of political expression left, there is an obligation to enter some kind of dialogue. Instead of lecturing Republican women on their political and moral failings as women we might pause to listen. Perhaps they could teach us to address those women for whom the myth of Mother Ireland is still a powerful enchantment. Perhaps they know better than academics, writers and pamphleteers how to expose and destroy that enchantment.

Feminism needs to address women in both communities in northern Ireland. It will not succeed in doing so by sentimentalising unionism on the one hand and scurrying away from the civil rights issues raised by the treatment of women prisoners on the other. If feminism abroad understands stripsearching as flagrant abuse of civil rights and deliberate sexual degradation, then it is not because it does not understand the circumstances, but because it does understand the principle. It is because it is not so obsessed with distancing itself from one form of political violence in northern Ireland that it has become blind to all others. The involvement of the Council for the Status of Women (CSW) in attempts to improve the appalling conditions suffered by women prisoners in Mountjoy Gaol last year was indicative of the potentially broad range of feminist concerns. What has been revealed about conditions there reminds us how poor the record of the Republic of Ireland is on civil rights. It is further proof, if it were needed, that where conditions are bad they are usually worse for women. If we could overcome our fear of losing our extremely tenuous hold on political respectability, feminism could launch a campaign for an improvement in conditions for women prisoners—of all kinds, north and south—and the suspension of practices which attempt to use women's sexuality to degrade them. Feminism has reason to fear hi-jacking by nationalist and republican groups, but it cannot allow that fear to paralyse it. Public identification of feminism with such causes and with an anti-pornography campaign which is also anti-censorship would not only raise feminism's profile among sectors of the public which have until now remained unswayed by feminism's arguments. It would allow it to build a base from which to launch the long, difficult campaigns looming—including that for the removal of the eighth amendment to the Constitution.

Moreover, it is time for feminism to ask if it has not already been hi-jacked by its more respectable political allies. Liberal forces in the Labour Party and to a lesser extent in Fine Gael may have been on our side in the battles on divorce and on the abortion amendment, but that support is in the end less significant than the failure of that support to be effective. They helped us to lose. The nomination of and support for Mary Robinson by Labour in conjunction with the Workers' Party, Greens and others was obviously more effective, but feminism cannot afford to lose any more ballots in Ireland and some caution is necessary.

Feminism cannot, in attempting to see women outside their traditional role as symbols of the nation, be content to merely impose a revised role on them, a role as victims of the nation or of history. The work of contemporary continental feminist thinkers, with its emphasis on the way in which we are produced by and produce the dominant culture and the internal complexities of any programme of cultural and psychological change, may offer a way out of the twin stereotypes into which any analysis of women in Irish culture so easily falls. An analysis which emphasises how deeply we are involved in patriarchal culture and in our idealisation as symbols of the nation denies us the moral high ground—we are not the innocent victims of Irish or any other kind of historical circumstance. Women are not, as Edna Longley suggests in her pamphlet, essentially more peaceable, less dogmatic, uninfected by bloodthirsty political ideologies. Women have been actively involved in every possible variant of both nationalism and unionism. They too have been prejudiced and brought their children up to be prejudiced. Women have supported and carried out violent actions. They have gained and lost from their involvement. If patriarchal history has portrayed us as bystanders to the political process, it has lied. We have always been implicated, even in our own oppression.

A Dangerous Consensus

Any analysis of feminism in Ireland needs to take note of an observation by Angela Carter, quoted by Clodagh Corcoran in her LIP pamphlet *Pornography: The New Terrorism:*

> The notion of a universality of human experience is a confidence trick and the notion of a universality of female experience is a clever confidence trick.

Irish feminism has sometimes perforce played such tricks. In the 1980s it appeared to progress, where it progressed at all, by stealth, disguising its demands for women in assertions of human, individual or civil rights. The problematics of asserting women's rights as an extension of 'universal' human rights (themselves only tenuously conceded by Irish political and religious culture) dominate Clodagh Corcoran's excellent essay on pornography. The analysis of the cultural and social significance of pornography will be familiar to readers of Andrea Dworkin and Susanne Kappeler. (The difficulties and shortcomings of Dworkin and Kappeler's work is outside the scope of a pamphlet such as this.) The factor which gives Corcoran's essay its wider significance for Irish feminism is its application, in a specifically Irish context, of the dangers inherent in concepts of universal rights or liberties which are blind to gender:

> Liberals intellectualise vaguely about 'freedom,' 'human rights,' 'freedom of expression.' They speak of these 'freedoms' as though they were a common experience for women, and hope we won't see through such hypocrisy.

> That the rights of man may be and are exercised in our society through the denial of the rights of woman is the fundamental lesson of pornography. It is a hard lesson for the Irish women's movement for it has derived support from and even argued its case in the protectively anonymous language of 'humanism.'

Clodagh Corcoran's image of the Irish public man, addressing 'large meetings on censorship,' pointing towards illusory freedoms, could be transposed onto Eavan Boland's portrait of the Irish literary man, trading 'in the exhausted fictions of the nation' and allowing 'these fictions to edit ideas of womanhood and modes of remembrance.' Such a writer is perceived by Boland as constructing his voice out of the silence of women:

> Long after they rejected the politics of Irish nationalism [Irish poets] continued to employ the emblems and enchantments of its culture. It was the culture, not the politics, which informed Irish poetry: not the harsh awakenings, but the old dreams.

> *A Kind of Scar: The Woman Poet in a National Tradition*

Those old dreams, 'Dark Rosaleen, Cathleen Ní Houlihan, the nation as woman: the woman as nation', have become for Irishwomen the sign of their invisibility, of 'the power of nationhood to edit the reality of womanhood.' Boland acknowledges that 'some of the poetry produced by such simplifications was, of course, difficult to argue with. Something was gained.' As a poet who still wishes to be part of the Irish tradition, Boland must nonetheless admit, 'what was lost was what I valued.'

It may be a shocking thought for some that the Irish woman reading Irish writing finds in it only a profound silence, her own silence. It is certainly a painful thought for an Irish woman writer and the talents of many of them must have been dissipated or lost in evading such pain. The exclusion of women was constitutive of Irish literature as it was constitutive of the Irish Republic. In her pamphlet Boland confronts that exclusion, but even her title, *A Kind of Scar: The Woman Poet in a National Tradition,* is testament to its disabling legacy. 'Mise Eire,' her own poem from which Boland takes that title, revised Pearse's poem of the same name. Pearse's refrain of 'I am Ireland' became, in Boland's poem, 'I am the woman.' The myth of Mother Ireland was countered by an insistent feminine subjectivity. Eavan Boland's LIP pamphlet counters another cultural cliché: Yeats's 'terrible beauty' is contrasted with a vision of 'terrible survival.' (The centrality of the Famine rather than the vagaries of nationalism to Eavan Boland's sense of her identity as an Irish woman writer is an interesting indication of the different shape Irish history may take when women have reconstructed their part in it.)

The common insight of Clodagh Corcoran and Eavan Boland is that even where Irish literary and political culture opposes the dominant ideology of church and state it often merely re-presents the emblems and the structures of that ideology in more 'enchanting' forms. One consequence of this is the cultural hegemony which the women's movement has found particularly difficult to shatter.

Rewriting the Script

If women are to renegotiate their relation to Irish culture, much work needs to be done. The work of analysing and theorising women's relation to Irish culture, of criticising and changing that relation, of providing a critical, political and historical context for Irish women's writing is an exciting and necessary task which, as yet, has scarcely begun. The work undertaken by feminist scholars elsewhere can be of invaluable assistance in this task and can expand the horizons of Irish sexual and national identity.

The American feminist critic, Nina Baym, has discussed the way in which nationalism influenced and often constituted the definition of 'American literature.' That definition was produced by (male) academics eager to legitimise not only American culture, but also their own status as professionals and the equals of their European counterparts. As Nina Baym points out 'the search for cultural essence' which ensued excluded women and ethnic minorities almost entirely, working on the basis that the experience of these groups is not 'normal', i.e. masculine, white, 'the same', and is therefore 'inessential.' On these criteria, the work of white, male and predominantly middle class artists was regarded as that which best expressed the essence of American culture. Work by such artists and writers was thus deemed to be not only the mainstream, but the best.

Baym identifies the myth of the artist as hero, struggling against the odds to create his 'own' work as the myth which legitimised the 'artist' for American culture, reshaping 'him' in the familiar mould of a culture which valorised action and 'truth' and was ambivalent about art and artifice. Art became macho. The writer became the prototypical hero, his writing a pioneering exploration of new territory which he made his own. Effectively, he became a literary imperialist.

The myth of the Irish artist is a different myth, but it is

equally masculine in its terms and equally concerned with the legitimation of a particular view of national culture. Two forms of the myth of the (literary) hero predominate. He may be a 'true son' of 'Mother Ireland': this view has very much gone out of fashion. The current myth of the literary-subversive-in-exile (epitomised by Joyce) is no less masculine in its terms, however, and has certain similarities with the American myth, for he too is a 'son' escaping from the 'nets' of 'Mother' church, 'Mother' Ireland and, perhaps, 'Mother' tongue.

If the male Irish writer must speak from this Oedipal place of exile, what position as speaking and writing subject is available to the Irish woman? According to Nuala Ní Dhomhnaill:

> We've all internalised this patriarchal thing. It would be a lie for me to say that I'm out of the woods, because I'm not.
>
> *Graph 1* (1986)

Ní Dhomhnaill here echoes the imagery of the French novelist and theorist Hélène Cixous. Cixous sees language as an agent of the internalisation of 'the whole patriarchal thing' and argues that 'as soon as women begin to speak...they're taught that their territory is black: because you are Africa, you are black, your continent is dark. Dark is dangerous.' The image of the feminine as a colonised territory has now become almost banal, but Cixous's association of language and colonialism is particularly resonant in an Irish context.

For both Ní Dhomhnaill and Cixous the language of patriarchy colonises women's self-concept and world view. It presents the masculine as the norm and the feminine as an aberration. Words abound for experiences which are exclusive to or predominantly those of men. The public domain, which was for so long the domain of men, is also the domain where discourse proliferates. The private domain, women's traditional 'sphere,' is very often the realm of the oblique and unspoken. (Compare, for example, the proliferation of technical vocabularies in the twentieth century—mechanical, electronic, computer languages and jargon—with the scarcity of words relating to the experience of childbirth.) How then can women use language, particularly how can women write, without succumbing to the inherent masculine bias in the languages of patriarchal cultures? According to Ní Dhomhnaill the woman must write—and the man who would break out of the strait-jacket of patriarchal repression and 'linguistic schizophrenia' must write—in 'the language of the Mothers' which she calls Irish.

This latter assertion has caused considerable controversy. Ní Dhomhnaill herself admits, 'there's a level of hurt involved in the language.' This is especially so for women. The question of Irish identity and the question of feminine identity often—as we have seen—have mutually exclusive answers. Moreover the political exclusion implicit in this valorisation of the Irish language is undeniable and runs the risk of a return to the same old insular Irishness. The most productive way to understand Ní Dhomhnaill's assertion is as an attempt to revise the significance of the language she chooses and to assert that she has a choice. The use of Irish by a woman poet to write in ways which challenge the basic assumptions and myths of patriarchy is an attempt to wrest authority, not only from patriarchy and misogynist myth, but from that formulation of national identity to which the Irish language and the silence of women were fundamental. That is an exercise which can only be beneficial to those many women writers in Ireland who do not see Irish as their mother tongue and who instead grapple with the problem of looking back through literary mothers who are as often as not Anglo-Irish and excluded from that narrow definition of Irishness which Ní Dhomhnaill challenges.

Analogies: The International Context

Women on either side of the political divide in Ireland share with the women of many developing countries the burden of the social and sexual conservatism which stifles societies which are insecure in their origins and haunted by civil strife. If we look for analogies to the position of Irish women, it might perhaps be to the Arab nations where, as in Ireland, women are too often the scapegoats of national and religious identity. We must be wary, however, that we, from our position on the margin of European culture, do not colonise other women's marginality, their history, literature and experience, for our own ends. European feminism poses certain problems for third world women who perceive it to be ethnocentric in its approach to the specific cultural and economic dilemmas of women in the developing countries. It is important to keep those reservations in mind, even as we look forward to becoming part of new European feminist movement.

We are moving towards a Europe which will be more integrated, but will nonetheless place feminism in a political context far more diverse than anything we have previously experienced. Political alignments and the locus of power are shifting and those changes offer opportunities to escape old political polarities. Ireland is not the only European country where feminism and nationalism are in conflict. It is worth noting that one of the first groups which demonstrated in large numbers against the new, united German state were women protesting at the threat to abortion and childcare facilities, previously guaranteed in East Germany. The resurgence of nationalism and ethnic strife in eastern Europe makes it more urgent than ever that feminism not only re-examines its relation to nationalism, but that it actively seeks to change the nature of national and ethnic identity and how we experience them. A particular construction of sexual identity has, in Ireland and elsewhere, given form and substance to national identity. Women have been denied a role in the life and history of nations and been reduced to symbols of the nation. As women claim and change their role and seek a different identity for themselves as women, they will also change the meaning of national identity. According to Eavan Boland, 'Irish poems simplified most at the point of intersection between womanhood and Irishness.' Irishwomen, now that they are breaking their silence, will complicate and change Irish culture at precisely that point of intersection. The double marginality of Ireland -European, but sharing a history and experience with post-colonial states elsewhere, never quite one thing or another—may yet provide a space in which Irish women can make and say something different of ourselves as women and of the many traditions which are our burden and our inheritance. No longer the territory over which power is exercised, women, in exercising power, may redefine the territory.

References
Baym, Nina. 'Melodramas of Beset Manhood: How Theories of American Fiction Exclude Women,' *The New Feminist Criticism*, ed. Elaine Showalter. London: Virago, 1986.
Boland, Eavan. 'Mise Eire,' *The Journey*. London: Carcanet, (1987).
Boland, Eavan. *A Kind of Scar: The Woman Poet in a National Tradition*

Dublin: Attic Press LIP Pamphlet, (1989).

Cixous, Hélène. (1976). 'The Laugh of the Medusa,' trans Keith and Paula Cohen, *Signs* 1.1: 875-99, 1976.

Corcoran, Clodagh. *Pornography: The New Terrorism*. Dublin: Attic Press LIP Pamphlet, 1989.

Eagleton, Terry. *Nationalism, Colonialism and Literature: Nationalism, Irony and Commitment*. Derry: Field Day, 1988.

Kearney, Richard ed. *Across the Frontiers: Ireland in the 1990s*. Dublin: Wolfhound, 1988.

Longley, Edna. *From Cathleen to Anorexia: The Breakdown of Irelands*. Dublin: Attic Press LIP Pamphlet, 1990.

Nandy, Ashis. *The Intimate Enemy: Loss and Recovery of Self Under Colonialism*. Delhi. Oxford: Oxford University Press, 1983.

Ní Dhomhnaill, Nuala. Interview with Michael Cronin, *Graph* 1 (Oct), 1986.

Riddick, Ruth. *The Right to Choose: Questions of Feminist Morality*. Dublin: Attic Press LIP Pamphlet, 1990.

Rousseau, Jean Jacques. 'Discourse on the Origin of Inequality', *The Social Contract and Discourses*, trans GDH Cole, rev. ed. JH Brumfitt and John C Hall. London: Everyman (2nd ed.) (1973).

A note on the author

Gerardine Meaney was born in Waterford in 1962 and educated in Kilkenny and at University College Dublin. She is a feminist critic and also writes fiction. Her stories have appeared in newspapers and journals, in the *Midland Review* (1986) special issue on Irish women's writing and in *Wildish Things: An Anthology of New Irish Women's Writing* (Attic Press, 1989). In 1986 she won a Hennessy Award for New Irish Writing. From 1988 to 1989, she was a Junior Research Fellow at the Institute of Irish Studies, Queen's University, Belfast and now lectures in English Literature in University College Dublin.

10
THE MISSING SEX
Putting Women Into Irish History

Margaret Ward, 1991

Where are the women?

We need to know how women disappear, why we are
initiated into a culture where women have no visible past,
and what will happen if we make that past visible and real.
If the process is not to be repeated again, if we are to
transmit to the next generation of women what was denied
transmission to us, we need to know how to break the
closed circle of male power which permits men to go on
producing knowledge about themselves, pretending that we
do not exist.

Dale Spender

The new history is coming; it's not a dream, though it does
extend beyond men's imaginations.

Hélène Cixous

In the past few years, I have become increasingly concerned
about what is happening to Irish history—with how it is
being researched, how it is being published, and with how it
is being taught. It might seem strange, if not perverse, to voice
such anxieties at a time when the production of Irish feminist
history seems at last to be coming of age, but my reluctant
and disappointed conclusion is that, despite all our efforts,
our foremothers remain in the margins, unknown to most,
managing, at the very best, to become a 'special option' in an
undergraduate honours course—and that only if there are
some very persistent women on the staff of that particular
history department.

There has been so much discussion over the political
direction of the various new history texts that have emerged
in recent years that now seems an appropriate time in which
to raise another, possibly more uncomfortable question
concerning those same histories: why are women not featured
more prominently within their pages? Those engaged in the
production of history have been mostly concerned with the
implications of 'revisionism'. It is a political controversy,

largely conducted by men, fuelled by those who want to distance the profession from any taint of nationalist sympathy, but what does all this mean for women? We seem to be invisible whatever the particular ideological view of the historian. Who are the people who make history? The argument rarely seems to touch upon the human content of the narrative. Conventional historiography has given us kings, with the odd queen thrown in, and rebellious chiefs and politicians, with the peasantry popping in and out of the picture. In the last couple of decades the working class has managed to shoulder its way on to the scene and the history of the Irish working class is now rapidly unfolding, thanks to the diligence of a new generation of historians. But it is all strangely women-free. Where are they? What have they been up to for the past few hundred years? Does anyone know or care, and can we get hold of the source material that will enable us to discover their hidden history? If we do, do we just 'add women and stir' and let the stew of Irish history thicken with this female addition?

Men have written women out of history, that is an undeniable truth, and it has occurred despite the fact that in many instances the history of women's struggles has been available for those who have had the inclination to look beyond their prejudices. Because women of previous generations, despite all the hurdles they have had to overcome, have written extensively about their own times. But the male `gatekeepers', to use Dale Spender's term, have ensured that works which challenge patriarchal structures (and practically any book by an outspoken woman would fall into this category) have difficulty in being circulated and are often rapidly out of print, not to be republished. It is only the advent of feminist publishing houses that has ensured the rediscovery of those countless works from our foremothers. In Ireland too, women wrote and were published (although admittedly in fewer numbers), but so far, despite brave efforts by feminist publishers here, lack of resources has hampered the task of reclaiming their work.

Written out of the textbooks
We live in a world so dominated by masculine values that the majority are unaware of anything remarkable or retrogressive in such a state of affairs. We can, I hope, still be shocked and

angered when specific instances are isolated and held up for scrutiny. In the case of history textbooks, it is only when the extent of women's relegation to the footnotes is clearly seen, that the urgency of the task of pointing this out becomes apparent. The professional historian's level of awareness concerning women's contribution to politics and society can only be described as abysmal. And the effects of this blinkered vision are not confined within the walls of academia. It certainly has repercussions on the topics that future graduates will regard as valid areas for research, but, more importantly, it also affects the world outside. Thousands of readers, eager to learn more about their past, have helped to put some history textbooks into the bestseller lists. Can they be blamed for believing that women have been passive subjects throughout the centuries, or censured for disbelieving those who try to argue that women also have a past that needs to be written about?

In the 1930s a new generation of Irish historians emerged. It is their legacy that we now confront. They described themselves as modern professionals, dismissing what they regarded as the antiquated nationalism of their predecessors. The new history was to be 'value-free' and scientific. F S L Lyons was moulded by this group, a leading light in the second wave of historians anxious to reveal a more complex scenario. His monumental work, *Ireland Since the Famine*, published in 1971, has, until very recently, been the standard text in undergraduate reading lists. Was the resolve to revolutionise our perceptions combined with any awareness that women might have had a history that, so far, had been all but forgotten? Would the revisors of history also revise the sex-blindness of the past generations? Would Lyons succeed in unearthing women's contribution?

Ireland Since the Famine
My remarks are confined to the period 1880-1922, both for reasons of brevity and also because this is the period when Irishwomen were at their most active in the political arena. Lyons does mention two organisations of women. The Ladies' Land League he castigates for their 'irresponsible' behaviour and Anna Parnell for her 'reprehensible' conduct. This is very strong language for the supposedly impartial historian, but he doesn't bother to elaborate on his judgements. The second organisation, Cumann na mBan, gets a footnote. Lyons tells

207

us that, due to its having followed the lead of Erskine Childers during the Treaty debates, it was dubbed 'the women and Childers party'. Not only is this an insultingly brief reference for a significant organisation, but the insult is compounded by the sexist nature of the reference. The women of Cumann na mBan are not given credit for possessing autonomous political views but instead have Childers credited as their leader. With regard to historical accuracy, nowhere in the Treaty debates is there any evidence to support this jibe. The six female members of the Second Dáil demonstrated an impressive ability to articulate their views, and one that certainly had no need of any male voice whispering prompts from the side.

No other women's group is considered to be part of 'Ireland since the Famine'. The only reference to the suffrage movement in the whole of this 300 odd-page text is the following, referring to Countess Markievicz: 'Interested above all in women's rights—it was the suffrage question that first caught her interest.' We know therefore that Lyons was aware of the existence of the Irish suffrage movement, but the inference is clearly that this has no significance for the historian—at least, not for that particular historian. As Mary Cullen has said:

> (Lyons) has made a judgement, whether consciously or unconsciously, that women's rights and feminist movements are not a significant part of Irish history in the sense that he judges nationalism, the cultural renaissance and the labour movement to be. It is also clear that he does not think his responsibility as a historian of this period of Irish history requires him to present feminism or feminist political action to the reader as part of that history.

This myopia leads to a distortion when the lives of those whose political careers straddled various different causes are assessed. As Cullen has put it, 'A woman like Markievicz may be seen as part of Irish history when she is participating in nationalist or labour political or military activity. She and other women are *not* seen as part of Irish history when they campaign in support of women's claims for civil and political rights.'

So women are not seen as part of Irish history, and neither are the causes they fought for. This male-oriented conscious-ness, which permeates the whole of the discipline, is, as Sheila

Johansson has described it, a kind of 'collective amnesia', and one which makes women 'vulnerable to the impositions of dubious stereotypes'. In countries with a less turbulent past, women are depicted as having remained outside the political arena. This is difficult to maintain in an Irish context, given the upheavals of the centuries, but popular culture has no difficulty in continuing to regard women as angels of the home, their political involvement confined to actions such as confronting the bailiff, or providing shelter for the fugitive. The former can be regarded as a defence of the family, while the latter remains within the domestic arena. It is a cosy and unchallenging romanticism. Without knowing what 'the flow of time' has meant to women, to their collective past, false judgements that have repercussions for the present continue to be made. The image of *Mother Ireland* reigns supreme.

Modern Ireland 1600–1972

Over the last few years a new name has emerged to carry on the mantle of revisionism. Roy Foster, the new guru of British academia, is now top of the reading lists with his ambitious survey, *Modern Ireland 1600-1972*. How does he compare with his predecessor? The women's movement had not established itself as a force within society at the time Lyons was writing. But the intervening years have witnessed some fundamental changes in Irish life, the result of sustained pressure by organised feminism. Surely all writing, on historical subjects just as much as on contemporary issues, must be sensitive to, and reflect society's changing priorities and emphases? Using that criterion, can we see changes in historical scholarship in the seventeen years that have elapsed between Lyons's survey and Foster's?

If we use references to the Ladies' Land League as an initial gauge, then Foster would appear to be more sensitive in his assessment of women's political contribution. He declares:

> Perhaps one of the most important and least recognised achievements of the Land League is that it provided a political baptism for a generation of radical Irishwomen who spoke on platforms, organized tactics, were denounced by the clergy and got arrested. Many of them would later be involved in the suffragette movement and Sinn Féin.

He is certainly more sympathetic than Lyons to Anna Parnell and the Ladies' Land League, but he has the advantage of having read Anna Parnell's long-lost manuscript history of the period. However, despite this, his assessment too is inadequate and distorted by a sexist bias. Foster claims Parnell doubted his sister's political acumen and suppressed the organisation, yet Anna's own evidence presents a very different picture. She was not a parliamentarian, but a radical nationalist with an acute awareness of where her brother's tactics were leading. Once the men were out of jail and controlling the movement again, the women were determined to dissolve their organisation, conscious of their vastly different aims and their use of very different methods to achieve those aims. But, just as no contemporary, not even a man as sympathetic as Michael Davitt, could really understand the significance of the short history of the Ladies' Land League, and its revolutionary potential, so no present-day (male) historian seems able to analyse the events of that time from the point of view of the women participants. The real legacy of the Ladies' Land League is that Irish women became aware that they needed to have their own organisation. Any other conclusion lets men off the hook for their conduct during that time.

Anna Parnell, as her manuscript demonstrates, was acutely aware of women's political powerlessness:

> Whatever the relative values of men and women may be, it is certain that the former cannot be done without, when it is a question of altering the status of a country. If the men of that country have made up their minds that it shall not be done, the women cannot bring it about.

Her unsuccessful efforts to get her manuscript published (she gave it to Helena Moloney, then editor of *Bean na hÉireann*, journal of the nationalist-feminist group Inghínidhe na hÉireann, to edit for her and the manuscript disappeared after a police raid), adds another dimension to our knowledge of women's disappearance from history. Every other participant in the Land War seems to have written a memoir and to have had no difficulty in getting it published. It took Anna Parnell, despite her incredible notoriety during the Land League era, 100 years to get into print. Significantly, it was an Irish feminist publishing house which recognised the importance of the work. Reading this account now gives enormous insights into the extent to which Irish history has been male history and she is illuminating on the question of the types of

political alliances that women activists might have taken—
following neither the path of fenianism nor parliamentarian-
ism.

Let us, for a moment, return to Roy Foster and the extent
of his inclusion of women in *Modern Ireland 1600-1972*. The
statement that some former members of the Ladies' Land
League would later become suffragettes is the only reference
to the suffragette movement to be found in his text. He omits
even a reference to the fact that in 1918 women won the vote.
Have we reached the post-feminist age when so obvious a
reference can be assumed? I doubt it. As with Lyons, despite
the fact that the suffrage movement was an all-Ireland, cross-
party, cross-class and cross-religion organisation of women
covering the whole of the thirty-two counties and which saw
thirty-six of its members imprisoned for their activities, it is
simply not regarded as important enough to be incorporated
into the main text. For some reason, the formation of the
Irishwomen's Suffrage Federation in 1911 is listed in his
chronology of important events, while Hanna Sheehy-
Skeffington's membership of the Irishwomen's Franchise
League is referred to only in a biographical reference to her.
That is all the attention that the feminist movement receives.
It remains a subject for the footnote only. My pleasure in
noting that Inghínidhe na hÉireann receives a significant
mention was qualified by my surprise in realising the almost
total absence of any mention of Cumann na mBan. It is simply
referred to as 'extreme' on one occasion and 'radical' on
another, while the context is unexplained. Was political antipathy to their views an explanation for this lack of interest?

This comparison of male sensitivities to women's role in
history seemed incomplete, so I decided to use a simple head
count in order to continue the process of evaluation. For the
period under discussion, fifteen references to individual
women appear in Lyons's index and thirteen in Foster's.
Foster has used more substantial biographical references as
footnotes, but against this, women rarely appear in the body
of his text. Lyons's bibliography lists eight substantial works
about women of the period. Basically, they are the extent of
scholarship at the time he was writing. He obviously
considered (and rightly so) texts like the Van Voris and
Marrecco biographies of Constance Markievicz to be
important works, but there was very little else available to be

211

commented upon. Now times have changed, and what is Roy Foster's assessment of the feminist research which has broken new ground since the publication of *Ireland Since the Famine*? Dana Hearne's edition of *The Tale of a Great Sham* is commended, but precious little else. No biographies are considered worthy of note; the pathbreaking *Women in Irish Society* is ignored. Rosemary Cullen Owens's invaluable history of Irish suffragism, which has formed the starting point for much research since its publication, is also absent. Perhaps I should be flattered to be dismissed in these words, 'The important topic of the Irish feminist movement in this period is nowhere treated adequately; see, in default of anything else, M Ward, *Unmanageable Revolutionaries.*'

Bibliographies, particularly in texts which are broad-ranging surveys, destined to be read by the general public and students alike, are important markers on the current state of scholarship. They serve a dual function: as a guide to areas of further study and as an assessment of the profession. The majority are methodical and uncontroversial, but a minority prove to be more revealing of the idiosyncracies of the compiler than of anything else.

Many other texts share the malecentrism and arrogance of *Modern Ireland*. It would be tedious to detail them all, but most figure prominently in undergraduate reading lists. I could mention writers like K T Hoppen, whose *Ireland Since 1800*, manages to avoid all reference to women (apart from one mention of Queen Victoria and another of Margaret Thatcher) but he is typical of so many. What is infuriating is the fact that it is one of the main works cited on the Trinity College reading lists, as it is doubtless on many more. I do, however, want to consider briefly one other male historian. (I don't want to imply that all women historians have automatically demonstrated an awareness of these issues, but they are not the ones who have written these influential all-purpose surveys.) My intention is not simply to indulge in invective but to emphasise the dangerous tendencies of contemporary scholarship and to spell out some of the implications of this for the future. Those I have singled out are not simply Ivory Tower academics: they are ever-willing to discuss contemporary issues, using their historical knowledge to add weight to their pronouncements, and all are regular contributors to both press and media. They have influence and for that reason should be all the more carefully scrutinised.

Ireland 1912–1985
J J Lee's recent work, *Ireland 1912-1985: Politics and Society*, was one I greeted with anticipation, as the author had been a contributor to *Women in Irish Society*, with an article entitled `Women and the Church Since The Famine' and he had also shown an awareness of women in *The Modernisation of Irish Society*, his book in the Gill and Macmillan series. The sub-title of his most recent book also gave reason for hope: 'Politics and Society' implied that this would not be an institutional account and nor would it take a narrowly political focus, the one exception when it might possibly be conceded that women, for various structural reasons, are not particularly visible. It was therefore with considerable disappointment that I discovered that there are in the book, which covers seventy-three years of Irish history, a mere five substantive references to women: principally, the extension of the franchise; the Constitution protests of 1937; ratios of female to male emigration, and mention of the Women's Peace Movement in the north and the Abortion Referendum. Very few women are referred to by name (nine for the period equivalent to Lyons and Foster) and those that are, tend to be defined in exclusively masculine terms: Kathleen Clarke is 'Mrs Tom Clarke' even though the reference is to her independent role as a senator; Lee complains that Mary Hayden's professorship of Irish History was unjustified and should have been given to Edmund Curtis; Eileen Lemass is Haughey's sister-in-law; and Maud Gonne is only referred to via the men in her life '(Seán) MacBride, son of Major John MacBride, executed in 1916, and of Maud Gonne, of Yeats fame'.

Lee could hardly be more hostile to the notion of women's autonomy. His bibliography reveals that he has read nothing on women that could have been incorporated into his text, lightening its excessively male focus. It is a very wide-ranging survey which includes many references to obscure journals and articles from European sources, untranslated into English. But, for women, only Ethna Viney's 1968 work on *Women in Rural Ireland* is listed. In a gesture of quite staggering arrogance, Lee lists his article from the MacCurtain and O Corráin work, but fails either to give the book a separate bibliographical reference or to list any other contributions from it. The only conclusion to be drawn is that he feels only his article has merit. This kind of attitude has dire repercussions for the future study of history. As I have said, bibliographies are statements of the 'state of the art', and are used by many as pointers to further research. If the growing body of work by women scholars is excluded, it remains invisible, known only to a small band of devotees, or those determined enough to go beyond the narrow confines of the academic world. The male 'gatekeepers' continue to do their job very effectively.

The teaching of history

The texts I have criticised are being written by academics, by professors who presumably set the tone for what occurs within their departments. What happens to their students? Do they spend three or four years studying `history' only to graduate as uncomprehending of the reality of women's lives and of women's contribution to historical events as they were when raw young freshers? Until there is a much greater availability of material on women's lives for teachers and students to use, what happens to those few who have emotionally or intellectually rejected the male-centred ethos that surrounds them? One young history student, desperate to learn more about women's role, commented to me of her experience in tutorials:

> ...there is a rather disconcerting void. To mention Inghínidhe na hÉireann, for example, in a tutorial on the nationalist revival, is like talking some exotic foreign language and receiving an accordingly blank response. The GAA and Yeats were almost totally responsible for everything, it seems.

What happens to anyone who wishes to undertake research into women's historical contribution? Is there anyone there to give encouragement, to offer pointers? Are there many women in roles of teacher, of supervisor of theses? Does it remain a battle for academic credibility, to prove feminist research is intellectually rigourous and valid? I hope that present-day graduates have an easier time than I had, when trying to convince the powers-that-be that they needed to undertake research on women, but when I see what stage mainstream history is at now, I don't feel overly optimistic. If women's studies are not integrated into the core curriculum of undergraduate study, then they are unlikely to figure prominently in research proposals. And, as the cycle continues and research findings trickle down to school level, so new texts will continue to have very little about women in them, and the next generation of school students will enter higher education with no awareness of women's role in historical events and no desire to continue and intensify their studies.

My feelings are endorsed by women historians within Ireland. Maria Luddy and Cliona Murphy, in a hard-hitting survey of the present state of historical scholarship, describe history in Ireland as: 'A narrative account of the doings of men, largely carried out by men, written by men and taught by men'. They go on to ask a number of pertinent questions:

> How many of the male historians in Ireland…take a good look at themselves and their departments and their subject matter? What is the ratio of male to female undergraduates? And how does this ratio reverse itself as one proceeds up the academic ladder? Where do all the enthusiastic female undergraduates go? Does their disappearance have any link with the invisibility of women in history?

They declare their belief that it is 'problematic for the discipline of history' that women who do manage to become professional historians are the ones who write women's history, making that history, if not inferior in the eyes of men, then at least a very separate history which simply reverses the norm so that women research and write it and read it and teach it to other women, while men can continue to ignore what is happening. In many departments now, that would appear to be the current state of 'women's studies'. The battle to get women's studies onto the curriculum is being won, but it has become a separate area of study and those who undertake research remain within this female ghetto, completely marginalised and unable to penetrate the prevailing male orthodoxies. Those rare women academics who have won recognition for their work from their profession as a whole, often find that it is their 'mainstream' work which wins the plaudits, while the critics remain silent about their other research—that which is concerned with women's issues.

Historical research

In Irish life, the relegation of the female is as prevalent in institutions of higher education as it is in the pub or the betting shop. Therefore, whereas some American or British male academics no longer regard it as effeminate or insignificant to publish research on women, it still seems inconceivable that any of the present generation of Irish male scholars will announce their intentions of embarking upon such a study. The academic world waits with great anticipation when it is announced that someone is preparing the official biography of Michael Davitt or W B Yeats, but what would the reaction be if one of these eminent persons was to announce that, to take some unlikely examples, his latest project was a comparative study of the British and Irish suffrage movements, or a biography of a notable female trade unionist? Ironically, their sexism precludes them from realising that in many countries today, feminist studies are in the vanguard and reputations can be made on the basis of original research in the area. It is an area ripe for a male takeover!

One British scholar who has made his reputation with his studies of European feminism is Richard Evans. Several Irish feminist historians have used the conceptual framework of his book, *The Feminists*, to analyse the radical content or otherwise of Irish feminism. In doing so, they have rightly pointed out his exclusion of Ireland, which is made all the more anomalous because of his inclusion of most European countries—encompassing Finland and Iceland for example— and his evaluation of the differing strengths of suffrage movements in Protestant and Catholic countries. Examination of the Irish experience would have been most enlightening (although it might have caused problems for his basic thesis), but presumably he assumed the Irish experience to be the same as the rest of Britain's. Ignorance of the rich amount of Irish primary source material is probably also part of the reason. When Evans published his book in 1977, little on the subject had appeared in print. It is another example of how marginal Irish women have been, in an historical sense, until very recently. And it again demonstrates how determinedly masculine the perspective of Irish historians has been.

Cliona Murphy's engrossing account of the Irish suffrage movement, which elaborates upon and develops some of the research of Rosemary Cullen Owens, is only the second book to appear on the subject. Ireland must be the only country in the western world to have such a paucity of print on such an important issue. Murphy's focus is the impact of feminism on Irish society in the early twentieth century. Her work sheds great light on such subjects as the role of religion, the mobilising of public opinion, the influence of the press: topics surely of general interest to all historians of the period. But will that book be read and its title added to undergraduate reading lists? The fact that it is published by the influential Harvester imprint will perhaps, given the elitist criteria of the academic world, enhance its chances. In her conclusion, Murphy says her study serves 'as an indicator of what as yet has to be done' and she makes a number of suggestions for further study: biographies of those women who played a role in the suffrage movement; thematic studies on, for example, the numbers of female doctors and female writers who became involved in the movement; analysis of the Munster Women's Franchise League and other non-militant groups which, so far, have had very little attention. As she says, 'much more work will have to be undertaken before a more balanced picture of Irish history will emerge in the history books.'

Why has the Irish suffrage movement suffered from such neglect by historians? Hanna Sheehy-Skeffington, a leading suffragist, calculated that, in proportional terms, it was as large as its British counterpart. It was certainly not concentrated in Dublin, because many towns and country districts also had suffrage groups and societies within them. Neither is there any difficulty with source material, as the Irish Citizen ran between 1912-1920 and the Irish movement often featured in the pages of British suffrage journals. It was also composed of educated women who wrote copiously. I think the explanation lies in the fact that to research the organisational history of women's struggles for their rights requires a total shift of perspective to a woman-centred consciousness, and this has needed a degree of self-confidence and intellectual combativeness that has, until recently, been difficult to imagine. But the process has begun, and as more material is unearthed, there should be increasing numbers of students eager to build upon the small foundations that have so far been constructed. The few studies of Irish suffragism that exist at the moment throw so much light on topics like the hold of religion, the degree of political contact with the international community, the influence of the press upon public opinion, and the effect of the Home Rule crisis upon unionist-nationalist relations, that I fail to see how any historian could be indifferent to understanding more about that particular aspect of our past.

Irish feminist history

Feminist historians are obviously in need of support—both intellectually and emotionally. An Irish Association for Research in Women's History, its members coming from north and south, has been formed in the past few years. Its annual conference in 1990 attracted a wide variety of women, both young graduates and those women who have lived through, and helped to make, history in the period between the 1920s and the 1940s. Through such continuities the pursuit of history becomes not an abstraction, but a search for a past in which we all share and which we all have a vested interest in understanding.

In 1987 an Irish Feminist History Forum was established, both as a group where those interested in women's history could pool their thoughts and findings and also to provide an impetus for the publication of new material. Their objective is, they say, to enable as broad a range of readers as possible to see that 'not only do Irish women have a history, but that it is a history which is vibrant and worth recording.' The first publication to emerge as a result of this initiative is *Women Surviving: Studies in Irish Women's History in the 19th and 20th Centuries*. As the editors explain, in all the articles women are:

> firmly planted within their own historical period. They are not living in a separate dimension as one might have supposed from…reading the traditional textbooks in Irish history…Their lives are firmly connected to, and dictated by, the political, social, demographic and economic happenings of the time. They are a part of history, not on the fringes of it.

The studies, which range from examining the role of nuns in society, women in workhouses, women as prostitutes, and as domestic servants, through to analysis of women in the suffrage movement and women's contribution to post-Independence politics, are valuable additions to our understanding of Irish society and important contributions to the underdeveloped field of Irish social history. They are also some of the first attempts at integrating women into the mainstream of Irish history, rather than simply fitting women 'into the empty spaces', which, so far, has been a necessary stage through which feminist history has been travelling.

Another pointer in demonstrating the sorry state of scholarship here, is the fact that in some countries scholars are complaining that histories of women have too often concentrated upon suffrage and other women's rights campaigns, to the detriment of social histories of the family, changes in domestic labour, the influence of class and sex on female oppression, etc. Practitioners in Ireland have a very long way to go before we could even begin to be critical in that sense, but Women Surviving is a brave attempt to move away from the more obvious areas of research, in order to develop a more complex picture of the totality of women's experiences.

What Irish feminist historians have criticised is not the clinging to women's rights preoccupations, but rather what they consider to be an excessive concentration upon nationalist history. Cliona Murphy attributes this to the fact that the new independent Irish state lauded those women who helped in the national struggle, creating folk heroines 'comparable only to ancient Gaelic queens', while the suffragists were viewed as unnationalistic, if not traitors, for putting women's issues before those of the nation. The latter is undoubtedly true, but it doesn't explain the fact that the nationalistic heroines were also by and large equally ignored by the historians, and it has only been in the past decade that any real assessment of their contribution has begun. Rather than get caught up in a feminist version of the revisionist debate, I would contend that nationalist and feminist women have fared equally badly when it comes to serious attention by historians, and that it is as important that the one movement gets recognition as the other. But I would accept that it has in a sense been easier to begin with the nationalist cause because its landmarks have already been defined and so the task becomes one of finding the evidence to describe the important role we all suspected, but could not document, that women had played during the various stages of the struggle against British rule in Ireland.

Putting gender into history

In writing this type of history, the goalposts do not change. It is not male-defined, because much of it is detailing women's autonomous contribution, but at the same time women continue to be the outgroup, fitting into categories and value-systems which consider 'man' as the measure of significance. Gerda Lerner has described this as 'contribution history': the movement in question—nationalist, unionist, labour, etc.—stands in the foreground of the inquiry while the contribution made by women is then evaluated. Women's own independent preoccupations and their fight against sexual oppression are not part of this scenario. Lerner regards this as 'transitional women's history', one step on from the first level of 'compensatory history' which looks for notable women, the women who achieved, rather than describing the historical experience of the mass of women. The writing of biographies falls into this stage, but not entirely so, as modern biographies attempt to situate the individual within the context of the period, and to give greater prominence to those who shared the lives of the better-known.

I don't want to dwell at length on the significance of these various stages, merely to use them as pointers to the current state of Irish historical research. What exists at the moment is assumed to be 'gender free' but the reality is that the experiences of men (and not usually working-class men) are dominant. It has therefore been male history, and a class-based history at that, which has determined what the important historical periods have been. What we have at present, in relation to a gendered history that takes women as well as men into account (and that only to a very limited degree), is 'contribution history'. There are some—very few—accounts of such subjects as 'women and Irish nationalism', and 'women and the trade union movement'. But we still have a long way to go in achieving general acceptance that gender is a legitimate category for historical analysis, and one that must be integrated into the textbooks.

What would be different if this were to happen? There must surely be a radical change in the writing of all history, because the feminist approach challenges the categories and the conventional periodisation of historians. The whole concept of periodisation—the important eras in history which have set the agenda for future generations—is called into question by advocates of a gendered history. Concepts we have accepted without question will have to be radically overhauled. Let us take one example, the period we describe as the Renaissance. Historian Joan Kelly has argued, in a seminal essay, that women had no such renaissance. Her analysis of the historical and literary sources for the period constructs a very different society from the one commonly presented. Her vastly different conclusions are a product of the fact that she begins by seeking to establish (and then to measure), 'loss or gain with respect to the liberty of women.' She found that women as a group, particularly upper and middle class women, experienced a contraction of social and political options in their lives as family and political life became restructured by the transition from feudalism to the early modern state. Noblewomen were increasingly removed from all public concerns and new constraints were placed on their personal and social lives, while women from the bourgeoisie found themselves disappearing into a private realm of family and domesticity. The Renaissance, that great period of cultural and political expansion, looks very different when viewed through feminist eyes:

> Renaissance ideas on love and manners...almost exclusively a male product, expressed this new subordination of women to the interests of husbands and male-dominated kin groups and served to justify the removal of women from an 'unladylike' position of power and erotic independence. All the advances of Renaissance Italy, its protocapitalist economy, its states, and its humanistic culture, worked to mould the noblewoman into an aesthetic object: decorous, chaste, and doubly dependent—on her husband as well as the prince.

Another, rather obvious example, is that of the various Reform Acts that gradually extended the franchise in Britain and Ireland. They conferred no benefits on women and in fact, once the word 'men' was legally defined so as to exclude women, it could be said that women's struggle for equality suffered a severe defeat, and one which occurred at the very time when the whole notion of 'democracy' was supposedly heralding the modern era of citizenship.

Maria Luddy and Cliona Murphy offer some suggestions for a list of significant dates for Irish women. This includes the establishment of religious communities in the early 19th century; the winning of educational rights for women in the middle of the 19th century; the impact upon women of the Contagious Diseases Acts of the 1860s; the development of the first suffrage groups and the opening up of local government to women. As they stress, the incomplete nature of their list is indicative of the limited amount of research that has been completed.

On issues of theory as well, a gendered history poses certain problems for historians. Proponents of modernisation theories assume an unproblematic advance for women, but, in the Irish context, what is 'tradition' and what is `modernisation'? Were women better off before or after the advent of colonial rule; did changes in the land tenure system mean that women became more isolated within the individual family? Is there a gulf between revisionist history and feminist history—the one legitimates colonial rule by portraying images of backwardness, the other has different indices of evaluation. Historically significant periods for women might be very different from what is now itemised in our history books. At the least, as Luddy and Murphy have said, we need to ask questions as to why events like the Act of Union, Catholic Emancipation or the various Land Acts should be as important for both sexes and for those of different class backgrounds. If there is a dichotomy of experiences between women and men and between women and men from different social groups, then this needs to be taken into account.

Joan Kelly has suggested that attitudes toward sexuality should be studied in each historical period because she considers that constraints upon women's sexuality imposed by society are a useful measure of women's true status. Could this method be used by Irish historians, and would it be an effective tool for evaluating change? Anthropological studies of the sexual order have revealed a consistent pattern regarding women's status: where familial activities coincide with public or social ones, the status of women is comparable to, or superior, to that of men; as we move along the scale to 'civilised' societies, domestic and public activities become more differentiated and sexual inequalities increase. Sexual inequality and the control of property are obviously linked, but sex and class relations are not the same. One of the primary tasks of feminist history is to extend this analysis of the relationship of the sexes to an understanding of the connections between changes in class and sex relations. It could further our understanding of the position of women in Gaelic society, the impact of Christianity on Ireland, changes of family structures pre- and post-Famine, not to mention the fairly dramatic changes in Irish life over the past couple of decades. This kind of synthesis stresses the interrelationships of women and men's lives, using inclusive historical perspectives in order to analyse their experiences. It is the hallmark of what is being posited as 'gendered history'.

Although no single approach or perspective can fit the complexities of the historical experience of all women, we do need to have new categories, to pose new questions, before the synthesis of a new universal history can be written. There is urgent need for self-criticism on the part of the historical establishment, coupled with a greater readiness to meet the need of their women students for a history which speaks to their lives, which has relevance to them. At a time when universities are competing for students, consumer demand should be voiced loud and clear. And no more heading off discontent through the stratagem of relegating women's studies to options for final year students. As an interim measure, until written material has been produced which will enable full integration of the experiences of women into the historical mainstream, women's studies should be on the core syllabus. It must be an essential area of study for both sexes because only then can women's lives be given validity and men's eyes opened to the reality of women's abilities.

Those of us who are feminist historians, inside or outside the academic world, know that there is no room for complacency with what we have achieved. A chill goes down my spine each time I remind myself that our first wave feminists at the turn of the century—despite all their books, journals, newspapers, arrests and martyrdom—a movement that attracted thousands to the cause of female suffrage, vanished without trace. It was buried by the male gatekeepers, and only exhumed through the diligence of a new generation of women activists. If we do not win this battle, then not only will our past as Irish women be forgotten about once again, but so too will our present, and contemporary accounts of the campaigns and sacrifices of the past decades will be in danger of the same fate. On the other hand, if we are victorious and male historians are forced to meet the challenge being posed by feminist scholars, they will never again be able to pretend that we do not exist!

References

Mary Cullen, 'Telling It Our Way', In Liz Steiner-Scott (ed.), *Personally Speaking*. Attic Press, 1985.

Mary Cullen, 'How Radical Was Irish Feminism?' In P J Corish (ed.), *Radicals, Rebels and Establishments*. Appletree Press, 1985.

Richard J Evans, *The Feminists*. Croom Helm, 1977.

R F Foster, *Modern Ireland 1600-1972* Penguin Books, 1989.

K T Hoppen, *Ireland Since 1800*. Longman, 1989.

Sheila Ryan Johansson, ''Herstory' As History: A New Field or Another Fad?'. In Berenice A. Carroll (ed.), *Liberating Women's History*. University of Illinois Press, 1976.

Joan Kelly, *Women, History and Theory: The Essays Of Joan Kelly*. University of Chicago Press, 1984.

J J Lee, *Ireland 1912-1985*. Cambridge University Press, 1989.

Gerda Lerner, `Placing Women In History: A 1975 Perspective'. In Berenice A. Carroll (Ed), *Liberating Women's History*. University of Illinois Press, 1976.

Maria Luddy and Cliona Murphy (eds.), *Women Surviving*. Poolbeg Press, 1989.

F S L Lyons, *Ireland Since The Famine*. Fontana, 1973.

Margaret MacCurtain and Donncha O Corráin (eds.), *Women In Irish Society: The Historical Dimension*. Arlen House, 1978.

Margaret MacCurtain, review of Catriona Clear, *Nuns in Nineteenth Century Ireland*; Anne Haverty, *Constance Markievicz*, Cliona Murphy, *The Women's Suffrage Movement and Irish Society in the Early Twentieth Century* in *Gender and Society* ,Vol.2 No.3 1990.

Cliona Murphy, *The Women's Suffrage Movement and Irish Society in The Early Twentieth Century*. Harvester Wheatsheaf, 1989.

Rosemary Cullen Owens, *Smashing Times: A History of The Irish Women's Suffrage Movement 1889-1922*.. Attic Press, 1984.

Anna Parnell, *The Tale Of A Great Sham* (ed. Dana Hearne., Arlen House, 1986.

Dale Spender, *Women Of Ideas*. Pandora Press, 1988.

Dale Spender, *Man Made Language*. (2nd edition) Pandora Press, 1990.

Acknowledgements

With thanks to Deirdre Clancy, Mary Cullen, Margaret McCurtain, Ailbhe Smyth, Liz Steiner-Scott and Paddy Hillyard for their comments and suggestions.

A note on the author

Margaret Ward's previous books include *Unmanageable Revolutionaries: Women and Irish Nationalism* (1983), *A Difficult Dangerous Honesty* (1987), *Twenty Years On* (1988) and *Maud Gonne: Ireland's Joan of Art*, (1990). She lectures in history at Bristol Polytechnic.

11

GLASS SLIPPERS AND TOUGH BARGAINS
Women, Men and Power

Maureen Gaffney, 1991

Introduction

This pamphlet is about power—specifically the place of power in the day-to-day intimate relationships between women and men. What in the old days used to be quaintly called the 'battle of the sexes'. Women wanted to be wedded. Men wanted to be bedded. To resolve the struggle, men had to tame their rebel hearts, domesticate their dreams, enter into the bondage of being good providers and, most likely, die in harness. That's how men saw it.

Women saw it differently. They found they had achieved a Pyrrhic victory. They had got their man all right, but the spoils of war eluded them. Instead of becoming heroines of true love and passion they were delivered into a life of drudgery and boredom. Sadly, only men had time to be heroes. The battle of the sexes settled down into sporadic cross-fire and occasional sniper attacks on the domestic front. But with the advent of the contemporary women's movement, renewed hostilities broke out. Women were demanding their rights. This time, the old-fashioned battle of the sexes had become a new and more sustained political struggle.

I want to argue here that the notion of power is central to this new sexual politics. Without power, sexual politics becomes a tragicomedy of manners, an elaborate set-piece where arguments about sexual destinies, roles and personalities float about, fully detached from the power relations that fuel them. Male power is obvious in male-dominated institutions. But the more close-up women and men get to each other in personal relationships, the harder it is for women to see, never mind confront, power in the relationship. And the more tempting it is for them to avoid the issue altogether.

First, I will be arguing that the struggle for power was prematurely abandoned in the second stage of the women's movement. Instead, many women were seduced by the cosier notion of a united front with men—a vision of the liberated woman and the new man walking hand in hand into an androgynous sunset.

Second, I will argue that in close relationships the exercise of power is not always obvious, but comes enmeshed and disguised in a complex matrix of personality patterns, expectations, interactions and deepseated psychological processes. This makes it all the more important for women, in their struggle for power, to understand the psychology of both sexes, particularly their own. I will attempt to show how traditional male-dominated psychology has constructed woman as problem and how feminist psychology has re-constructed an altogether stronger new woman. Finally, I will suggest how an understanding of the new psychology of women can help women to make power their own.

Power means different things in different contexts. It can refer to the ability to dominate others—to control and limit their actions. Alternatively, it can mean to 'empower'—the capacity to influence and help others (and oneself) to grow and develop. Or power can be a psychological trait—the possession of a strong and forceful personality. Finally, power can be socially structured—the capacity bestowed by society to determine your own and other people's economic, social and political fate. My own preferred definition is the simple one offered by feminist psychologist Jean Baker Miller[1]: power is the capacity to produce a change, that is, to move anything from point A to point B. This can include acting to create movement on a large scale in the economic and political arenas. But it can also include creating change in our personal relationships and even in the way we think and feel.

I

Waiting for the new man

For most of us, the issues of sexual politics are encountered in their most dramatic and intimate form in marriage and long-term close relationships. While much of what I have to say here will be couched in terms of marriage, it will be clear that it applies equally to other types of close relationship.[2]

However, many sociologists argue that the legal status of a marriage changes the nature, particularly the power balance in a close relationship—a point I will be returning to later. In any event, marriage is the relationship that most of us end up in: the institution that most symbolises the hopes, expectations and fantasies that men have about women and women have about men.

But the kind of relationship in marriage that a lot of people are looking for frequently remains more in the realm of ideal than reality—something the sociologists and psychologists have been busily confirming for us in the last few years. Is this simply a matter of human frailty? Men and women united in suffering? Experiencing pain in about equal measure? Nothing to be done, perhaps, except heave a little philosophical sigh?

Not really. Because there are two marriages in every union. One for the man; and one for the woman. And these two marriages don't always coincide. Studies[3] show that men find marriage more satisfactory than women, and their satisfaction does not decrease over time (as women's does). When a man expresses dissatisfaction with his marriage, he is more likely to be reflecting discontent with his general life situation, mainly his job, than he is with his relationship with his partner. Yet, when a husband is unhappy, then the couple is unhappy. Everybody suffers.

For a woman, regardless of educational level, just getting married and being married is a very important source of emotional gratification—not to mention the economic and social pressures to be married. While marriage is secondary to a man's self-esteem, it is primary to a woman's. When a woman is dissatisfied with a marriage, the unhappiness spreads to all areas of her life. But curiously it does not seem to affect her partner. He can still pronounce the marriage happy (since he's happy) and, with impeccable male logic conclude that his partner must be imagining things or simply looking for trouble. The unhappy woman can only turn to her women friends, her mother, housework or God for consolation.

The sociologists argue that simply because marriage is more important to a woman than it is to a man, a man has more power in marriage. A woman is going to be more willing to make adjustments, even to the extent of narrowing and denying aspects of her own personality, in order not to

227

displease her husband. A woman learns from an early age how to please a man. Before marriage, she learns to psyche him out. She learns to become sensitive to his thoughts and feelings. After marriage, keeping him happy can be a full-time job. Literally.

The exorbitant price women pay for love and marriage is now well documented. Married women have worse mental health than either single men or married men. Interestingly, married men do better than single men. Most significantly, single women do best of all, experiencing the least psychological distress. More married women than single women feel they are about to have a nervous breakdown and they suffer more phobic reactions, depression and feelings of passivity. In middle age, more married women than single women are alcoholics. It is true, of course, that marriage tends to protect people in general from suicide. But it protects women less.

Do men prefer to marry the more psychologically frail women? Or do women start out psychologically healthier than men and does marriage reverse this state of affairs? Either way, the conclusion is subversive. When it comes to mental health and marriage, the great irony is this: women want marriage more than men but men do better out of it.

You might think that results such as these showed at the very least that something was wrong in the state of marriage. All the mental health experts (usually male) however, weighed in with another, less subversive explanation: the problem was women. A vast literature on women's personality grew up, documenting their dependency, their immaturity, their natural tendency to depression and other ills of the psyche.

And their natural superiority in caring for children was both the problem and the solution. Dr Spock, the natural law, and the civil service ban on married women working were all of one mind: women's place was in the home. And women's boredom and dissatisfaction were nothing that a bit of flower-arranging, creative cooking and voluntary work would not sort out. A bit of psychological adjustment here. Some self-improvement there. And the truly feminine woman could rock the cradle and thereby rule the world.

The new man
With the advent of the women's movement, and the exposure

and rejection of 'the problem without a name', in Betty Friedan's *The Feminine Mystique,* the focus shifted to men. At first, the problem was defined simply. Women were oppressed by a male-dominated society. They had to fight for their right to work, to get control of their fertility and to be heard. The solution was to wrest control from men.

For an honourable while, women busied themselves raising their consciousness and demanding their rights. But then something happened. Having got so far down the feminist road, women became preoccupied by how to change men. Men's personality and masculinity gradually got more and more attention. The 'problem with men' began to be relocated in their personalities rather than in the power structures in society. In some circles, among more radical feminists, masculinity acquired a reputation which hovered somewhere between wilful immaturity and downright skullduggery. Patriarchy was women's enemy, right enough. And didn't all men support patriarchy to some extent? War between the sexes was inevitable. World evil was laid at men's door. The sisters and the sociologists pinned it all on men.

But the more tenderhearted of the feminists advanced what they believed to be a more psychologically sophisticated analysis and proposed a united front with men. Men, the new line went, were not the oppressors. It was the male role that was the problem. Not men in person, as it were. Breaking out of sex-role stereotypes, rather than challenging men's power, became the solution. Men needed to become more intimate, understanding, gentle; more involved with babies and the home. The concept of the new man was born. Androgyny became the new age destiny. The next wave of the modern women's movement was heralded as women and men working together fighting the real oppressor—rigid sex roles. Sexual perestroika was declared and sexual glasnost the way forward.

There was a surge of interest in men's problems—the demands, constraints and burdens of the whole masculine endeavour. How could men be expected to turn into lady confessors, angels in the house and mothers' helpers if, at the same time, they were to be successful at work, sturdy oaks to their families and able to evoke a full sexual response in women?

There was a flurry of academic interest in the circumstances which had pushed men into this terrible dilemma and a major excursion into psychoanalysis to find an answer. The explanation went like this: for both boys and girls the earliest and most primitive experiences of attachment and identification are with a woman, the mother. The basic struggle to separate and become an individual is a struggle with her. But a boy, at about age two, has to turn to another person, his father, to find a male identity. The result is that boys feel angry at being cast out by the mother, but at the same time feel threatened by their tendency to identify with her. They try to deal with this conflict by becoming independent and strong and by controlling their subversive soft feelings. These efforts are the beginning of the legendary rigid male ego boundaries. As they grow up, boys continue to be vigilant against any urges to yield to the passive feminine side of their identification, something which would threaten the very foundations of their sense of masculinity and self. They become highly motivated to prove over and over again that they are indeed male and not female.

Because masculinity is vulnerable and difficult to achieve, it also needs a heavy support industry to keep it from backsliding. Fathers and peers feel obliged to keep up the pressure on young boys to act in a suitably masculine way. In addition, men and boys seem to need an endless supply of nurturance and emotional support, mainly from women, to maintain this acquired taste we all have for masculinity as we know it.

Well, this analysis went down quite well with men. At last women were beginning to see the strain they were under. And how they needed to regain the lost, denied part of themselves in a dependable relationship like a marriage. Men were more than ready to acknowledge that they too were victims (maybe more so if the truth were known); that they also wanted to be full, authentic human beings. They freely admitted that in the past they had been maladaptive. Yes, they were exhausting themselves and putting themselves into an early grave competing with one another, oppressing women, despoiling nature, and losing touch with their feelings and with the higher things in life. And getting ridiculously preoccupied with silly things like power, status and filthy lucre.

There was a great deal of talk about male role strain, male dilemmas, the stress of trying to live up to the male image, and the crisis in masculinity. Now, thanks to the women's movement, men could freely admit their inadequacies. At last it was clear that all these problems men and women were having getting on together were not really men's fault at all. Nor were they the fault of women. In fact, they were nobody's fault. It was the male sex role that was the problem. Thank God someone had shouted stop. Women breathed a sigh of relief. The propaganda war had been won. Now we were all in this together.

Defining the male role as the enemy meant that men could approve of feminism as a struggle against traditional sex roles. Just the same as men's own struggle, really. The solution? Men had to become more expressive, more vulnerable; more in touch with their own feelings. They had to be more sensitive to women, try to understand her angle on every issue. Get out of pinstripes and into softer lines. They had to share roles with women, particularly their wives. The prodigal son, husband and father, had to return to his rightful place: the bosom of the family.

Armistice

In the beginning everybody was quietly optimistic. Research on sex differences was showing that there was not much difference between the sexes after all. By the end of the 1970s, it had been confirmed that men were more physically aggressive than women. Women (but not little girls, interestingly) were found to be a bit more dependent than men. Men had better spatial skills, while women had better verbal skills. In practically everything else, the differences between the sexes were inconsistent (and turned out more often than not to be the result of experimental bias and stereotyped expectations rather than innate differences).[4] And sure we could all live with a few differences. There was room for all types. Men, it was reported, were doing a little more housework. Sharing the care of babies was proceeding nicely too. Loads of earnest studies showed that men could be just as nurturant as women. They had the ability to change nappies and feed the baby. Their ever-increasing presence in the delivery room, solemnly timing contractions, was heralded as the beginning of a sea-change in the true shared caretaking of children. So we all sat down and waited for the arrival of the new man. It was only a matter of time.

While we were waiting, researchers went back and found that even though men had the ability to look after the babies they were not, by and large, doing so.[5] They played a lot with the children and were less authoritarian than a previous generation of fathers, but the executive responsibility for childcare still rested with mothers. If women were at home, they still ran the show. If women were out at work they still organised the childminder and took time off when the kids were sick. On the domestic work front the news was dismal. Country after country was scoured by social scientists looking for the equal partnership actually in operation. But even in Eastern Europe, where the majority of women worked, it was still women who did the lion's share of the housework.

On the emotional front, the news was not so good either. The traditional bargain in marriage was being changed. In the old days, the rule was that men were the good providers. They kept their wives and families by the sweat of their brow. In return, men expected a lot of domestic tender loving care and peace and quiet to pursue a few hobbies. Now, with the new style marriage, women were also breadwinners and were anxious to share the burdens and pressures of economic family life which had once fallen entirely on their husbands. Now, please, could they get a bit of emotional intimacy in return? But men remained stubbornly attached to the idea of being in emotional control. The new man was not quite ready to come out of the closet.

Sexual inequality and power

Waiting for the new man and helping him find himself as a way of changing sexual politics had a fatal flaw. The issue of power was forgotten. In fact, even the issue of politics was forgotten. What had started as a revolutionary enterprise had become a kind of grand-scale therapy instead. Part of the explanation for this can be found in the broader history of the last two or three decades. The first stage of the women's movement happened in the heady 1960s, when politics, struggle and liberation from oppression were still fashionable issues. In the more sober, conservative 1980s we had time to look again at the fall-out from the counter-culture. And it became clear that it had often amounted to little more than an extension of privileges for the already powerful. In the second stage of the women's movement, the struggle became more specialised. Women in business tried to fight their corner. Women in politics did their bit. Women academics started women's study groups. Piecemeal progress was made (though generally by those who were already privileged). The basic politics often got lost. Hanging over the whole enterprise was the big, unfinished business: When were men going to change? When were men going to free up women at home and change their way of relating so that women could begin to realise their full potential? Women found themselves, once again, doing what they have always done: playing the waiting game with men.

The problem with a concept like the new man is that it implied that the problem with men is their personalities. The problem with men is their power. Look at the traditional definition of masculinity: courage, inner direction, aggression, autonomy, mastery, adventure, toughness of mind and spirit. Enough to set a woman's heart on fire? In reality, it has much more to do with being dominant in the power structure than with male personality as such. Just read that list of qualities again—and think of Margaret Thatcher.

Of course, most individual men are not all that powerful. The power structures in our society are organized in hierarchies. Men have to fight their way up these hierarchies—in politics, in business, in the unions, in sport. Even when they do not actually get to the top, their eyes are always on the next step. A lot of their energy goes into maintaining whatever place they already have on the various hierarchies in their lives. Whether he is one-up or one-down is a major motif in male psychology.

Inevitably, men bring all their skill and practice in power dealings into their relationships with women. They don't, by and large, do it consciously or maliciously. They do it automatically. For example, they do it by assuming from their earliest youth that whole families will be organised around their work and careers, freeing them to move house when they need to, and allowing them to work the long and unsociable hours necessary for promotion. More importantly, they assume that their wives' task is to ensure that family life runs smoothly so that they can face the world of work and competition feeling confident and unhindered. Such male assumptions are based on the idea of the service of others, and may be supported by traditional ideology or even violence. The idea that other people should service your needs is part of being powerful. And it is women who do most of the servicing of men's needs.

Men, whether of the old or new variety, cannot and will not liberate women. It is not in their interest to do so. Because it is in the nature of power and privilege that if one group gets more of these scarce commodities, there will be less for the rest. Men, true veterans in the pursuit and retention of power, know this. For example, an increase in women's participation at work will mean greater competition for men. More rights for women in family life inevitably means a lessening of privileges for men. It is not that men are instinctively against women in some simple-minded way. They are just determined to hold on to their access to power and privilege. It's a tough old world out there, men say. And you have to keep your eye on the ball. It is women who must do the real struggling.

Sexual politics does not mean a moral crusade—promising to be a good girl and to do it better than men. Neither does it mean a crusade to improve men. Nor does it mean waiting for the new man. The new man will not be created from the tender, therapeutic rib of woman. Rather, when the fight for sexual equality is well and truly won, it's the New Man who will come to the negotiating table. Men will change, all right. But only when they have to.

II
Women, psychology and power

The struggle for sexual equality is quite evidently political and economic. But it is also, very significantly, psychological. Feminist psychology has played a major role in equipping us for the next stage of the struggle for equality by constructing the new woman. The new psychology of women reinterprets and redefines women's identity, positively reframes their special qualities, and provides a new understanding of their experiences and ways of relating with the world. Most importantly, it elucidates how power has shaped much of the psychology of both women and men.

Jean Baker Miller's hypothesis[6] is that much of what happens to women can be understood in terms of their social definition as unequals, just like other groups who have been similarly designated as unequals on the basis of class, race or religion. The difference in the case of women is that they have lived with men in intimate and intense relationships, thus altogether clouding the picture. As in any unequal power situation, the dominant group defines the subordinate group as defective or inferior in some way. Thus, just as whites labelled blacks as less intelligent, men have labelled women as less intelligent, less rational, not strong enough, not having whatever the culture currently defines as necessary to take the reins of power.

Dominant groups also assign one or more acceptable roles for the subordinate group. Acceptable roles typically involve providing services that no dominant group wants to perform for itself (for example cleaning up the dominant group's waste products). On the other hand, the functions that a dominant group prefers to perform are carefully guarded and closed to subordinates. Within the entire range of human possibilities, the most highly valued activities in any particular culture will tend to be kept in the domain of the dominant group, the subordinates getting the less prized activities. Margaret Mead observed that in every known society, men's activities were regarded as more important than women's, notwithstanding what these activities were. When identical activities are performed by women, they automatically lose their status.

There is a certain acceptable psychology for subordinates: submissiveness, passivity, dependency, lack of initiative in thinking, deciding and acting. These traits make subordinates pleasing and non-troublesome to the dominant group. These traits also justify the group's subordinate status. The descriptions suggest a certain childlike quality, evoking the idea of immaturity, helplessness, and the need to have an eye kept on them in case they get up to some mischief. That's the benign version of the relationship. Of course, there is also a more sinister version, involving force, pressure and ultimately the threat of violence.

The dominant group do not like to be reminded of the inequality. They prefer other explanations: that the dominant and subordinate groups are engaged in a common enterprise; that the subordinate group could not manage without this relationship; that the subordinate group actually prefer it this way (usually, it is suggested, because they can't or won't take responsibility); or finally that this is the way nature intended it to be. A kind of white man's burden.

A remarkable bit of reasoning when you think about it: that a 'weak' group should be protected by being in the control of a strong group. After all, the same end could surely be better accomplished by controlling the strong group to make sure they don't exploit the 'weaker' one. And this suggests who might have made the arrangements in this way. Examining the relationship between men and women, the same pattern of rationalisations can be detected. Men are not impressed by arguments about their alleged power over women. The hardliners prefer to think of themselves as over-burdened breadwinners. Many men may indeed work harder to support their families. Still, when pressed, they will also acknowledge that they would not turn down promotions, choose to earn less money, or compromise the pursuit of their dream—even if they had no families to support.

Simone de Beauvoir was especially wary of male logic in this area, warning that husbands 'even though of comparatively mediocre ability' will dominate their wives in argument. 'In masculine hands,' she sternly concluded, 'logic is often a form of violence, a sly kind of tyranny.' Or, as Germaine Greer put it more matter-of-factly: male logic has a hidden agenda, and arguments with men are simply disguised *Realpolitik*.

One of the consequences of the almost automatic denial of dominance is that the dominant group is frequently taken by surprise at the first expressions of anger and faint stirrings of rebellion in the subordinates. The dominants are alternately amazed, wounded, fearful and angry. After all, they protest, they were only doing what was best for everybody. In a marriage breakdown, for example, the husband will often appear genuinely and utterly mystified by the depth of the wife's anger and resentment, even though to an outsider the problems in the marriage may be entirely obvious. Husbands in such situations will often try desperately to find an explanation in terms of 'outside influence', an *agent provocateur*—the wife's mother or, more frequently, her female friends.

Subordinates frequently do not speak out about their oppression for fear of retaliation. So they will often resort to disguised and covert resistance. They may have to be overtly pleasing to the dominants, but this docile and charming exterior can contain a powerful hidden defiance. The consequence is that the dominants are deprived of real knowledge of the subordinates. The subordinates meanwhile know an awful lot about the dominants. They have to.

Women, for example, become adept at doing little dances around their men: reconnoitring the territory, looking for smoke signals, testing how the 'mood' is today, if it is a good time to make a request; behaviour in women which historically has been alternately praised and disparaged as 'feminine intuition' or 'feminine wiles'.

A consequence of all this is that subordinates are deprived of knowledge of themselves, simply because they are so busy knowing the dominants on whom their survival depends. They are also deprived of many opportunities to experiment with other ways of being and acting, because so much of the public realm of the dominants is closed off to them. Not surprisingly, also, subordinates tend to absorb many of the negative myths about their inferior status, so their self-esteem may be low. Deep within, they may feel less important than or inferior to the dominant group. They may feel their only option is to imitate the dominants, to deny their own identity. Revolutionary movements often have to start by raising the self-esteem, and consequently the aspirations, of the oppressed group. In this respect, feminist psychology has played a quietly revolutionary role for women.

Psychological construction and reconstruction
Feminist psychology has now begun to cut through the thicket of traditional 'female' psychology—a largely male-inspired vision of woman as problem, burdened by any number of psychological deficits, strange syndromes and vague female disorders. That is, of course, when women got any look-in at all. Because a truly extraordinary amount of psychology was and is about men. This might come as a surprise to those who think of men's studies as a relatively recent phenomenon, a type of academic spin-off from the long-running saga of women and their woes. Yet this fact, like much else about men and women, is hidden because psychology calls men's experience 'human experience'. At least, that is, before the advent of serious feminist scholarship.

All the giants in psychology, right back to Freud and before, implicitly adopted male life as the norm, and tried to fashion women out of this masculine cloth. This gave rise to two problems. First, women did not always fit the male pattern. They messed up the theories. So psychologists had to set about explaining how women were different from men. This largely took the form of documenting how deficient

237

women were when measured against the male standard. Whether the focus of enquiry was individual differences, sex roles, or masculinity and femininity, the same problem emerged. Women's psychology and femininity became code words for a range of diagnoses—all of them depressing.

Second, there was the problem of explaining why men were more successful than women by almost any worldly standard of status and achievement. The explanation required the identification of a whole host of new female syndromes. Studies found women to be more conforming, more susceptible to persuasion, less assertive and less authoritative than men. Women were more likely to suffer from 'learned helplessness' and to believe that outcomes are determined by forces external to themselves, like luck or fate or chance.

'Fear of success' became one of the most extensively studied psychological theories about women's behaviour. Variants of this theory are still appearing. Recently, we had the 'impostor phenomenon', which describes how women, even when they have succeeded in the world, live in fear and dread that it is all a mistake—that they don't deserve their success and will be eventually 'found out'. And if women somehow manage not to fall prey to the 'impostor phenomenon', they may instead develop the 'Cinderella complex', that is, the fear of independence, and the hope that finding a man to take care of them will make them happy.

Study after study showed that low status, low competence and low success were inseparably linked with the notion of femininity. Nevertheless, mainstream sociologists remained convinced that whatever the negative psychological fall-out for women individually, the pursuit of femininity was 'functional' to the extent that it served to mould women for their major roles as wives and mothers. Just as the pursuit of masculinity was equipping men to be good providers. As Barbara Ehrenreich[7] sardonically observes: 'God gave women uteruses and men wallets.' For the most part, the fact that this traditional 'female' psychology was a classic account of the psychology of powerlessness was ignored. As was the fact that 'femininity' could be understood as the limiting of all goals and activity to a confined end—that is, to service and please men. A type of psychological corset that, in Jessie Bernard's phrase, deformed women—a psychological foot-binding that kept them in their place and made them sexually pleasing to men.

It is sobering to observe that in societies very different in place and time, masculinity has traditionally been no different from general success in whatever is valued in each society. And this very often simply comes down to power of some kind: power over nature, power over resources, or power over others both inside and outside the society. In particular, a common element in all variants of the male role is the habit of power over women. Feminist scholars point out that all this talk of roles serves only to obscure the power relationship between the sexes. As one feminist remarked, you may as well talk of 'slave' roles and 'owner' roles, 'boss' roles and 'worker' roles.

Freud and the feminist challenge

There were also stirrings of feminist rebellion in the psychoanalytic camp. Scholars like Nancy Chodorow[8] and Carol Gilligan[9] were beginning to mount a feminist challenge against the orthodox psychoanalytic account of the differences and relationship between the sexes. Freud, who had dared to enter the dark basement of the unconscious, who had not flinched from tackling civilisation and its discontents, gave up on women. 'What do women want?' he asked querulously. 'Women', he concluded, were a 'dark continent'. This, of course, did not stop him from building his entire theory of human development around the experiences of the male child, culminating in the Oedipus complex.[10]

In the classic Freudian account, boys and girls start off the same, their primary attachment and identification being with their mother. But, by about the second year, they discover the penis. And thereafter, nothing is ever the same (you can see already that this is a male theory). It was self-evident to Freud that a girl, finding out she had no penis would, of course, want one, and subsequently define herself and her mother as lacking, inadequate, castrated. The boy, on the other hand, observing the plight of the 'castrated' females, develops an understandable fear that the same fate will befall him. A nice symmetry here. Penis envy for the girl. Castration anxiety for the boy.

But the problem was that while castration anxiety got you somewhere, psychologically speaking, penis envy was on a hiding to nowhere.

Orthodox Freudian theory went (still goes) like this: little boys desire their mother but fear their father's jealousy and vengeance. For a boy, the ultimate threat is castration by his father. The resultant fear puts paid to his Oedipal longings. He gives up his mother, identifies with his father and thereby joins the society of men. The successful Oedipal resolution becomes the bedrock of his conscience, his desire for mastery and achievement. Girls, on the other hand, deprived by nature of the Oedipal Complex and hence of the chance of a clean-cut and emphatic Oedipal resolution, stay dependent on the mother. Girls, deprived of this psychological scaffolding, are vulnerable to all kinds of psychological ills: like being overly-emotional, dependent, narcissistic, masochistic, and altogether unable to scale the dizzy heights of male ideals and achievement. So, only boys can achieve the end point of psychological development or maturity, which Freud saw as autonomy and psychological separateness.

Nancy Chodorow has argued that Freud's conception of maturity is a male one, shaped by male preoccupations, and that women achieve a different and no less mature end-point in their development. What Freud saw as difficulties in women's development, Chodorow sees as strengths. For example, because the primary caretaker is typically female, this means that for a girl the experience of attachment and identification can be fused. In other words, her sense of identity as a person and as a female are built upon her primary attachment to her mother, who is also the same sex. This does not mean, as Freud would have it, that women have weaker ego boundaries than men. An equally good way of interpreting it is that girls grow up with a sense of continuity and similarity to their mother, a relational connection to the world. As Chodorow[11] says of women: 'For them, difference is not originally problematic nor fundamental to their psychological being or identity. They do not define themselves as not-men, or not-male, but as "I, who is female".' The strong attachment of girls to their mothers means that they emerge from childhood with a basis for empathy built into their definition of self—in other words, with a strong basis for experiencing others' needs as their own. This is the source of many psychological strengths in women. Women are the keepers of relationships, the live-in therapists, the kin-keepers, the developers and nurturers of others' psychological growth.

Another fundamental of psychoanalytic theory was tackled by Carol Gilligan—the view of giants in psychology, such as Freud, Kohlberg and Piaget that women's moral or conscience development was (once again) deficient compared to men's. Most women, it seemed, do the right thing only in order to help and please other people. They are more influenced by feelings than by reason. A woman's conscience, Freud declared, was never 'so inexorable, so impersonal, so independent of its emotional origins as we require it to be in men.'

Gilligan believed that such a conception of moral development reflected what was important to men. She challenged the view that if women were different in the way they made choices, this implied they were deficient. She found that women did indeed reason differently, but in no less a complex or mature way than men. For women, moral problems and moral choices arise because of conflicting responsibilities and require solutions that take account of context and circumstances—reflecting the ethic of care. In contrast, men often see moral problems arising from competing rights that require formal and abstract solutions—the ethic of justice.

Carol Gilligan traces these differences to the contrasting patterns of psychological development for the two sexes, particularly the notion that separation is central to a man's identity and attachment to a woman's.

In response to a request to define themselves, for example, women describe a relationship—their identity being in that connection to others. When men define themselves, the response is more sharp-edged. The male 'I' is defined in separation. Their standard of self-assessment is developed through work and their status is defined in relation to others. A man begins with a sense of responsibility towards himself, a responsibility he takes for granted; then he considers the extent to which he is responsible for others. Proceeding from a premise of separation, but recognising that he has to live with other people, he seeks through his ethic of justice to minimise interference and hurt, by limiting action and restraining aggression. A woman, on the other hand, proceeds from a premise of connection, of responsibility for others—and then considers the extent to which she has a responsibility to herself. For her, responsibility signifies response. An extension, rather than a limitation, of action; an act of care rather than aggression.

But, there is, of course, a downside. Just as men's identity is built on separateness and is therefore threatened by intimacy and the fear of being swamped, rendered helpless and unmanned by soft feelings, women's identity is threatened by any break in attachment. The danger for women is losing their own sense of self in others' needs. Their fear is being separate, which is experienced as abandonment. Thus, men have more problems with relationships, women with individuation. As a consequence, issues of dependency, intimacy, danger, achievement, aggression and responsibility are all construed and experienced differently by the two sexes.

Other things being equal, this might cause minor tensions and misunderstandings between the sexes. The problem is that because men have power and cultural hegemony, they are able to install their particular psychological perspective in institutions, social relations and personal relationships, to mould the world in their image. Men, preoccupied by the need to remain separate and different from women, for example, can extend these preoccupations into childrearing practices and the rigid cultural demarcation of male and female territories. Thus, it is fathers rather than mothers who sex-type children, and who enthusiastically enforce traditional expectations of appropriate dress and behaviour for boys and girls.

Likewise, because males feel obliged to repress feminine qualities in themselves, they come culturally to reject and deprecate whatever they believe is feminine in the social world. The part of the world assigned to women is, therefore, marginalised—the day-to-day rearing of children, the serving of food, the routine keeping clean of bodies, houses, and souls. At the same time, all the power and decision-making relating to this women's sphere is located in the 'real world'—largely controlled by men.

Conclusion

While the feminist remapping of the dark continent has provoked a paradigm shift in traditional male psychology, it has also caused some anxiety for women. There is the worry, for example, that the new psychology of women may be misunderstood as an essentialist view of men's and women's nature—i.e. the notion that differences between the sexes are innate. And that this may be used once more to keep the two sexes firmly in their separate and unequal spheres. How can women grasp the reins of power in the 'real' world, for example, if they are going to remain wedded to the caring-and-sharing image of themselves?

But in reality it is not women's strengths—their ability to connect and care—that are impeding women's progress. It is the fact that such strengths coexist with powerlessness and inequality. As soon as women begin to act on the basis of their own particular strengths and inclinations, for example in committing themselves to close relationships and parenthood, they are led into emotional and financial dependency. It is only when women become more powerful that they will be able to act on those qualities without losing sight of their own needs and make the world a more woman-friendly place.

There is no absolute consensus among feminist scholars on the true nature of the differences between men and women. But on some points, at least, there is agreement. Research to date indicates, for example, that women and men have the same basic psychological repertoire. From that repertoire, women and men tend to select different actions. It is also becoming clear that gender is not a static category, but is better understood as a process of social interaction—influenced by choices and social pressures, of course, but primarily a way of structuring relations, especially power relations, between the sexes. So, it is really more a question of 'doing' gender rather than 'having' gender. How much choice and natural inclination enter into this complex process is something that will only become fully clear when power has been removed from the equation. As the philosopher Janet Radcliffe Richards suggests, you cannot know 'nature' apart from its context: 'The reason we do not know about the nature of women, and of course men, is not that we have seen them in the wrong environments, but that we have not seen them in enough different ones. You know something about the nature of iron, if you know that it looks grey, feels heavy and is cold to the touch, but you know far more if you know that if it is left in a damp place it will rust, if it is stroked with a magnet it will become a magnet itself, if it is heated enough it will melt, and so on.'[12]

Maybe we will find that many of the differences between women and men have nothing to do with gender at all, but are simply the different exigencies and themes, virtues and failings of two different worlds, however we label them: the world of work and the world of the family; the public sphere and the private sphere; agency and community; reason and feeling; Yin and Yang; a philosophical bifurcation as old as man and woman themselves. That would be OK too. What women want is not to be forced to personify just one of those worlds. Women want the power to be able to experiment with many possible selves. Maybe men do too. But that is another day's work.

This is where the issue comes back to power. Many of women's demands involve expanding the environments in which each of the sexes has traditionally operated. To achieve that social change requires power. And it is not at all necessary to base the case for that social change on arguments for or against the supposed essential sameness of men and women, or indeed the supposed superiority of women. Even if women and men are truly different, that still does not mean there cannot be equity and justice in the relations between them.

To effect such social change, women must make power their own. Yet power is a threatening concept for many women. When they try to take control of their lives they are often accused of being selfish. And because of their responsiveness to others, their pull towards self-denial in the service of others, women are mortally afraid of being selfish. The accusation has extraordinary resonance for them because it undermines their core identity as people who care about attachments. To be selfish is to destroy connection. Thus, the first step for women is to empower themselves by learning to act on the basis of their rights as well as their responsibilities. Women need to get used to identifying their own interests and to introduce these interests in negotiating issues within relationships.

Confronting power, trying to change its balance, means conflict. Between dominants and subordinates, conflict is inevitable. Many social scientists now acknowledge that 'the ancient war between the sexes (is) a pivotal notion'.[13] And often, this conflict is entirely out of proportion to what women are actually demanding. Many women leave relationships rather than face the conflict with their threatened and enraged partners. It is in the nature of things that those in power interpret any demands from subordinates as threatening—the thin end of the wedge. Indeed, men often react to women's reasonable demands as if they were tantamount to the dismantling of sex itself—hence the fantasies of 'castrating women', unmanned men, and impotence (in all senses of the word) at the prospect of women being 'on top'. It is as if dominants cannot conceive of there being anywhere else to be except on top or underneath.

Women have a different experience of power. They equate power in themselves with giving, making possible—connected up with the ethic of care. This notion of power is rooted in their experience of both sides of the dominance-subordinate relationship. With men, women act as subordinates; with children they act as dominants. But the nature of women's relationship with children is, in Jean Baker Miller's formulation, one of temporary inequality. Their role is to empower the child to grow in strength and capacity so that the child can make the journey from unequal to equal, that is, to the status of fellow adult.

Not that women can afford to ignore men's version of power. If women want to know in a practical way how this kind of power works in daily life, and what it achieves, they need only observe men. Male psychology is an exquisite study in how to acquire and hold on to power. Women cannot choose to bypass this kind of power on their way to a more woman-influenced world.

Women no longer want to have to choose between relationships and personal achievement—a choice men have never had to make. That will require fundamental changes: equal opportunity and equal pay at work; and on the home front, shared household responsibilities and childcare to enable women to pursue their own achievement goals. But women also want change at a psychological level—not just equality in close relationships but more opportunity to fulfil their own particular goals of increased intimacy, communication and commitment.

To individual women, these issues within relationships are often experienced as unique personal dilemmas. Yet, nowhere is the old feminist war cry—the personal is political—more relevant. Because as individual women find ways around these dilemmas, they are radically changing the nature of marriage and of society itself. In most western countries, for example, more and more women are choosing to delay marriage and parenthood until their careers are established, and to view childrearing as an interlude in their lives—albeit an extremely important one—rather than as a lifetime job in itself. Increasing numbers of women are combining motherhood with full-time or part-time work. And there has been a dramatic increase in the number of women who never marry at all, in the number of cohabiting couples, and in the proportion of married couples who choose to remain childless.

Finally, there has been an exponential increase in the number of couples divorcing—with women being much more likely to take the initiative. Indeed some sociologists are now coming to the conclusion that putting a relationship on a legal footing, ie getting married, inevitably leads to less equality and power for women; and that forgoing children may be the only means, given male resistance to women's demands, by which women can achieve full equality in marriage and the workplace. John Scanzoni and his associates report that women in cohabiting relationships with no children are more insistent on equality than are married women, and are more willing to terminate the relationship if the partner becomes too dominant. And this holds true even when these women get married later.

But once children arrive, the power balance changes for women generally. Women find then that they have less power in decision making, and a more traditional division of labour emerges. Women who were formerly equal partners become 'junior partners'; those who were 'junior partners' are demoted to being 'helpmates'—while their partners now become 'head of the family'. Most significantly, even when the children get older and these women resume employment, the ideology, power distribution and household division of labour do not shift back to the old equality.

The women who are most likely to leave unsatisfactory relationships are those with full-time work, who have not interrupted their careers during the marriage, who earn more money and who have a strong preference for equal relationships. They are also the ones who are least likely to remarry. Divorced women without full-time, well-paid jobs are the ones most likely to remarry. But even the latter report that second marriages entail less exploitation than first marriages, and they claim that they push more openly for influence and resist dominance more strongly than before. It is ironic that it should be women, who are so passionately committed to close relationships, who are now storming the

246

Bastille of marriage. It is a measure of their desperation and powerlessness to negotiate within close personal relationships. But it is also a measure of their passionate commitment to equality.

In their struggle for equality women are often accused of tearing the family apart, of killing off the idea of love, of bringing the bargaining of the marketplace into the bosom of the family. The implication is that consensus, stability and cooperation are the hallmarks of the 'normal' family. The reality is that families already live with a remarkable degree of struggle, dissension and general disenchantment. And social scientists are now beginning to discover that much of that conflict stems from the deep divisions in values and power between the sexes. The traditional family, however, chooses to send this struggle underground.

In modern relationships, however, women have brought the battle between the sexes openly on to the societal stage. In the process they have discovered something about the quest for true love. Living happily ever after has very little to do with fitting into tight glass slippers fashioned by a demanding Prince Charming. It has much more to do with Cinderella becoming one tough bargainer.

Notes
Detailed referencing of the large number of studies on which this pamphlet is based would be impractical. I have confined myself to the more important texts in feminist psychology, along with a number of key review articles.

1 Jean Baker Miller, 'Women and Power', Work in Progress, No. 1 Wellesley: Stone Center Working Paper Series, 1982.
2 The issue of power and same-sex relationships is outside the scope of this pamphlet. Much could be learned about gender and power, however, by studying gay and lesbian relationships, in which power imbalances are not gender-based.
3 Jessie Bernard, *The Future of Marriage*, (2nd ed). New Haven: Yale University Press, 1982.
4 K Deaux, 'From individual differences to social categories: analysis of a decade's research on gender.' *American Psychologist* 39 (2), 105-116, 1984.
5 S Coverman and J Sheley, 'Change in men's housework and childcare time, 1965-1975.' *Journal of Marriage and the Family* 48, 413-422, 1986.
6 Jean Baker Miller, *Towards a New Psychology of Women* (2nd ed), London: Penguin, 1986.

7 Barbara Ehrenreich, *The Hearts of Men: American Dreams and the Flight from Commitment* , London: Pluto Press, 1983.
8 Nancy Chodorow, *The Reproduction of Mothering*, Berkeley: University of California Press, 1978.
9 Carol Gilligan, *In a Different Voice*, Cambridge, Mass: Harvard University Press, 1982.
10 Much of the traditional theorising on gender, and some of the new scholarship, is largely based on the experience of white, middle-class Western people. It ignores the fact that the construction of gender can be influenced by race, class and culture. See, for example, the critique of Carol Gilligan's work in the special issue of *Signs: Journal of Women in Culture and Society*, 11(2), 1986.
11 Nancy Chodorow, 'Feminism and difference: gender relation and difference in psychoanalytic perspective', *Socialist Review* 46, 42-64, 1979.
12 Janet Radcliffe Richards, *The Sceptical Feminist*, London: Pelican, 1980.
13 J Scanzoni, K Polonko, J Teachman and L Thompson, *The Sexual Bond: Rethinking Families and Close Relationships*, Newbury Park, CA: Sage, 1989.

A note on the author

Maureen Gaffney qualified in psychology at University College Cork and completed her postgraduate studies at the University of Chicago. She now works as a Senior Clinical Psychologist with the Eastern Health Board and is a Research Associate in Trinity College Dublin, and a member of the Law Reform Commission. She has presented several RTE television series and contributes regularly to radio on topics of psychological interest.

12

REPULSING RACISM
Reflections on racism and the Irish

Gretchen Fitzgerald, 1992

I have spent most of my life living in countries where I have been perceived, at least initially, as being different, often in a derogatory sense. For over forty years I have carried with me, like a dull ache, both the reality and the imminent possibility of being found unacceptable on the basis of culture and the colour of my skin. This has shaped and marked me. My perspective on racism in Ireland is personal, rooted in my own experience and in the knowledge I have gained from living in Ireland for more than twenty of those forty years.

I use the terms black and white for convenience, without specifying the diversity within these categories, though being of Asian origin, I obviously recognise it.

Prejudice and Discrimination

Racial prejudice is prejudice against people who look, speak, dress, or behave differently from 'us' because of their ethnic origins or culture. We are all guilty of racial prejudice, whether we are Indian, Irish or European. Such prejudice is often based on ignorance or fear, particularly when there is little contact between people of different nations or ethnic groups. This frequently gives rise to a mythology of popular misconceptions and generalisations. We are all familiar with stereotypes in film and drama of the drunken Irishman or the inscrutable Chinese. Such prejudice has existed for centuries. With the advent of colonialism, racial prejudice evolved into an ideology of racism. The concept of superior and inferior races based on a hierarchy of skin colour was formulated. This was further compounded by the existing hierarchy of male superiority to female inferiority becoming 'rationalised' in theories based on perceptible differences between the sexes and the consequent division of labour and economic power.

Racism: the background

Between the sixteenth and nineteenth centuries, first the Portuguese and Spanish and then the Dutch and British, set out in search of new lands, colonising new territories in pursuit of wealth and cheap raw materials. (Human beings, as slaves, were included in the latter category.) The colonisers were motivated by the ever-increasing needs and appetites of Europe after the industrial revolution. Dazzled by the abundance of resources they found, they were blind to the already existing developed societies, the established trade links and the industries they came upon. Europeans destroyed the social fabric, culture and customs of communities in South America, Africa, Asia, the West Indies and the Pacific. Moral and spiritual approval for these activities was provided by the Christian churches. Hard work and service to the crown were made paramount virtues. The Christian churches followed the merchants and state servants into the colonised lands, adding their 'spiritual mission' of conversion (forced or otherwise) to the European process of 'civilising the savages'.

European institutions of various kinds—legislative, administrative and bureaucratic—were assumed to be infinitely superior to local ones, which they either replaced or were grafted on to. As the colonisers saw it, they needed to impose their institutions in order to better control the local populations and more efficiently organise the export of resources. It was considered to be in the interests of local communities to absorb and adapt to the new cultures, either voluntarily or by force. Through this process of political and economic power racism as an ideology evolved, supported by the work of writers, philosophers and scientists.

The eighteenth and particularly the nineteenth centuries gave rise to a plethora of theories to support the ideology of racism. These were based on the premise that 'white' people were biologically superior to people of any other colour. Ethnic groups were examined, evaluated and compared to the 'white' races. The shape of European skulls was declared to be more suited to intellectual thought. A crude hierarchy of races based on colour—white, yellow, brown, black—was defined and justified. Where colonial societies dominated indigenous populations, the hierarchy was made more complex by the interweaving strands of race and gender, resulting in four other categories: white men; white women;

black men, who threatened white women and dominated black women; black women, who were seen as powerless, subservient and acquiescent in their subservience to the other three categories.

Insisting that certain groups of people are mentally, morally and physically superior to others because of their skin colour or some other biological feature, in turn leads to the insidious categorising of individuals on the basis of their 'natural' type and origin. So if one is considering a Scandinavian and an Indian for the same job, one may conclude before ever meeting either of them, that the Scandinavian will be more efficient. Such bio-social theories contend that physical features and intellectual and moral capabilities are transferred genetically and dictate all the relevant characteristics and traits of individuals belonging to the 'natural' type group.

This categorising by 'known natural' type is applied to men and women also. Men are seen as physically stronger, and independent. Women are seen as the primary carers of the very young, dependent and more suited to domestic labour. Women perform domestic labour, not because it requires essentially feminine skills, but because historically and culturally specific roles have been attributed to women.

This thinking came to threaten Europeans themselves through fascism, the aim of which was to literally eliminate all those perceived to belong to inferior races. And it was only after the culmination of such thinking in the holocaust that the notion of biologically superior races became morally unjustifiable.

After the second world war, UNESCO gathered together a group of scientists to examine the issue of racial hierarchies. They concluded that race was more a social myth than a biological phenomenon. Certainly the human race is characterised more by its similarities than by the wealth of differences in skin colour and ethnic origin which are often mistakenly equated with 'race'.

But theories of biological superiority persist. Most of us have been brought up to believe that there are many different races, all biologically determined on the basis of real or perceived differences. From this it is but a small step to conclude that variations in physical features, culture and behaviour are based on innate biological differences. So, Irish people are all lazy, as are Africans, while Germans are cold!

251

Such prejudiced generalisations, and categorising by racial or national typology, has further implications. Some white Europeans are considered to be inherently superior to all others. Friction and antagonism between 'superior' and 'inferior' nations therefore becomes inevitable. Yet the culture and beliefs of groups of people, even in countries which are ethnically homogeneous (and few are), have evolved over many centuries and were in process long before national boundaries were defined.

In 1965, the United Nations, in the *International Convention on the Elimination of All Forms of Racial Discrimination*, defined racism as 'any distinction, exclusion, restriction or preference based on race, colour, descent or national or ethnic origin...' But words are not sufficient to remove feelings of superiority which have been lodged in the European psyche for generations or the reciprocal feeling of inferiority created in others. Only if existing global economic and power relations, established on the basis of racist thinking, are radically altered, will racist practices lose their attraction and diminish.

For me, the term racism denotes the relations of power by which one group dominates another because of ethnic or cultural differences. Racism is reinforced and combined with other forms of prejudice and discrimination based on class, gender and religion.

Whether we are the victims or the practitioners of racism (and each of us can find ourselves in either category at one time or another), we must change both our thinking and our behaviour in order to develop anti-racist practices. We need to monitor our conscious and unconscious attitudes if we are to bring about individual and collective change.

The Irish—victims and practitioners

Does racism exist in Ireland? Most Irish people if asked this question would tend to answer 'no'. They might also point out that the Irish have been and continue to be the victims of racial discrimination. As early as the seventeenth century plans were drawn up to make Ireland Britain's bread basket using Irish resources for the benefit, not of the nation, but of the British Crown. While historians disagree about the causes of the Famine (1845-48) certain facts remain. During each year of famine millions of pounds worth of food, mainly cattle and grain, were exported to Britain. Food was also imported and available to those who had the cash with which to purchase it.

This situation in Ireland in the nineteenth century has its parallel in many third world countries today. (A term more accurate than 'third world' is people from Latin America, the Caribbean, Asia and the Pacific (LACAP). I have specifically used the term 'third world' here because, in the context of oppression and discrimination, the people of LACAP countries have been relegated to third place in the economic and political pecking order of global power.)

The Irish were considered by their British colonisers to be an inferior race and were regularly depicted as such in cartoons where they were compared to chimpanzees and 'blacks' and regarded as little better than 'savages'. Ireland is no longer a colony, but discrimination against the Irish in Britain, the United States and other countries to which the Irish have emigrated, is well documented. In Britain this persists in relation to accommodation, employment and social acceptance. The 'No Irish Need Apply' signs were once as familiar to Irish emigrants as is the experience of black men and women in Ireland today being told that the flat is 'already let' when they look for accommodation, or the experience of black men, of being refused entry to discos in Dublin. Despite their history, the Irish abroad quickly realised that they could benefit from the situation of institutionalised white superiority by allying themselves with those in positions of dominance and took an active part in racial conflicts against other minorities in the United States and Australia. In recent years many Irish people have emigrated to South Africa. I still remember the day a college colleague excitedly told me of his plans to emigrate to South Africa, without once acknowledging that by his action he would be openly supporting the apartheid regime.

Experiencing racism does not prevent one being racist oneself. This applies to the Irish at home and abroad at every level—individually, institutionally, and nationally. Irish society is predominantly white. It is often assumed to be monocultural, traditional, at ease with itself. Discontent, discrimination and oppression between rich and poor, men and women, people of different ethnic, cultural, sexual and religious orientation, while acknowledged, are still largely seen as the concern of small minorities. The emerging struggle of minority groups for equal rights and protection against discrimination in Ireland has its parallel in the feminist movement. After long and hard battles sexism is now at least recognised as existing, though we have not yet managed to free Irish society of sexist thinking and behaviour. Racism is still struggling to be recognised as an inequity.

Historically, Irish people have discriminated against and attacked the Jewish community, with incidents recorded in Cork and Dublin in the nineteenth century; including a pogrom in Limerick. More recently fascist groups have also indulged in anti-semitic activities, producing magazines and stickers which are abusive to Jews. Discrimination against Jews based on cultural differences is also common on an individual basis.

Ireland's missionary tradition has meant that Irish people have played their part in reinforcing and continuing the effects of colonialism mentioned earlier. While Irish missionaries have brought many positive things to the inhabitants of previously colonised countries, there is little doubt that the Christian churches, by introducing what they believed to be a superior code of beliefs, values, educational system, language and lifestyle, created an elitist and divisive structure within communities visited by missionary groups.

I come from Goa, a former Portuguese colony which in the sixties became part of India. St Francis Xavier, whose body is ceremoniously exposed each year on his feast day, brought Catholicism to Goa. As a child I read with fascination and horror about the Inquisition taking place in Goa at the same time as it did in Spain and Portugal, with its subsequent forced conversions. I assumed that the majority of Goans were Catholics, dominating as they did the social and institutional fabric of the region. With some surprise I discovered only in my early adulthood that two thirds of Goans were actually Hindus.

One of my worst experiences of racial discrimination, and one which I still find deeply painful to recall, was when I was between five and eight years of age, in a primary school run by an order of Irish nuns in India. The convent school was a fee-paying one and set in idyllic surroundings. Perhaps unintentionally, it contained a large proportion of white and 'Anglo-Indian' children. The white children were either resident or expatriate English or fair-skinned Parsis; the 'Anglo-Indian' children had some claim to superiority and whiteness through descent. There was little room for someone like me who was not only dark but, unfortunately (then), the darkest skinned in my class. My abiding memories of those years are the beauty of the place contrasted with the abysmal misery to which I was reduced by vicious taunting and endless bullying. The memory is relived each time I hear of a black child at school in Ireland being treated in a similar way.

My experience of racism in Ireland began as a student. In a small city where black women were virtually non-existent I was particularly conspicuous on and off campus. My middle-class, black femaleness was perceived as 'exotic', 'exciting', 'dangerous'. I was stared at, often to the point of rudeness, particularly when walking through the college canteen, a torture I soon gave up. I also stopped attending some lectures, for the same reason. My social relations with other students became limited and distorted. Those men who asked me out were seen as the 'daring few' and fell into three categories. The first were genuinely interested in me as a person; these were in a minority. The second, bluntly, were dominated by lascivious intent. The third, largely through ignorance, patronised or trivialised both my colour and my sex. Acute shyness, the strangeness of living in a new culture, and the lack of a clear understanding of how to deal with what I was encountering meant that, for the most part, I retreated into solitary loneliness. My feelings of inferiority and unacceptable 'difference' did not disappear when I began work in Ireland, or later when I married an Irishman; although by this time my social milieu was largely accepting of me and therefore afforded me some protection against experiencing racism. I discovered that my knowledge of 'white' culture, whether literary, philosophical or historical, was assumed by those around me. However, the continuing significance or usefulness to me of my own culture and customs was of little interest to them. This sense of not belonging and of not being fully understood made me question for many years whether I had the right to bring a child, whose cultural origins would be as complex as my own, into such an unthinking society.

Ireland's traditional missionary role of proselytising has been largely replaced by charity and development work abroad. The approach to both is now generally more enlightened than when I first came to Ireland. I was horrified then to find school children still 'buying black babies'. The traditional missionary role and charity and development work are, however, fundamentally flawed by misconceptions.

There is still a belief underlying most Irish overseas

development aid activities that we are not only better off but also more knowledgeable and intellectually or academically superior to people in third world countries. 'Black people are uncultured, ignorant, stupid and lazy and must be helped to think and do what is in their best interests.' Though this is no longer openly stated, it is difficult to gain any other impression from the publicity materials and campaigns launched by many fund-raising agencies in Ireland. Visual images and accounts of living conditions and disasters project black people as passive victims who do little or nothing for themselves. A few development organisations are attempting to return respect and responsibility to black people.

For the Irish development worker the existing construct poses a dilemma which is becoming more openly recognised. As one worker said in a recent newspaper interview: 'It is impossible to live and work...without daily coming up against the racism inherent in both one's personal attitudes and in the nature of most aid programmes in the country...On a personal level one tends to prejudge or classify people on the basis of colour. White is seen as wealthy, well-educated, powerful and "civilised", whereas black is considered to be poor, uneducated, unimportant, simple and naïve...These preconceived prejudices are usually only broken down by establishing real social relationships...' (Sunday Business Post, 8 December 1991). The last sentence is particularly affecting. It can be difficult for development workers, who are invested, on arrival, with an innate superiority and who socialise within an expatriate network, to establish anything more than superficial relationships with local people. The elastoplast of do-gooding, for so long the institutionalised and religious salve of the Irish conscience, is no longer seen as enough.

Racism in Ireland today

One often comes across the following line of argument in relation to racism in Ireland: if Irish people have unconsciously perpetrated racism overseas and continue to do so, it is understandable, one might say, given the historical context. At least Irish people are not racist in their own country today. Or they can't be since there is only a small number of black people in Ireland. So the argument and myth usually run. Firstly, the fact that there is a (small) indigenous black Irish population here is not usually recognised.

Secondly, the resident black population of African, Asian and Middle-Eastern origin has increased in recent years, certainly much increased from the time I first arrived in Cork and was told by people that I was the first black woman they had ever met, the only black people they had met or seen having been male clerics.

While statistics and research are scant, there is no shortage of evidence of racism experienced by members of these minorities, both at the hands of institutions and in situations such as finding accommodation or employment. Unfortunately, organisations like Harmony, The Anti-Racist Coalition, and ICOS (Irish Council for Overseas Students) who monitor racist behaviour, do not have the resources to carry out much-needed research and to provide statistics.

Racist attitudes and behaviour against travellers, Ireland's largest ethnic minority, are, however, well documented. Opinions amongst Irish people vary—one misconception being that all travellers are descended from people who were displaced from the land in the eighteenth and nineteeth centuries. Travellers are still not officially recognised as an ethnic minority, although the state has now implicitly recognised them as a distinct and identifiable group in recent legislation, notably The Prohibition of Incitement to Hatred Act which came into effect in 1990. Travellers have been discriminated against from as far back as the sixteenth century, when an act was passed to prevent 'tynkers and pedlars' from moving from one town to another. At the time of writing, Dublin County Council is proposing to prevent travellers from other parts of the country moving to Dublin. Such a proposal in relation to any other group of Irish residents, those from Cork or Sligo, would rightly be regarded as outrageous and would make news headlines.

There are an estimated 21,000 travellers in Ireland, who have a distinct identity, culture and lifestyle, of which the characteristic of nomadism is the most controversial and the one least accepted by Irish people. It is usually referred to as the 'problem of itinerancy' or vagrancy and is viewed as illegal. The prejudice and discrimination against travellers is similar to that practised by white people against black people. Travellers' skin colour does not protect them from racist thinking and behaviour, which is based on the ethnic and cultural differences between Travellers and 'settled' Irish people.

Let us first take the question of prejudice. How many of us personally know, socialise or can count a traveller among our friends? Ask this question of the Irish in relation to black people. Many Irish people may never have seen a black person, owing to the small number of black people in Ireland. The same reason surely cannot be given for our lack of familiarity with travellers. Yet generalisations about travellers based on minimal contact abound. There are frequent protests by residents throughout the country whenever a halting site is to be built in their area. Generalisations, made on the basis of distant observations and myth, allow us to relinquish personal and collective responsibility for our society's behaviour towards marginalised groups.

Travellers are Irish and in some people's memories are regarded as part of the cultural fabric of rural Ireland where they went from place to place, working and then moving on. The collapse of the economic base of the traveller community in the past thirty years has meant a shift from a rural to an urban base. This has resulted in an intensified experience of racism. Now, even though they are Irish citizens, travellers are denied access to many of the basic rights accorded all citizens in relation to accommodation, education (less than twenty per cent of traveller children attend secondary school), health, employment, social welfare, even the franchise. The Irish state makes it virtually impossible for travellers to fully avail fully of these rights and still preserve their culture and lifestyle.

Institutionalised racism is illustrated by the statistics which reveal the systematic exclusion and oppression of travellers, eg, a high infant mortality rate, short life expectancy, frequent hospitalisation, high unemployment and widespread illiteracy.

Women travellers bear a double burden of oppression. They are discriminated against by men who, as in settled society, hold the balance of power in the traveller community. Discrimination which settled women experience in relation to education, employment and domestic labour is felt even more acutely by traveller women. Traveller women, like settled women, bear the burden of domestic labour and responsibilities. Their domestic situation is made more difficult, however, by the quality of their accommodation and lack of access to water, sanitation, electricity, refuse collection, shops, launderettes and super-markets. Thus traveller women are discriminated against by settled society and by traveller males, while settled women fail to realise the common oppressions they share with their traveller sisters.

How racist are Irish insititutions?

Institutional racism exists most visibly where racial discrimination is sanctioned by the constitution or laws of a country and legitimised in the authority of state institutions. The most extreme form of institutional racism is the apartheid system in South Africa which is now being slowly dismantled. This form of segregation, based on the colour of skin of different groups of people, led to a small (white) minority considering themselves superior to and holding economic and political power over the (black) majority. Another extreme form of racism is segregation of a minority to a limited area or territory, such as the reservations for Indians in North America, and homelands for the blacks of South Africa and aboriginal peoples of Australia.

Where does Ireland stand on anti-racist legislation? In the *Harmony Report: Racism in Ireland*, Marian Tannam states that 'In spite of having made human rights a central part of its own constitution, Ireland has played a disappointing role in the international human rights movement. In 1971, Seán McBride commented that the failure to act then to become involved in the world struggle against racism 'puts in question our sincerity when one professes loudly our attachment to the ideals of human liberty'.'

Ireland has no comprehensive body of anti-discrimination legislation. The Prohibition to Incitement to Hatred Act (1990), makes it illegal for neo-Nazi and fascist groups to prepare or possess materials or recordings of a racist or similarly offensive nature in Ireland. Until then Ireland was being used as a base from which to publish and distribute such material to Europe. The passing of this Act enabled Ireland to belatedly ratify two International Covenants—one on Economic, Social and Cultural Rights (1966) and one on Civil and Political Rights (1966).

However, Ireland is still not in a position to ratify the *UN Convention on the Elimination of All Forms of Racial Discrimination* which it signed in 1968, and which, if ratified, would mean that individuals and groups in Ireland would be afforded legal protection against discrimination.

An Anti-discrimination Bill being prepared by The Irish Travellers Movement, the Dublin Travellers Education and Development Group (DTEDG), and The Irish Council for Civil Liberties (ICCL) will be submitted to the Department of Justice in 1992. The Bill, while focusing on the travellers, aims to set out the principle of equality for all groups. The Labour Party has published a Private Members Bill on equal status. The aim of the Bill is to outlaw discrimination against individuals and groups on any grounds including sex, colour, race, nationality, ethnic origin, disability, age and sexual orientation, with the exception of positive discrimination. Existing equality legislation in relation to employment refers only to sex-based discrimination and does not extend to discrimination on the basis of ethnic or cultural differences. The EEA (Employment Equality Agency) has no remit in this area.

Aliens, immigrants, refugees and the Department of Justice

Irish immigration law is governed by the Aliens Act (1935) and the Irish Nationality Acts (1956 and 1986). These acts establish two categories of persons—citizens and aliens. Anyone who does not fulfil the conditions for citizenship within the terms of the Irish Nationality Acts is in the residual category of aliens.

The Aliens Act and subsequent orders and regulations virtually determine the status, rights and obligations of aliens in this country. There are relatively few legislative Acts that discriminate against legally resident aliens; those which do, affect political participation, jury service, and entry to officership in the defence forces.

The situation is different in relation to immigrants. The Department of Justice has very wide discretion under the Aliens Act to enforce, by orders and regulations, restrictions on the entry, landing, freedom of movement, expulsion and deportation of aliens in the state.

In the late 1980s there was an increase in immigrant litigation in this country which focused on the constitutional rights of aliens, many of whom relied on the family law provisions of the Constitution, culminating in a landmark Supreme Court judgement in the case of Fajujonu v. The Minister for Justice, 1990. In this case an infant plaintiff, an Irish citizen, sued the Minister for an infringement of her family rights under the Constitution. The alleged infringement was the making of a deportation order against her father who was an alien. The Supreme Court held unanimously that 'where an alien has lived for an appreciable time in the state and has become a member of a family within the state containing children who are Irish citizens, those children have a Constitutional right to the company, care and parentage of their parents within that family'. The judgment went on to say that where a family is constituted of alien parents and children who are Irish citizens, the state can force the family to leave only if it is satisfied that the interests of the common good and the protection of the state and society are so predominant and overwhelming as to justify such an interference.

The Fajujonu judgement is significant for two reasons. Until then there was a belief that where a policy question was involved natural justice and fundamental rights would be less likely to apply. The judgement also laid down for the first time that where the Department of Justice finds against the plaintiffs, reasons must be provided for the decision.

International agreements concerning refugees have not been given effect in Irish law. All applications for refugee status and political asylum are determined by the Department of Justice. No information is available as to what criteria the Department applies to applications for refugee status and political asylum. There are no clear, public and enforceable procedures in relation to refugees, and the Irish refugee or asylum-seeker has no protection under Irish law.

There are an estimated 400 Vietnamese here, some refugees from Chile, and a very small group of Iranian Bahais. None of these refugees has entered the country through the discretion of the Department of Justice. They are here consequent to special invitation from the Minister of Foreign Affairs and international pressure.

Influence of education and the media

Two other institutions play a major role in fostering racism: the education system and the media. Both need to be considered in the light of *who* has access to them and what information and messages they choose to transmit.

Where access to education is concerned, I have already pointed out that less than twenty per cent of traveller children attend secondary school. Education currently provided in many Irish schools neither affirms nor addresses the distinct identity of travellers, nor does it challenge the racism that travellers experience.

The prevailing ethos in primary, secondary and third level schools and colleges is as inherently racist as it is sexist. The formal curriculum itself, particularly in the areas of history and geography, needs to be closely examined and overhauled. In Ireland today, it is possible to do a primary degree in history and never once in three years discuss racism or western colonial exploitation, even in relation to the racism Irish people have experienced as part of their own history, never mind that experienced by third world countries.

To really combat racism in the education system, new inter-cultural materials need to be introduced. Innovative ways of teaching, which bring pupils into contact with ethnic and cultural minorities, should be devised, ways which emphasise positive rather than negative aspects. At present there is little that helps to educate students about these differences; still less that ensures that the thinking of future generations will be permeated with anti-racist awareness and practice as surely as it is permeated with racist thinking at present.

To bring about such a change requires political will, resources and understanding of our global interdependency. Apart from the DTEDG there is hardly any organisation in Ireland providing specific anti-racist materials for schools. Some overseas development organisations state that there is an underlying anti-racist ethos in their development education materials which challenge assumptions about third world countries and other minorities. Many of the recommendations of the European Parliament *Report on Racism and Xenophobia*, deal with action the EC should take in combating racism through education. The Report recommends that:

> Member states introduce teaching against racism into the curriculum of their primary schools as a compulsory subject.
>
> (Recommendation 71)

> Member States step up the support that education can provide for the campaign against racism, anti-semitism and xenophobia through the teaching of human rights and history at school, through teacher training and university research.
>
> (Recommendation 73)

262

There is no code of practice on racism and the media in Ireland. Guidelines on race reporting are, however, issued to NUJ (National Union of Journalists) members in Britain. It has been said that the media are not directly racist in their reporting of news items in Ireland, though individual instances of racist reporting have been documented. However, implicit in much media reporting and advertising, when closely scrutinised, is the continued assumption that western culture is superior and black culture is inferior. It is evident in reports on political regimes which western cultures find unacceptable and in so-called documentaries where women, particularly, are often portrayed as subservient with little or no social, economic or political independence, in sharp contrast to the 'liberated' western woman who may well be doing the reporting.

Juxtapositions of this kind are particularly noticeable in advertising and fashion features on television and in magazines, where visual images convey the sophistication of the 'white' woman in contrast to the 'primitive nature' of the blacks surrounding her. A favourite image is that of the vulnerable white woman, more often than not dressed in virginal white, with the presence of a black man nearby or in the background, implying threat or danger. Such images are inextricably invested with highly charged sexual, racial or class meanings. They might not set out to be explicitly racist, but they are part of a familiar everyday imagery through which racism is expressed.

In order to establish how balanced and fair media coverage is in relation to ethnic groups, the information and images transmitted about, to and from ethnic groups need to be examined. No such analysis of the Irish media has ever been undertaken.

The *Evrigenis Report* maintains that: 'Information about minorities is quite often biased, dwelling at length on the misdemeanours of some members of minority groups, giving poor coverage to the problems of such communities and ignoring almost all their achievements...' It continues: 'Whilst acknowledging that the media can play a positive role in forming knowledge about ethnic communities, it is undeniable that currently overall media presentation perpetuates a negative image of these communities.' The report then recommends 'that a campaign be conducted to raise the awareness of media professionals of the importance of their role in eliminating racial and xenophobic prejudices, particularly through appropriate treatment of the news'.

Ireland within the EC

The advent of a single European market within the EC is supposed to allow the freedom of movement of goods, services and people within the member states. This entails harmonisation of policies and legislation. Harmonisation of policies in relation to freedom of movement has become a contentious issue. Racism is increasing in Europe and there is also a marked increase in neo-Nazi and fascist movements. This has been matched by an increase in representation of democratically elected extreme right-wing parties in many EC countries. In Germany, members of ethnic groups have been moved into hostels in large numbers to protect them from violent attacks. In Britain, where 7,000 racial attacks are reported a year, it is estimated that there is under-reporting of attacks by a factor of ten. The Eurobarometer survey on racism in 1989 found that one in three Europeans felt that there were too many non-nationals in their country. A sizeable minority felt the presence of immigrants in their country was a negative factor for the future. At the same time, one in four EC citizens were in favour of improving or at least maintaining the rights of immigrants. Most people were in favour of harmonising immigration legislation within the community, rather than member states making unilateral decisions in relation to immigrants.

While on the face of it harmonisation seems to make good sense, there is a fear among many that it will lead to more restrictive policies being practised by some member states in preference to the more liberal ones of others. In bringing about harmonisation, international conventions, inter-governmental coordination and human-rights issues are of key importance.

The main groups working on inter-governmental coordination on harmonisation are the TREVI (Terrorism, Radicalism, Extremism and Violence Initiative) and the Rhodes Groups. Both groups have come under considerable criticism from anti-racist organisations. The TREVI Group, originally set up to combat terrorism, proposed standardised solutions for policing national frontiers which included regular checks on migrants, refugees and asylum seekers. The

Rhodes Group arbitrarily drew up a list of fifty-nine countries whose nationals, it decided, would require an entry visa for any of the twelve member states. They also excluded the UN High Commissioner for Refugees from discussions within the group of coordinators when refugee matters were being discussed, in violation of both the Treaty of Rome and the UN Convention and Protocol on the Status of Refugees.

It has been mooted that a common immigration policy, while desirable, is not essential before internal frontiers are abolished, and that non-Europeans living in the EC would be able to circulate freely through the community although they would not always have the right of residence. It is difficult to see how this distinction could be made, without creating a stratum of second-class citizens who, without nationality but legally resident in a member state, would be more vulnerable to random identity controls because of their skin colour. One has only to go through Dublin airport any day of the week to see that this situation already exists, with black people regularly being singled out for identity checks.

The twelve member states of the European Community have a total population of 320 million. Approximately six million of these are from developing countries. The Federal Republic of Germany (FRG), pre-unification, had the highest percentage—5.2 per cent of non-EC migrants. Ireland and Italy have the lowest with 0.5 per cent and 0.2 per cent respectively. Known incidents of harassment and violence in Ireland are low compared to some other countries but, considering the small number of groups of people here from other countries, it is not particularly encouraging. Rather, it is felt that if there were more foreigners here, particularly non-Europeans, 'racism and xenophobia could reach dangerous levels' (Report on the Findings of the Committee of Inquiry into Racism and Xenophobia, 1991).

Racism not only exists but is a major social, moral and political problem in Europe. It is up to each of us to deal with our individual ignorance, fear and racist tendencies. Collectively, we need actively to influence the role Ireland plays in ensuring that we live in a society which respects fundamental rights and rejects all forms of discrimination.

Fostering racism

Cultural roots do not necessarily and simply mean belonging to a particular country, city, town or community. They are an internal state, an inner-self. As children we develop a databank or blueprint of family memories, experiences, symbols, commitments and values. These we apply to individuals, places, lifestyles and shared moral and social mores. Our individual culture becomes a map of meaning which helps us to make sense of our lives. We identify with the culture or distinctive way of life of a group or class, as it is manifested in institutions, social relations, systems of belief, the use of objects and materials. All these are initially invested with the meanings, values and ideas of our blueprint. With increased experience, knowledge, and exposure to new things and people, we add or subtract from the subscribed norms of the blueprint. As we grow older, we graft our own memories and experiences on to it. The childhood blueprint is our essential repository, our most inner self. But it evolves as our ideas, beliefs, and values change and as we ally with like-minded people within a local, national or more extensive global framework. Thus, culture is not a static mantle of values, beliefs and behaviour but a mixture of all that we have experienced and thought about that makes life meaningful to us.

This has particular personal relevance for me as a black woman born in India with a mixed Portuguese, British and Indian culture, who has chosen to spend my adult life in Ireland and raise a family here. Skin colour and sexism have been paramount in the evolving of my blueprint. My inner-self has been defined and constantly redefined by and for me, in relation to the 'superior white other'. Being perceived as inferior has left me with an abiding sense of inadequacy and guilt which is only slowly decreasing. I have often been subjected to a type of inverted racism which disregards the cultures which have formed me. Because I am middle-class, do not speak English with a broken accent and do not wear any particular national costume, I am often regarded as 'not really Indian', 'not Irish', a 'West Brit', 'not coloured, because you're like us'. What is perceived as an identifying feature about me is used, consciously or unconsciously, to discriminate by either inclusion or exclusion. There is an assumption among many Irish people that those whose skin colour is different 'aspire' to adopt a 'superior, less primitive' culture.

Each of our identities is made up of an intertwining of such factors as ethnic origin, culture, class and gender. To discuss any one of these characteristics in isolation without reference to the others is to grossly over-simplify the complexity and enormity of the discrimination problem.

Historically, the struggles of black people and women for emancipation are related. White women initially looked at the slavery of black people in order to understand and interpret their own domination. Parallels and comparisons of subordination were drawn. American feminists in the 1960s adopted much of the language and non-violent tactics of black activists in the civil rights movement. These interconnections have since had an uneasy and often fraught alliance.

In Britain, a lack of true understanding of black women together with a focus on cultural customs such as the dowry system and arranged marriages have led to bitter divisions between white and Asian feminist women. Black women have experienced white feminists as quick to criticise and direct, but less keen to listen and learn. Black women have experienced the women's movement as narrow and reluctant to expand and incorporate other visions and realities.

The women's movement in Ireland has scarcely begun to address these issues. For me, the divisions which have characterised the politics of feminism in relation to black women first need to be recognised and then overcome. This can only be done if one moves from sympathy towards recognition of other realities, which in turn will lead to the formation of alliances to lend weight to political actions. Thus, in Ireland, Traveller and black women need to ally with settled white women to achieve solidarity and strength in order to win collective battles.

To do this we need actively to search out points of common reference and collaborate on shared actions and interactions. These must recognise and accept the differences, aims and ideals of all those who have been marginalised by the single, double and triple oppressions of class, gender and race.

References and further reading

Banton, M. and Harwood, J. *The Race Concept*. Newton Abbott: David and Charles, 1975.

Bourne, J. *Towards an Anti-Racist Feminism*. London: Institute of Race Relations, 1984.

Cashmore, E. *The Dictionary of Race and Ethnic Relations*. London: Routledge and Kegan Paul, 1984.

Community Workers Co-op, *Women and the Community*. Dublin: Co-options, 1989.

Community Workers Co-op, *Racism, Co-options*. Special Edition, Dublin: APSO, 1990.

Committee of Inquiry into Racism and Xenophobia, *Report on the Findings of the Inquiry*. Luxembourg, 1991.

The Courier, *Dossier: Immigration.* Number 129, 1991.

Crowley, N. *Racism and the travellers.* Dublin: DTEDG, 1991.

Eager, B. *The Situation of Aliens, Migrants and Nomads in Ireland.* Dublin: DTEDG, 1991.

Evrigenis Report, European Parliament working document report, Document A2-160/85, Luxembourg, 1985.

Eurobarometer, *Public Opinion in the European Community.* Special Edition on Racism and Xenophobia, Brussels: EC, 1989.

European Parliament, *Report on Racism and Xenophobia.* 1991.

Harmony Report, *Racial Discrimination in Ireland: Realities and Remedies. March,* 1990.

Husband, C. ed., *Race in Britain—Community and Change.* London: Hutchinson, 1982.

Links 21, White Lies—*Racism and Underdevelopment.* Oxford: Third World First, 1984.

Miles, R. and Phizachlea, A. *White Man's Country: Racism and British Politics.* London: Pluto Press, 1984.

NGO-EC Liaison Committee, *Code of Conduct—Images and Messages Relating to the Third World.* Brussels, 1989.

'Olé, Olé, Olé, - Racism in Dublin',*In Dublin*: 2-15 August, 1990.

Pontifical Commission, 'Iustitia et Pax', *The Church and Racism— Towards a More Fraternal Society.* Dublin: Veritas, 1989.

Tannam, M. *Racism in Ireland—Sources of Information.* Dublin: Harmony, 1991.

UN International Convention on the Elimination of All Forms of Racial Discrimination, 1965.

UNESCO, *Sociological Theories. Race and Colonialism.* Paris: Unesco, 1980.

Ware, V. *Beyond the Pale—White Women, Racism and History.* London: Verso, 1992.

Acknowledgements

Thank you to all those who gave me information and support, particularly to APSO, the Agency for Personal Service Overseas; Róisín Conroy, Gráinne Healy, Ailbhe Smyth and all at Attic Press; Niall Crowley, John O'Connell, Killian O'Donnell, Vivienne Rooney and my closest collaborator, Lynnea Fitzgerald.

A note on the author

Gretchen Fitzgerald was born in India. She attended schools in India and Britain and first came to Ireland to take an honours degree in Philosophy and Economics at University College Cork. For the last number of years she has worked with APSO, the Agency for Personal Service Overseas, prior to which she worked with Dublin County Council, the (former) Health Education Bureau and Trócaire.